T0388536

CRISIS MANAGEMENT, DESTINATION RECOVERY AND SUSTAINABILITY

The COVID-19 pandemic brought travel to a halt, and the global tourism industry has been one of the sectors hit hardest during the pandemic. This book looks at how the tourism industry can enhance its resilience and prepare for future crises more effectively.

The book provides insights into the economic, social, geopolitical and environmental implications of the COVID-19 pandemic on the tourism and hospitality industries and the responses in diverse international contexts. It highlights key concepts and includes cases with real-life applications. The book also discusses future research directions in a post-pandemic scenario.

This book will be an invaluable resource for practitioners in the areas of tourism and crisis management and for readers to compare and contrast tourism destination recovery and crisis management practices through different research methodologies and settings.

James Kennell is Reader in the School of Hospitality and Tourism Management at the University of Surrey in the United Kingdom.

Priyakrushna Mohanty is Assistant Professor in the Department of Business Administration (Tourism), Christ University, Bengaluru, India.

Anukrati Sharma is Head and Associate Professor of the Department of Commerce and Management, University of Kota, Kota, Rajasthan, India.

Azizul Hassan is a member of the Tourism Consultants Network of the UK Tourism Society.

CRISIS MANAGEMENT, DESTINATION RECOVERY AND SUSTAINABILITY

Tourism at a Crossroads

Edited by James Kennell, Priyakrushna Mohanty, Anukrati Sharma and Azizul Hassan

Routledge
Taylor & Francis Group

LONDON AND NEW YORK

Designed cover image: Getty Images

First published 2023
by Routledge
4 Park Square, Milton Park, Abingdon, Oxon OX14 4RN

and by Routledge
605 Third Avenue, New York, NY 10158

Routledge is an imprint of the Taylor & Francis Group, an informa business

British Library Cataloguing-in-Publication Data
A catalogue record for this book is available from the British Library

ISBN: 978-1-032-28234-3 (hbk)
ISBN: 978-1-032-28235-0 (pbk)
ISBN: 978-1-003-29583-9 (ebk)

DOI: 10.4324/9781003295839

Typeset in Bembo
by Apex CoVantage, LLC

CONTENTS

FIGURES

TABLES

EDITOR BIOGRAPHIES

Azizul Hassan is a member of the Tourism Consultants Network of the UK Tourism Society. Dr Hassan has been working for the tourism industry as a consultant, academic and researcher for over 20 years. His research interest areas are technology-supported marketing for tourism and hospitality, immersive technology applications in the tourism and hospitality industry, and technology-influenced marketing suggestions for the sustainable tourism and hospitality industry in developing countries. Dr Hassan has authored over 150 articles and book chapters in leading tourism outlets. He is also part of the editorial team of 25 book projects from Routledge, Springer, CAB International and Emerald Group Publishing Limited. He is a regular reviewer of a number of international journals.

James Kennell is Reader in the School of Hospitality and Tourism Management at the University of Surrey in the United Kingdom. He carries out research on a range of issues in events, tourism and hospitality, with a specific focus on how politics and policy affect the governance of these industries. He has published a number of articles, book chapters and other papers on these topics and is a co-author of the core undergraduate textbook *Events Management: An Introduction* (Routledge). James is a regular contributor to a range of media and has been interviewed for BBC News, BBC Radio 4, The Guardian, China Daily and other outlets.

Priyakrushna Mohanty is Assistant Professor in the Department of Business Administration (Tourism), Christ University, Bengaluru, India. He is also U.G.C. Senior Research Fellow at the Department of Tourism Studies, Pondicherry University, India. He is an awardee of the prestigious Travel Corporation (India) Gold Medal for his outstanding performance in the Master's Degree in Tourism Studies programme at Pondicherry University. He also holds a Master's Degree in Commerce along with three PG Diploma Degrees in Rural Development, Research

Methodology and Teaching Skills. He served the Indian Railway Catering and Tourism Corporation, Ltd., for two years, after which he was recruited to be a guest faculty member in the Department of Tourism Studies, Pondicherry University. He has published more than 15 articles and chapters in both international and national journals and edited books. Dr Mohanty is passionate about the academic areas of tourism sustainability, sustainable livelihood, technology and tourism, along with gender issues in tourism development.

Anukrati Sharma is Head and Associate Professor of the Department of Commerce and Management, University of Kota, Kota, Rajasthan, India. She is Director of the Skill Development Centre of the same university. She is also Dean (Honorary) of two faculties, Tourism and Hospitality and Aviation and Aerospace, at Rajasthan Skill University (a Government State University) in Jaipur. Her doctorate from the University of Rajasthan is in Tourism Marketing, and she completed her dissertation research focused on the progress and prospects of tourism in Rajasthan. She has two postgraduate degree specialties – one in International Business (Master of International Business) and the other in Business Administration (Master of Commerce). Her special interest areas are tourism, tourism marketing, strategic management and international business management. A member of 17 professional bodies, she has attended a number of national and international conferences and presented 45 papers. She has been invited to talks, lectures and panel discussions in different countries, such as Sri Lanka, Nepal and Turkey. Dr Sharma handles training sessions at the Rajasthan Police Academy, Jaipur, on such topics as change management, communication skills, gender discrimination, and personality development.

CONTRIBUTOR BIOGRAPHIES

Lwazi Apleni is Lecturer at the University of Zululand's Department of Recreation & Tourism. He is responsible for teaching and learning at both the undergraduate and postgraduate levels. His other duties include research, university service and community engagement. He received his Junior Degree (Tourism Management) at WSU in 2011. He also holds a master's degree in Management Sciences (cum laude) obtained from the University of Science & Technology Beijing in China. Lwazi is currently reading his PhD at the University of Johannesburg. In his PhD, Lwazi diagnoses 'Sustainable Local Economic Development (LED) through Tourism in Selected Eastern Cape District Municipalities'. As someone who is currently occupying academic territory, Lwazi was named Emerging Researcher of the Year at the Annual UniZulu's Vice-Chancellor Academic Excellence Awards. Additionally, from 2013 to the present, he has contributed 19 manuscripts on approved scholarly platforms (one policy brief, 11 journal articles and seven book chapter articles).

Manpreet Arora is Senior Assistant Professor of Management in the School of Commerce and Management Studies, Central University of Himachal Pradesh Dharamshala, India. With around 20 years of teaching experience, she has varied areas of interest. She is a gold medalist at the undergraduate level and a distinction holder at the postgraduate level. Her areas of research interest include accounting and finance, strategic management, entrepreneurship, qualitative research, case study development, communication skills and microfinance. She has been guiding research at the doctoral level. Having published more than 25 papers in various journals of national and international repute (including SCOPUS, WOS and Category Journals), she has also worked as content developer of MHRD '*e-PG Pathshala*' Project and OER's for IGNOU. She has written 30 book chapters in national as well as international books, handbooks and volumes published with

Routledge, CABI, Apple Academic Press, IGI, Taylor and Francis and Springer Nature, among others. With four edited books in her credit, she is a persistent researcher in the field of management.

Gonçalo Barbosa is a first-cycle tourism student at the Universidade Portucalense Infante D. Henrique. Professionally, he has experience in catering in one of the most popular tourist spots in Portugal, Ribeira do Porto, where he stayed for more than three months. He is currently a student representative for the tourism course as well as a member of the student council of the Department of Tourism, Heritage and Culture.

Charles Bladen has dedicated his 35-year career to the consumer experience industries, graduating with a degree in Hospitality Management, Marketing and Education. Since 1987, he has successfully performed in operational and management roles in hospitality, tourism, events, services and digital marketing organisations, mainly with responsibility for a variety of projects and international brands. Charles has designed, delivered and managed training, education and professional development programmes, as well as supervising research projects at undergraduate and postgraduate levels both in the UK and internationally in Europe, Asia and the USA. Regarded as an expert in experience design and experiential learning, Charles also publishes in a variety of leading journals and professional contexts and is lead author of the bestselling book 'Events Management: An Introduction', published by Routledge. He is also regarded as a specialist in the application of business simulations and other digital technologies. In addition to his professional and scholarly activities, Charles is a campaigner for a better understanding of neurodiversity in professional settings and is an artist and poet.

Carol Callinan is a psychologist and education specialist with 18 years' experience in applied research and higher education. Her work explores constructivism, social constructionism, knowing and knowledge growth. Her focus on developing an appreciation of multimodal communication, particularly non-verbal modes, and the influence that this has for understanding engagement, learning and interaction contribute to a more holistic appreciation of lived experiences. She is particularly interested in the application of this work to industry. Carol leads a programme that draws together psychology and education and supervises research projects in a number of areas at both undergraduate and postgraduate levels. Carol has developed and delivered educational programmes and training that explore inclusion, diversity and special educational needs and disability and is widely published.

Emine Cihangir is an academic in the Tourism Department at Van Yuzuncu Yil in Turkey. In addition to her Bachelors and Masters degrees, she has a PhD in Corporate Professional Management from Marmara University in Istanbul. She has professional experience in hotel management and has published papers on several aspects of tourism in Turkey.

Kübra Cihangir-Çamur is Associate Professor in the Urban and Planning Department at the Gazi University of Ankara. She has publication experience in the structure of tourism entrepreneurship and the planning of tourist destinations (e.g., Bodrum).

Jaime Coelho is a first-cycle tourism student at the Universidade Portucalense Infante D. Henrique.

Xolile Dlamini-Mnisi has been a lecturer at the Tshwane University of Technology, Mbombela Campus, for the past 9 years. She is currently the coordinator for the Adventure Tourism Management course, and she lectures in adventure leadership and adventure operations subjects. She has a Masters in Tourism and Hospitality, a degree in Adventure Tourism and is currently pursuing her PhD study in tourism and curriculum development. She has attended several conferences and presented papers nationally as well as at international conferences. She has co-authored a few articles with colleagues and is also a reviewer with the journal of hospitality and tourism. Her main passion is learning and teaching.

Francisco Antônio dos Anjos is Professor at the University of Vale do Itajaí, Brazil. He is coordinator of the Graduate Program (Master's and Doctorate) in Tourism and Hospitality at UNIVALI and President of the National Association for Research and Graduate Studies in Tourism. He works in the field of tourism where he develops research with funding from CAPES, FAPESC and CNPq. He leads the research group PLAGET-Planning and Management of Tourist Space. He participates in the scientific boards of several scientific tourism journals. From 2017 to 2018, he served as Assistant Secretary of Tourism, Culture and Sport of the State of Santa Catarina Brazil. He coordinates the Iguassu International Tourism Forum.

Sara Joana Gadotti dos Anjos is Professor of the Postgraduate Masters and Doctoral Program in Tourism and Hospitality at the University of Vale do Itajaí, Brazil. She was Editor of the Revista Brasileira de Pesquisa em Turismo – RBTur (2012–2017). Sara is Regional Editor for South America of the Journal of Hospitality and Tourism Insights, a member of the editorial board of the Journal of Destination Marketing & Management, Revista de Cultura e Turismo – Cultur, Tourism Vision and Action and Applied Tourism. She is Regional Vice President of the South America International Tourism Studies Association. Her research interests include innovation, motivation, human resources, tourist behaviour, management of destination excellence, hotel management and quality service.

Marta Fernandes is a first-cycle tourism student at the Universidade Portucalense Infante D. Henrique. She had a short experience working in event management and worked as a server at a coffee shop.

Ana Carvalho Ferreira is a master's student in Tourism Management at the IPCA's Higher School of Hospitality and Tourism (in Barcelos, Portugal). Her main lines of research are tourism management, tourism marketing and virtual tourism. She has completed advanced studies in tourism management.

Mahender Reddy Gavinolla is Assistant Professor at the National Institute of Tourism and Hospitality Management, India, and guest lecturer at Vidzeme University of Applied Sciences, Latvia. His research area includes sustainable tourism and heritage management.

Mireia Guix is a lecturer in tourism at the University of Queensland, Australia. She has consulted for the United Nations Environment Programme, the European Commission, the Inter-American Development Bank and national tourism government agencies, such as VisitScotland and the Catalan Tourism Board. She collaborates worldwide in sustainable destination planning projects, cooperation projects and event management. Her research focuses on corporate social responsibility, sustainability accounting and communication for the hospitality and tourism sectors. She has experience in teaching responsible tourism and sustainability-related topics at several universities.

Shuaibu Chiroma Hassan is Senior Lecturer in Isa Kaita College of Education, Dutsinma, Nigeria. He has an MSc in International Tourism and Hospitality Management from the University of Bedfordshire, a Higher National Diploma and National Diploma in Catering and Hotel Management and a Postgraduate Diploma in Education. He is a Fellow and Member at the Institute of Management Consultants (Nigeria), a member of the World Tourism Network and a member of the National Association for Technical and Vocational Educators (Nigeria). His areas of interest include heritage tourism, tourism marketing, event management, food and nutrition, hospitality management and the history of cultural heritage, amongst others. He has written journal articles, conference papers and book chapters on these subjects and reviews for conferences/journals.

Unathi Sonwabile Henama is Senior Lecturer in the Department of Tourism and Event Management at the Central University of Technology in Bloemfontein. He had formerly lectured at the Tshwane University of Technology in Pretoria. He has a PhD from Mid Sweden University and a Master's from the University of the Free State. He has written numerous articles and presented research papers at both local and international conferences. He is the leading tourism commentator in South Africa and is regarded as an authority on tourism matters. His views are highly sought after by TV, print and online news outlets.

Sarah Hussain is the Head and Associate Professor, Department of Tourism and Hospitality Management, Jamia Millia Islamia (A Central University) in New Delhi, India. She holds a PhD degree in hospitality. Previously, she served as the Principal of Banarsidas Chandiwala Institute of Hotel Management & Catering Technology, New Delhi. She has chaired the India International Hotel, Travel &

Tourism Conference (2019) and co-chaired the International Conference on Transformational Tourism (2020). She brings immense experience in imparting hospitality education and is considered an authority in hospitality management (Rooms Division Management, Revenue Management, Research Methodology, Hospitality Marketing & Sales, and Business Communication).

Shantanu Jain completed his graduate studies (B.Sc. H&HA) from the Institute of Hotel Management, Bhopal & post-graduate studies from (M.Sc. HA) from the National Council for Hotel Management & Catering Technology, Noida, where he was awarded 3rd in Academic Excellence for 2017–18 & 2018–19. Research is Shantanu's passion, and he has 21 papers & 5 book chapters published in UGC Care, International & National journals & conferences. He has also been invited to 7 webinars as a guest speaker. At present, he is pursuing his 2nd post-graduate qualification in travel and tourism management (MTTM) from IGNOU and is currently employed with the Institute of Hotel Management, Hyderabad as an assistant lecturer. Shantanu loves collecting die-casts and enjoys progressive music.

Vitor Roslindo Kuhn is a professor of Gastronomy at Universidade do Sul de Santa Catarina, Brazil. He has experience in the field of tourism, with an emphasis on gastronomy, working mainly on the following topics: confectionery, lodging, American pasta, dietary restrictions and multiple regression.

Roshan Lal Sharma is Professor in the Department of English at the Central University of Himachal Pradesh, Dharamshala, Himachal Pradesh (India). He has been a Senior Fulbright Fellow at the University of Wisconsin-Madison (USA) and an Honorary Fellow at the Institute for Research in the Humanities (IRH) at UW-Madison from 2007–08. He has authored *Raja Rao's Shorter Fiction* and *Walt Whitman – A Critical Evaluation*; co-authored *Som P. Ranchan: Dialogue Epic in Indian English Poetry* (Pencraft International, 2012); and co-edited *Mapping Diaspora Identities: India and Beyond*, and *Communication, Entrepreneurship and Finance: Renegotiating Diverse Perspectives* (2018), and *Envisioning Effective Management Communication* (2019), and *Communication Perspectives in Modern Businesses*. He has more than seventy-five published papers and book chapters to his credit on mystical poetry, Indian Writing in English, comparative literature, literary and cultural theory, folk theatre, and diverse dimensions of communication. He is a member of the editorial board of the Review of International American Studies (RIAS), a peer-reviewed international journal.

Jesús Amparo López-Vizcarra majored in Tourism at the Autonomous University of Baja California (UABC, Tijuana, Mexico), with a Master's Degree in Education. She has been a professor at the School of Tourism and Marketing at the Autonomous University of Baja California, Tijuana campus, Mexico, for the last 15 years.

Simiso Lindokuhle Mabaso is a lecturer at the Durban University of Technology in the Department of Ecotourism, Riverside Campus. His duties include lecturing Ecotourism Development, Ecotourism Management to the Diploma and Advanced Diploma students. He is involved in curriculum development and community engagement. He previously worked for TUT, UKZN and Durban Tourism. Some of his duties at Durban Tourism include assisting emerging tourism entrepreneurs within the Durban jurisdiction area by providing guidelines in terms of business registration, advising them on the right platforms, marketing their businesses for Durban tourism and creating promotional material to promote their businesses. Gathering information on major tourism activities in Durban for compiling the promotional guide for Durban to present Durban as a prime destination, making sure that promotional guides are available across the country and international through partnerships with South African embassies across the world, South African Tourism and Tourism KwaZulu Natal, to make sure that Durban is well presented across the world. Presented at two international conferences and published papers from those presentations.

Petrus Mfanampela Maphanga is Tourism Technical Assistant within the Department of Tourism Management at Tshwane University of Technology, South Africa. He holds a Master of Management Sciences. He has co-published articles and book chapters published by Emerald Publisher in 2020 and Taylor and Francis Group Publisher in 2020. He is currently pursuing doctoral studies in Tourism from Tshwane University of Technology, South Africa. His research focuses on sustainable tourism development and cultural tourism, as well as rural tourism.

Rekha Maitra is employed with DAV Centenary College, Faridabad, as Associate Professor in the Department of Travel and Tourism Management. She worked with Jai Hind College, Mumbai, as an adjunct professor. Rekha has 18 years of teaching experience in the hospitality and tourism industries. Her area of expertise is housekeeping, front office, & tourism. She has made 19 publications in journals, books and magazines. She received the Indian Hospitality Congress's Aspiring Researcher of Tourism and Hospitality 2014 Award. She was on the editorial board of ARC, International Journal of Research in Tourism and Hospitality (IJRTH) and Asian Mirror International research journals. She was associated with Tata McGraw Hill Publications, Oxford Publications, and Sage Publications as a book reviewer.

Carla Sousa Martins has a Master's in Tourism Management from the IPCA's higher school of hospitality and tourism (in Barcelos, Portugal). Their main lines of research are tourism management, tourism marketing and virtual tourism. She also has advanced studies in hotel management and she is a PhD student.

Anindya J. Mishra is a full professor of sociology at the Indian Institute of Technology, Roorkee, India. His research interests include social gerontology, sociology of health and sociology of work. He has to his credit about 30 papers in reputable national and international journals, in addition to contributing significantly to various anthologies/conferences. Currently, he is also engaging in a project sponsored by the ICSSR.

Neha Mishra is pursuing her Ph.D. in Sociology from the Indian Institute of Technology Roorkee, India, and has completed her master's in Sociology from Jawaharlal Nehru University, New Delhi. Her broader area of research is social sustainability, tourism and risk analysis. As a Ph.D. research scholar, she has participated significantly in various conferences and seminars. She has also contributed chapters in books and communicated papers to reputable journals related to her field.

Jorge Carlos Morgan-Medina majored in Tourism at the UABC (Mexico). Made a postgraduate in Planning and Managing of Tourist Space (University of Alicante, Spain) and another in Sustainable Human Development (Central European University, Hungary). Has a Master's Degree in Public Management of Tourism, Sustainability and Competitiveness (International University of Andalusia, Spain) and an Advanced Studies Diploma (University of Barcelona, Spain). Has a Ph.D. in Territorial Planning and Regional Development (University of Barcelona, Spain). Has been a professor at the UABC for the past 25 years; national and international lecturer and keynote speaker; visiting professor; author of journal articles, books and chapters.

Oswaldo Muñoz Rubio has a master's in information technologies management from the Instituto Tecnológico y de Estudios Superiores de Monterrey – México. He is a specialist in Educational Management, Institución Universitaria Politécnico Grancolombiano – Colombia and a University Specialist in Integration of Information Technologies in Organizations, Universidad Politécnica de Valencia – España. He was a telecommunication engineer at the Universidad Santo Tomas – Colombia, a professional in Business Management at the Universidad Industrial de Santander – Colombia, and a research teacher on the research seedbed of education and tourism at Via Investigations, Corporación Universitaria Minuto de Dios.

Eva Pelechano-Barahona has a PhD degree in Business Administration, and she is a professor in the Department of Economics and Business (Administration, Management and Organization) of the Rey Juan Carlos University. Her research interests are part of strategic management of the company in particular: knowledge management, intellectual capital, inter-organisational networks and strategic management of technology and innovation. Eva's research activities include numerous publications in national and international scientific journals. Some of these journals are included in the Journal Citation Reports or indexed in prestige databases as Technological Forecasting and Social Change, International Journal of Technology Management, Interscience, Innovar, Cuadernos de Economía y Dirección de la Empresa, Revista Europea de Dirección y Economía de la Empresa, Journal ESIC –Market, Journal of Intellectual Capital and The Journal of High Technology Management Research.

Catarina Silva Pereira is a master's student in tourism management at IPCA's higher school of hospitality and tourism in Barcelos, Portugal. Her main lines of research are tourism management, tourism marketing and virtual tourism. She has completed advanced studies in hotel management.

Madiseng Messiah Phori is a tourism lecturer in the Department of Tourism Management at Tshwane University of Technology in South Africa. He holds a Master of Management Sciences, specialising in Hospitality and Tourism, from Durban University of Technology in Kwa-Zulu Natal, South Africa. He is currently in his final year completing doctoral studies in Tourism from Tshwane University of Technology. His research focuses include community-based tourism, sustainable tourism development, heritage and cultural tourism, rural tourism, and safety and security in tourism.

Dr. Makhabbat Ramazanova is Assistant Professor at the Department of Tourism, Heritage and Culture and a researcher at the REMIT-Research on Economics, Management, and Information Technologies of Portucalense University, Portugal. Her main research interests are sustainable tourism, tourism and water, ICT in tourism, and tourism planning and development. She has published in international journals such as International Journal of Tourism Cities, Tourism and Hospitality Management, European Journal of Tourism Research, Tourism Planning and Development, Journal of Tourism Development, in book chapters Routledge, IGI Global, Springer and in several international and national conference book proceedings.

Adriana Guillermina Ríos-Vázquez majored in Tourism and in Law (Autonomous University of Baja California, Mexico). She has a master's degree in Marketing (Autonomous University of Aguascalientes, Mexico) and a Ph.D. In Global Development Studies (UABC, Mexico). She also has a postgraduate qualification in Mexico-United States Studies (El Colegio de la Frontera Norte, Mexico) and worked as an officer of Mexico's Ministry of Foreign Affairs for more than 17 years. She has been a professor-researcher at UABC for the past 22 years, where she has been a lecturer and co-author of articles, books and chapters. Her research interests are in: Social Sciences, International Relations and Cooperation, Security and Transborder Global Dynamics, Public International Law, Tourism and Marketing.

Erick Sergio Andrés Rodríguez is a Tourism and Hotel Business Manager from the Corporación Universitaria Minuto de Dios Uniminuto, and Researcher from the Education and Tourism Seedbed Research Route that belongs to the research group of Science, Environment and Sustainable Ecological Tourism-CAYTES.

José-Luis Rodríguez-Sánchez, Ph.D. is Lecturer in Business Administration and Organization at Rey Juan Carlos University, Madrid (Spain). His research interests include strategic alliances, cooperative agreements, mergers and acquisitions, and human resources management. His research has been published in the International Journal of Hospitality Management, Finance Research Letters, the International Journal of Environmental Research and Public Health, the International Journal of Manpower, the Journal of Organizational Change Management and Frontiers in Psychology, among other journals.

María Angélica Rojas Bernal is Magister in Education, Pontificia Universidad Javeriana and Specialist in the development of pedagogy and creativity at the Francisco José de Caldas District University, as well as Tourism and Hotel Administrator at the National Unified Corporation of Higher Education. She is Research Professor of the research group Science, Environment and Sustainable Ecological Tourism (CAYTES) of the Minuto de Dios Uniminuto University Corporation.

Mehmet Şeremet's academic background includes both bachelor's and master's degrees in Geography from Turkey and also a PhD from Plymouth University in the UK. His current post is that of Associate Professor in Geography at Van Yuzuncu Yil University in Turkey. He has published several papers in UK-oriented journals, including JGHE, IRGEE and Geography.

Lauren A. Siegel is Lecturer at the University of Greenwich in the United Kingdom. She has previously completed her PhD at the University of Surrey in the UK and her master's from the Hong Kong Polytechnic University. Her research focuses on behavioural science, peer influence and the use of technology for socially sustainable practices. She originally hails from the United States, which you can easily tell from her accent.

Anubha Mahender Singh is a research scholar in the Department of Tourism and Hospitality Management, Jamia Millia Islamia (a Central University), in New Delhi, India. She had previously worked in the capacity of Lecturer at the National Institute of Tourism and Hospitality Management. She has taught food production courses at the collegiate level and specialises in Continental cuisine. Her area of research is food tourism and gastronomy tourism. She is the corresponding author of the article.

Bruno Barbosa Sousa is a professor at the Polytechnic Institute of Cavado and Ave (IPCA, Portugal) and Head of the Master Program – Tourism Management – PhD Marketing and Strategy. He is a CiTUR research member. He is author or co-author of several papers and his research interests include tourism management, marketing and strategy. He serves on the editorial board of several peer-reviewed scientific journals and is an ad hoc reviewer of several peer-reviewed scientific journals. Member of the scientific committee of several national and international congresses and conferences.

Uglješa Stankov is Full Professor in the Department of Geography, Tourism and Hotel Management, Faculty of Sciences, University of Novi Sad. His main research areas are the strategic role of information technology in tourism and mindful tourist experiences. He actively cooperates with researchers and professional organisations from around the world and participates in several international projects. He has published more than 160 scientific papers and four books.

Thais González-Torres, Ph.D. is Lecturer in Business Administration and Organization at Rey Juan Carlos University, Madrid (Spain). Within the field of business and management, her lines of research range from interorganisational relationships to innovation in services and entrepreneurship, among others. She has published articles in prestigious academic journals in Business, Management, Hospitality and Tourism, and Education, highlighting the International Journal of Hospitality Management, Hospitality & Society, Tourism Review International, Finance Research Letters, and International Journal of Environmental Research and Public Health.

Rolando Torres Aguilera is Administrator of Tourism and Hotel Businesses at the Corporación Universitaria Minuto de Dios Uniminuto, Technologist in Tourism Guidance National Learning Service SENA, Specialist in design of tourism projects, Researcher of the Education and Tourism Seedbed Research Route, and a member of the research group Science, Environment and Sustainable Ecological Tourism-CAYTES. He is the CEO of the Worldwide Travelers Networks, SAS Travel Agency, and a member of the Executive Board of the Tourism Sector Council.

Đorđije A. Vasiljević is Associate Professor at the University of Novi Sad, Faculty of Sciences. His research interests are in geoconservation, geoheritage, geodiversity, geotourism and geoparks.

Peter Vlachos (BA, Toronto; MA, Toronto; MBA, East London; PhD, Greenwich) is Principal Lecturer in Marketing, Events, and Tourism at the University of Greenwich, UK, where he oversees the international portfolio for tourism, hospitality and marketing studies. His chief research interests are in place identity, urban and regional development, and the 'experience economy'. Peter's observations on the London 2012 Olympics were widely reported in the international press. His recent and forthcoming publications include gastronomic tourism in Albania, the professionalisation of the live events industry in Greece, and marketing ethics in music festivals. He reviews for journals including *Enlightening Tourism. A Pathmaking Journal*, *Urban Design International*, *International Journal of Tourism Cities*, and *International Journal of the Sociology of Leisure*.

Miroslav D. Vujičić is an associate professor at the University of Novi Sad, Faculty of Sciences. He is the main evaluator for impact assessment of the European Capital of Culture Novi Sad 2022. His main field of interest is decision-making processes, project management, product development, and cultural tourism, and he has proficiency in data gathering, analysis and interpretation of mathematical and statistical methods. He has published 36 research papers in Scopus-indexed journals and has more than 486 citations in the Scopus database. Programme Leader, PhD in Management and Business (Tourism). RVP for Eastern Europe in the ITSA Network. Departmental deputy head for international projects and student and staff mobility. A member of the Department Accreditation team, he has experience in creating study programs and managing quality assurance. He is an experienced project manager, as he participated in more than 20 international projects (H2020, Erasmus+, COSME, IPA INTERREG, COST, RCC and others).

Isabella Qing Ye is a lecturer in tourism & events at the University of Greenwich, UK. Her research and teaching predominantly focus on tourist behaviours and interpretation, geographies of cultural landscape, sustainable tourism, and critical studies in tourism and hospitality. She is a member of the Council of Hospitality Management Education (CHME) and the Association for Tourism in Higher Education (ATHE), as well as an expert panel member on the Binna Burra Foundation, Australia.

PREFACE

This book was conceived in the teeth of the global COVID-19 pandemic. The last two years have seen a predictable explosion in research into the impacts of the pandemic on the tourism and hospitality industries, much of it speculative or based on forecasting. Now, as initial waves of the pandemic abate and we benefit from vaccines, antiviral drugs and the bitter experience of managing a health crisis, is a useful time to reflect on how destinations, businesses and communities around the world coped with COVID-19. We hope that this book, through its combination of introductory chapters that set out the key concepts necessary for 'bouncing-back' in the post-pandemic recovery period and its broad range of international case studies from Asia, Europe, Australasia and North and South America, offers some practical insights of value to researchers, students and managers in the tourism and hospitality industries. As a team of editors, we are incredibly grateful to the editorial and production teams at Routledge for supporting this project. In particular, we thank Yong Ling Lam and Kendrick Loo for their guidance and patience as the book came together.

ACKNOWLEDGEMENTS

James Kennell

For my daughters, Lyra, Aphra and Evelyn.

Priyakrushna Mohanty

To the late Sephali Ma'am for teaching me English and life!

Anukrati Sharma

I would like to thank Lord Sai Baba for his blessings. I would like to thank my parents, Prof. J.P.N. Sharma and Mrs. Rekha Sharma for their unconditional support. I am thankful to the University of Kota, especially my team of faculty and students of the Department of Commerce and Management of the University of Kota, Rajasthan, India. I am thankful to my lovely daughter Viddushi Choudhary for all her love and support.

Azizul Hassan

I am thankful to my wife Sharmin and my boys Ehan and Rehan.

INTRODUCTION

Tourism at a crossroads

James Kennell, Priyakrushna Mohanty,
Anukrati Sharma and Azizul Hassan

Introduction

The impact of the COVID-19 pandemic on the global tourism and hospitality industries has been profound (Sharma et al., 2022; Sigala, 2020). Not since the terrorist attacks in New York in September 2011 have we seen global travel impacts as wide-ranging and as severe. Tourism and hospitality have shown incredible resilience in the past, with international arrivals recovering quickly after crises and periods of restructuring and diversification providing opportunities for entrepreneurship, product development and the emergence of new destinations (Beirman, 2021). The COVID-19 pandemic, however, is proving longer-lasting than the previous period of crisis. After emerging in China in late 2019, the virus has spread to every corner of the globe, but it has been experienced differently in different destinations. Some countries adopted severe lockdowns, while others took a more laissez-faire approach, at least initially (Cheng et al., 2022). Vaccines and other medical interventions that can prevent or mitigate the impacts of the pandemic have also been unequally distributed. National interests and corporate power have undermined the potential for a truly global approach to the pandemic, with vaccine nationalism undermining efforts to distribute medicines to the developing world (Wagner et al., 2021). The pandemic is not yet over, although the worst may have passed for many richer countries.

The diverse applications of travel bans, lockdowns and vaccination programmes mean that international travel is restarting uncertainly, and not all markets or destinations are yet fully integrated back into the global tourism and hospitality market. Many tourists, too, are apprehensive about their future trips, whether for reasons of health security, worries about the quality of experiences in destinations, accommodation and restaurants, or simply because of the new inconveniences and costs associated with travel (Fedeli et al., 2022). Despite these negatives, many people see

DOI: 10.4324/9781003295839-1

the pandemic as an opportunity to 'reset' tourism and hospitality and to consider anew how the industry can become more sustainable and make a more meaningful contribution to development (Stankov et al., 2020).

It is necessary for governments, local authorities and destination management organisations to find innovative and effective ways of responding to this significant crisis. Many businesses in tourism and hospitality are now facing a chronic human resources crisis caused by staff taking leave for illness, migrant staff returning to their original home countries, and many workers choosing to leave the industries altogether for more secure employment (Baum et al., 2020; Chen, 2021). In the face of this, many tourism and hospitality businesses have become more innovative, accelerating the rollout of technology and developing creative new service approaches (Chang et al., 2022; Mohanty et al., 2020).

Governments and their agencies across the world have intervened heavily in the tourism and hospitality industries, imposing new laws and regulations as well as providing financial support (Kennell, 2020). As the world learns to live with COVID-19 and to adjust to the 'new normal', it will be necessary to formulate effective policies and strategies that are based on evidence from the varied international experience accumulated by the tourism and hospitality industry during the pandemic (Škare et al., 2021). Researchers and educators have a role to play in this. Carrying out research that reflects deeply on these issues (Filep et al., 2022), and explaining its findings through publications and teaching will help to inform not only policy, but also the actions taken by businesses as we enter the post-pandemic period.

This book has the aim of gathering together examples of this research and presenting them in a way that will be useful for researchers, students and practitioners in tourism and hospitality, as well as policy-makers. There are important lessons to be learnt from this research, not just for the pandemic response but for future crises of different kinds. The book contains research from five continents and a mixture of chapters that focus on national case studies and those that take a more global perspective.

Overview of the book

The first section of this book provides an overview of the key principles that it is necessary to understand for the recovery of the global tourism and hospitality industries: first, the idea that tourism is at a crossroads, with multiple potential development paths ahead; second, the concept of crisis management; third, the principles of destination recovery; and fourth, the role of sustainable development.

Vujičić et al. (2023) examine how the COVID-19 pandemic could influence the acceptance of alternative pathways of post-pandemic tourism development. Under alternatives, this chapter considers not just alternative forms of tourism as a consequence of alternative consumer lifestyles but also all alternative ways of organising and conducting tourism businesses.

Vlachos (2023) explores and unpacks the concept of 'crisis', the impact of crises in tourism and hospitality settings, and policy responses. The chapter begins by considering the similarities and differences between human-made and natural-occurring crisis conditions, with numerous historical and contemporary examples. Then, a conceptual typology is formulated to distinguish between one-off and recurring (cyclical) crisis conditions, the scale of their impacts, and their influence on short- and long-term planning and development.

Bladen and Callinan (2023) propose that whilst pre-pandemic tourism and hospitality research has generally focussed on broader destination-marketing concepts, post-pandemic attention should be paid to the remedial and other post pandemic actions required by stakeholders to facilitate recovery and ongoing tourism destination effectiveness. Emphasis is placed on the strategic application of the psychological formation of tourist perceptions, with key attention to the role of social constructionism, semiotic design, and nudge theory in destination brand marketing messages.

Dos Anjos et al. (2023) approach the concept of sustainable development from the perspective of its intertwining with mobility, connectivity, technology and management during the pandemic period. In this scenario, two issues linked to the current crisis are highlighted: governance and sustainability, relating to the ability of destinations to manage risks, and the challenges for the management of tourism services, given the need for destinations to develop recovery activity that supports sustainable tourism.

The second section of the book presents 14 separate case studies. Twelve of these are from countries spread across five continents, while a further two take a more global perspective on issues affecting tourism at the crossroads.

The first chapter, by Henema at al. (2023) presents the first case from the global South. They show that in the absence of international tourism arrivals due to the COVID-19 pandemic and lockdowns, South Africa looked to domestic tourism for recovery. The local savings culture of *stokvels* is shown to have great potential in promoting domestic tourism expenditure if targeted marketing and packaging are undertaken for the stokvels economy to support the tourism value chain in South Africa. Stokvel tourism can create a new pool of domestic tourists to support South Africa's recovery whilst institutionalising the habit of holidays.

A second African case study is given by Hassan (2023). The chapter identifies marketing strategies adopted by Nigerian tourism organisations, destinations and managers during and after the coronavirus pandemic to enable them recover from this economic shock. SWOT analysis is employed to assess the internal and external environments of Nigerian tourism organisations in order to suggest the right marketing strategies for recovery. The chapter reveals new innovations, tools and marketing strategies employed by various governments, universities, agencies, tourism firms and marketing organisations during the pandemic periods through collaboration

Chapter 7 by Mishra and Mishra (2023) utilises Ulrich Beck's concept of the 'risk society' to analyse the type of risks created by the COVID-19 pandemic in the tourism industry and its impact on different sections of society that are dependent on the tourism sector. Using a case study of the famous hill station in India,

'Mussoorie', the chapter concludes that the COVID-19 pandemic has created risks that have intensified class, caste and gender differences in society in India, thereby impacting the lives of vulnerable sections of the population.

Arora and Lal Sharma (2023) draw attention to a global phenomenon: the relationship between Millennials' travel behaviour and their cohort's quest for spirituality. Millennial tourists have been severely affected during the pandemic due to heavy financial and other losses. This chapter explores millennials' quest for spirituality and spiritual well-being, also taking into account their interest in religious tourism, which at times could lead them to mystical experiences to help them escape from the drudgery of life during the post-pandemic period.

In Chapter 9, Cihangir-Çamur et al. (2023) explain that many scholars have tried to reveal the COVID-19 pandemic's interplay with the capacity of different societies to overcome, adapt and be resilient in the face of a rapidly evolving challenge. To this end, the Turkish experience and response to COVID-19 is presented and analysed from policy, planning and management perspectives. This chapter provides a critical viewpoint on how far Turkey's experience mirrors or differs from its rivals in terms of its crisis management plan and, in particular, its use of marketing strategies in the recovery process.

Ye and Guix (2023), in Chapter 10, also argue for the importance of localisation or locally led recovery, which has been increasingly recognised as advantageous in strategic crisis management and resilience building. A case study of the Binna Burra Lodge, Australia's longest-established nature-based resort, illustrates the complex effects of back-to-back disasters and the powerful occasion for sensemaking initiatives as part of an innovative localised recovery. The authors argue that locally led recovery provides a holistic, grounded approach; it provides an opportunity to give stakeholders a voice and return agency over their adaptation to systemic disruptions.

The case of external quality accreditations for hotels in Spain is the focus of the next chapter, by González-Torres et al. (2023). Customer trust in hotels and other tourism services can be seriously damaged by the effects of epidemic outbreaks, such as COVID-19, if quality standards are not maintained and improved by eliminating any uncertainty that the customer may have. This study examines the role and usefulness of external certifications related to the COVID-19 pandemic. The results revealed that large hotel chains prefer to develop their own quality procedures while using external certifications as a potential marketing tool to attract health-conscious tourists in the post-pandemic period.

In Chapter 12, Maitra and Jain (2023) explore the phenomenon of online education in hospitality settings, which became ubiquitous during lockdown periods across the globe. Using a survey of various hotel management institutes across India, they focused on evaluating the effectiveness of online learning as a substitute for hospitality courses. Findings suggest that faculty commitment to online education is a significant factor in its success; faculty should give personal attention to students as they face network issues, buffering, less visibility on mobile screens, chaos and connectivity problems.

The chapter by Barbosa et al. (2023) is concerned with addressing the importance of food delivery applications in the tourism and hospitality industry at the time of the COVID-19 pandemic from the perspectives of consumers in Portugal. To achieve the objective of the study, mixed methods were used with both qualitative and quantitative techniques and numerous insights were produced relating to restaurant business consumers and the reasons for their use of digital tools during the pandemic, and how this can capture the attention of consumers as a potential strategy to recover the industry and support crisis management in the future.

Also looking at the hospitality industry and the challenges that its workforce continues to face during this period of crisis, Siegel (2023) uses the case of the North American city of New York to identify pandemic-related stressors, including dangerous working conditions, low wages, job uncertainty and burnout. Agreeing with studies conducted prior to the pandemic, social support is a strong recommendation made in this chapter to help combat occupational stress; however, it is not a one-size-fits-all solution in a post-pandemic scenario. This study stresses the regional variance of occupational stress, which is dependent on local social and cultural factors as well as the agendas of regional decision makers.

In Chapter 15, a South American case study from Colombia is presented by Torres Aguilera et al. (2023). It presents the farmer's organisation, 'Building the Future of the Jardín Municipality, Antioquia', who sought in tourism a way to overcome challenges in a sustainable way. Based on this case, this chapter seeks to determine whether community tourism is a sustainable development strategy for agricultural communities post-COVID-19.

The next chapter draws on research carried out at the Mexico–USA border. López-Vizcarra et al.'s (2023) study revealed a clear relationship between the hotel occupancy slowdown in the border city of Tijuana and violence through the last period before the COVID-19 pandemic and a more obvious impact during the health emergency due to this phenomenon. Furthermore, it was found that the COVID-19 pandemic impacts on hotel occupancy can be solved by applying risk management programs in their planning, especially by using supply chains as the main tools.

Chapter 17 by Sousa et al. (2023) takes a global perspective to examine the emerging contexts in which VR and AR have surfaced in hospitality and tourism research, and whether in a post-COVID-19 landscape, there is interest and opportunity for cutting-edge technologies in contributing to destination recovery. From an interdisciplinary perspective, this chapter aims to present contributions to marketing, virtual tourism and pandemic management.

The final case study chapter, by Mahender Singh et al. (2023) highlights a vital area of the pandemic response that has been under-researched to date, that of the ways in which this has impacted chefs and their culinary practice. Using an Indian case study across multiple destinations, the study reveals how these key stakeholders in the hospitality workforce have adapted their practice to meet the regulatory and legal changes that have formed a part of the pandemic response and how they anticipate this developing in the post-pandemic period.

Conclusion

This book aims to provide both conceptual and practical guidance for researchers, practitioners and students considering how to support the recovery of the tourism and hospitality industries in their destinations. We hope that the book will be included in the reading list of undergraduate and postgraduate programmes of study and that the insights generated by each case study suggest practical steps that can be taken to support a sustainable recovery.

References

Arora, M., & Lal Sharma, R. (2023). Searching for a Break from the Drudgery of Daily Din: Analyzing Millennials' Quest for Spirituality and Well-being during the COVID-19 Pandemic. In J. Kennell, P. Mohanty, A. Sharma, & A. Hassan (Eds.), *Crisis Management, Destination Recovery and Sustainability: Tourism at a Crossroads*. Abingdon: Routledge

Barbosa, G., Coelho, J., Fernandes, M., & Ramazanova, M. (2023). The Use of Food Delivery Applications in the Restaurant Industry during the COVID-19 Crisis: Consumers' Perspectives. In J. Kennell, P. Mohanty, A. Sharma, & A. Hassan (Eds.), *Crisis Management, Destination Recovery and Sustainability: Tourism at a Crossroads*. Abingdon: Routledge

Baum, T., Mooney, S.K., Robinson, R.N., & Solnet, D. (2020). COVID-19's Impact on the Hospitality Workforce – New Crisis or Amplification of the Norm? *International Journal of Contemporary Hospitality Management*.

Beirman, D. (2021). *Tourism Crises and Destination Recovery*. London: Sage.

Bladen, C., & Callinan, C. (2023). Destination Recovery: Recovery of the Post-pandemic Tourism Destination Economy. In J. Kennell, P. Mohanty, A. Sharma, & A. Hassan (Eds.), *Crisis Management, Destination Recovery and Sustainability: Tourism at a Crossroads*. Abingdon: Routledge

Chang, Y.S., Cheah, J.H., Lim, X.J., Morrison, A.M., & Kennell, J.S. (2022). Are Unmanned Smart Hotels du jour or Are They Here Forever? Experiential Pathway Analysis of Antecedents of Satisfaction and Loyalty. *International Journal of Hospitality Management, 104*, 103249.

Chen, M.H. (2021). Well-being and Career Change Intention: COVID-19's Impact on Unemployed and Furloughed Hospitality Workers. *International Journal of Contemporary Hospitality Management, 33*(8), 2500–2520

Cheng, S., Zhao, Y., Kaminga, A.C., Wang, X., Zhang, X., & Xu, H. (2022). COVID-19 Containment: Comparisons and Suggestions for Global Response. *Inquiry: The Journal of Health Care Organization, Provision, and Financing, 59*, 00469580221086142.

Cihangir-Çamur, K., Cihangir, E., & Şeremet, M. (2023). Turkey's Tourism Recovery Process during COVID-19: Policy, Planning and Management. In J. Kennell, P. Mohanty, A. Sharma, & A. Hassan (Eds.), *Crisis Management, Destination Recovery and Sustainability: Tourism at a Crossroads*. Abingdon: Routledge.

dos Anjos, F.A., Gadotti dos Anjos, S.J., & Kuhn, V. (2023). Sustainability and Destination Recovery: Alternatives to Overcome the Crossroads of the Pandemic Crisis. In J. Kennell, P. Mohanty, A. Sharma, & A. Hassan (Eds.), *Crisis Management, Destination Recovery and Sustainability: Tourism at a Crossroads*. Abingdon: Routledge

Fedeli, G., Nguyen, T.H.H., Williams, N.L., Del Chiappa, G., & Wassler, P. (2022). Travel Desire Over Intention in Pandemic Times. *Annals of Tourism Research Empirical Insights, 3*(2), 100051.

Filep, S., King, B., & McKercher, B. (2022). Reflecting on Tourism and COVID-19 Research. *Tourism Recreation Research*. DOI: 10.1080/02508281.2021.2023839

González-Torres, Rodríguez-Sánchez, J-L. T., & Pelechano-Barahona, E. (2023). Building Trust among Tourists in the Post COVID-19 Period: The Role of External Quality Certifications. In J. Kennell, P. Mohanty, A. Sharma, & A. Hassan (Eds.), *Crisis Management, Destination Recovery and Sustainability: Tourism at a Crossroads*. Abingdon: Routledge.

Hassan, S.C. (2023). Innovative Marketing Strategies During Tourism Recovery in the Post COVID-19 Period in Nigeria. In J. Kennell, P. Mohanty, A. Sharma, & A. Hassan (Eds.), *Crisis Management, Destination Recovery and Sustainability: Tourism at a Crossroads*. Abingdon: Routledge

Henema, U.S., Alpeni, L., Phori, M.M., Maphanga, P.M., Mabaso, S.L., & Dlamini-Mnisi, X. (2023). Inducing Domestic Tourism through Stokvels in South Africa: Post-COVID-19 Tourism Recovery in the Global South. In J. Kennell, P. Mohanty, A. Sharma, & A. Hassan (Eds.), *Crisis Management, Destination Recovery and Sustainability: Tourism at a Crossroads*. Abingdon: Routledge

Kennell, J. (2020). Tourism Policy Research after the COVID-19 Pandemic: Reconsidering the Role of the State in Tourism. *Skyline Business Journal*, 16(1), 68–72.

López-Vizcarra, J.A., Morgan-Median, J.C., & Ríos-Vázquez, A.G. (2023). Recovery of Hotel Occupancy Using Risk Management of Supply Chains in the COVID-19 Pandemic Context at the US–Mexico Border. In J. Kennell, P. Mohanty, A. Sharma, & A. Hassan (Eds.), *Crisis Management, Destination Recovery and Sustainability: Tourism at a Crossroads*. Abingdon: Routledge

Mahender Singh, A., Mohanty, P., Hussain, S., & Gavinolla, M.H. (2023). COVID-19 and Changing Realities in the Food & Beverage Sector: Exhibiting the Indian Chefs' Perspective. In J. Kennell, P. Mohanty, A. Sharma, & A. Hassan (Eds.), *Crisis Management, Destination Recovery and Sustainability: Tourism at a Crossroads*. Abingdon: Routledge

Maitra, R., & Jain, S. (2023). Judging the Resilience of Online Learning for Hospitality Courses During COVID-19. In J. Kennell, P. Mohanty, A. Sharma, & A. Hassan (Eds.), *Crisis Management, Destination Recovery and Sustainability: Tourism at a Crossroads*. Abingdon: Routledge

Mishra, N., & Mishra, A. (2023). The COVID-19 Pandemic and Risk Analysis in Tourism Destinations: Insights from Queen of Hills 'Mussoorie'. In J. Kennell, P. Mohanty, A. Sharma, & A. Hassan (Eds.), *Crisis Management, Destination Recovery and Sustainability: Tourism at a Crossroads*. Abingdon: Routledge

Mohanty, P., Hassan, A., & Ekiz, E. (2020). Augmented Reality for Relaunching Tourism Post-COVID-19: Socially Distant, Virtually Connected. *Worldwide Hospitality and Tourism Themes*, 12(6), 753–760. DOI: 10.1108/WHATT-07-2020-0073

Sharma, A., Hassan, A., & Mohanty, P. (Eds.). (2022). *COVID-19 and the Tourism Industry: Sustainability, Resilience and New Directions*. Abingdon: Routledge

Siegel, L. (2023). The COVID-19 Pandemic and (Re)considerations of Occupational Stress in New York City's Hospitality Industry. In J. Kennell, P. Mohanty, A. Sharma, & A. Hassan (Eds.), *Crisis Management, Destination Recovery and Sustainability: Tourism at a Crossroads*. Abingdon: Routledge

Sigala, M. (2020). Tourism and COVID-19: Impacts and Implications for Advancing and Resetting Industry and Research. *Journal of Business Research*, 117, 312–321.

Škare, M., Soriano, D.R., & Porada-Rochoń, M. (2021). Impact of COVID-19 on the Travel and Tourism Industry. *Technological Forecasting and Social Change*, 163, 120469.

Sousa, B., Martins, C., Ferreira, A., & Pereira, C. (2023). Virtual Tourism and Digital Communication in the Context of the Post-pandemic Scenario. In J. Kennell, P. Mohanty,

A. Sharma, & A. Hassan (Eds.), *Crisis Management, Destination Recovery and Sustainability: Tourism at a Crossroads*. Abingdon: Routledge.

Stankov, U., Filimonau, V., & Vujičić, M.D. (2020). A Mindful Shift: An Opportunity for Mindfulness-driven Tourism in a Post-pandemic World. *Tourism Geographies*, *22*(3), 703–712.

Torres Aguilera, R., Rodriguez, E.S.A., Rubio, O.M., & Bernal, M.A.R. (2023). Community-based Tourism as a Post COVID-19 Development Strategy in Agricultural Communities. In J. Kennell, P. Mohanty, A. Sharma, & A. Hassan (Eds.), *Crisis Management, Destination Recovery and Sustainability: Tourism at a Crossroads*. Abingdon: Routledge

Vlachos, P. (2023). Crisis Management: Managing Tourism in the Face of Adversity. In J. Kennell, P. Mohanty, A. Sharma, & A. Hassan (Eds.), *Crisis Management, Destination Recovery and Sustainability: Tourism at a Crossroads*. Abingdon: Routledge.

Vujičić, M.D., Stankov, U., & Vasiljević, D.A. (2023). Tourism at a Crossroads – Ignoring, Adopting, or Embracing Alternative Pathways for More Sustainable Post-Pandemic Tourism Development. In J. Kennell, P. Mohanty, A. Sharma, & A. Hassan (Eds.), *Crisis Management, Destination Recovery and Sustainability: Tourism at a Crossroads*. Abingdon: Routledge

Wagner, C.E., Saad-Roy, C.M., Morris, S.E., Baker, R.E., Mina, M. J., Farrar, J., & Grenfell, B.T. (2021). Vaccine Nationalism and the Dynamics and Control of SARS-CoV-2. *Science, 373*(6562), eabj7364.

Ye, I.Q., & Guix, M. (2023). Restore, Reorient, and Reinvigorate: A Localisation and Sensemaking Approach to Crisis Recovery. In J. Kennell, P. Mohanty, A. Sharma, & A. Hassan (Eds.), *Crisis Management, Destination Recovery and Sustainability: Tourism at a Crossroads*. Abingdon: Routledge.

SECTION 1
Key concepts

1

TOURISM AT A CROSSROADS – IGNORING, ADOPTING, OR EMBRACING ALTERNATIVE PATHWAYS FOR MORE SUSTAINABLE POST-PANDEMIC TOURISM DEVELOPMENT

Miroslav D. Vujičić, Uglješa Stankov and Đorđije A. Vasiljević

Introduction

With the rapid spread of COVID-19, the globalised world has been confronted with an urgent threat of infection and significant mortality rates. The world was stunned by the graphic images of the disease's victims and the Chinese government's unexpected response and actions (Gössling et al., 2020). Western society, on the other hand, developed a sense of urgency following media reports from northern Italy. In the absence of a vaccine or known therapy, these stories exposed a new danger: the incapacity of one of the world's most advanced health systems to deal with such a large-scale disaster. Global audiences were forewarned that the best approach to deal with the current circumstances was to maintain social distance and minimise their connections with others. This sparked active citizen participation in an attempt to safeguard themselves and others, converting this disease into a community concern, resulting in the anti-COVID-19 catchphrase 'we are all in this together' (Harris, 2020; Radojević et al., 2020).

When the pandemic started, the travel and tourism industry was among the first to get hit. This showed the global audience how vulnerable the tourism industry is to sudden changes in visitor flows (Dwyer et al., 2010; Gössling et al., 2020). Indeed, the COVID-19 pandemic generated the most severe decline in the history of the tourism sector (Becker, 2020). Many voices emphasise that in the long term, tourism will evolve as a result of the severe structural damage that has already been done (Chang et al., 2020). Simultaneously, other voices have been heard, such as those who argue that, as capitalism's once-stable and rigid rules crumble in front of our eyes, a movement toward a more human-oriented view of the world should/could arise (Ateljevic, 2020). Indeed, the pandemic crisis provided a fertile ground

DOI: 10.4324/9781003295839-3

for the development of alternative pathways for future tourism development. For the most part, these alternatives would go ignored (Stankov et al., 2020).

Under alternatives to the course of tourism development so far, we do not consider just alternative forms of tourism or consumer lifestyles, seen as a niche market category, but, most importantly, we think of all alternative ways of organising and conducting tourism businesses. Here we could pinpoint, for example, the inclusion of alternative fuels for transportation of tourists and goods, the adoption of circular economy principles, water-saving, reduction of plastic and other waste, all the way to alternative approaches to a grassroots movement, mindful leadership, and similar. Many of these approaches are discussed thoughtfully in the tourism-related literature. However, their importance arises in times of global crisis, such as the COVID-19 pandemic.

The pandemic has already erected several impediments to long-term tourism development in the post-pandemic world. These are related to a lack of sustainable travel options, a lack of sustainability information and openness throughout the booking process and, ultimately, a lack of activities to support sustainable development at a destination during a holiday. The changes brought about by the imposition of travel restrictions and by direct dangers to health caused by the virus have restructured tourism business activities and the tourism experience itself. These changes influence the basic pillars of tourism that position it as one of the main drivers of sustainable economic development and the industry that leads to positive change in many destinations. The COVID-19 pandemic has threatened that progress unlike any challenge so far in modern society. Thus, to sustain tourism businesses in these challenging times and to allow the positive outcomes of traveling both for tourists and tourism providers, there is a need to develop an overall understanding of the issues brought by the pandemic (Chang et al., 2020; Galvani et al., 2020; Gössling et al., 2020; Higgins-Desbiolles, 2021).

To support the need for rethinking tourism in a post-pandemic world, this chapter contributes to the current stream of academic reflections on COVID-19 by highlighting the importance of incorporating alternative approaches to tourist development. Thus, the chapter does not emphasise the benefits of using a particular alternative approach in doing tourism-related business but discusses raising awareness and turning the spotlight on them to catch the momentum brought to the table by the pandemic. As a result, we base our study on the growing push for revisiting current economic systems in Western society. To establish a vital agenda for long-term sustainability, many of these initiatives might stimulate a new generation of tourists, resulting in a more meaningful tourism industry. This chapter will elaborate on three possible courses regarding the role of alternative approaches in tourism development.

Post-pandemic tourism developments

After COVID-19, many researchers and institutions are speculating about how quickly the tourism industry will recover as well as what its future will look like. Some believe it will carry on its current, largely unsustainable course, while others believe it will undergo a positive, sustainability-driven transformation (Ateljevic, 2020; Lew et al., 2020; Sigala, 2020). However, the post-pandemic transition is defined by a period of uncertainty, according to recent media reports. It is during this time that new viral mutations, periodic lockdowns, unequal distribution, and lack of vaccination are all factors that come into play. Other factors include concerns about vaccine safety and effectiveness, as well as the appropriateness of vaccination doses (Stankov & Filimonau, 2021). When the Omicron variant virus strain initially arrived, some countries panicked and closed their borders, only to later realise that the record rise in infections would not be as devastating as prior waves of COVID-19.

In such circumstances, tourist demand is continually shifting throughout the turbulent post-pandemic transition era, both in terms of market dynamics and in terms of travel motivations (Kock et al., 2020; Vujičić et al., 2020). This raises questions about the global tourist industry's future. Diverse tourist hotspots and tour operators have different long-term plans and visions for their businesses. In many countries, decision-makers are eager to put the past behind them and restore trust in tourism (European Travel Commission, 2021). Nevertheless, in light of the virus's actual spread, travellers and tourism operators also must take precautions and maintain a high degree of awareness at all times, especially in the case of chronic illnesses.

Nevertheless, if a complete economic and social collapse is ruled out, three possible futures can be envisioned: (1) things return to normal and operate following current norms ('back to normal'); (2) a 'new normal', governed by new rules, emerges; and (3) society and the economy undergo fundamental transformations (Hideg, 2020; Jahel et al., 2021). A new global economic order necessitates that all players in the tourism industry become more resilient and that corporate transformation is encouraged to adapt to this new reality (Sharma et al., 2021). Here, the growing segment of consumers interested in alternative approaches and lifestyles may catalyse the future, allowing for more responsible tourism development (Stankov et al., 2020).

Alternative scenarios of tourism development

Based on the course of tourism development in the post-pandemic period, we envision three scenarios regarding the role of alternative pathways in tourism development.

The first scenario implies no room for meaningful inclusion of alternative approaches into mainstream tourism development policies. Moreover, the tourism business will remain as usual, mostly ignoring alternative pathways. The second implies the broader adoption of alternatives with a new normal agenda set for tourism. This scenario explores an idealistic alternate future where many useful, but currently alternative, pathways are fully embraced in everyday life and tourism.

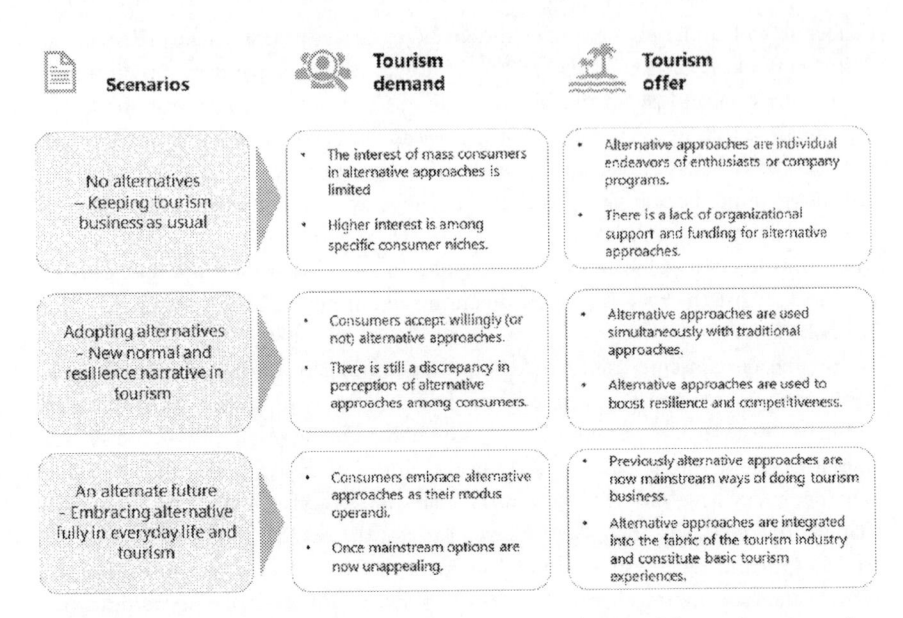

	Scenarios	Tourism demand	Tourism offer

FIGURE 1.1   Main characteristics of scenarios for the inclusion of alternative approaches to tourism devolvement

No alternatives – keeping tourism business as usual by ignoring alternative pathways

Researchers and practitioners in the tourism industry, who are known for their curiosity, pro-activism and agility, began brainstorming possible anti-COVID-19 solutions almost immediately (Dragin et al., 2022). Destination management and marketing organisations have activated their social responsibility mode, urging people to stay at home and dream of a time when things will return to normal (Lyman, 2020). There have been several special issues devoted to this in tourism-related journals, which have asked experts to analyse the harm that has been done to the business and plead for rapid emergency-driven solutions. In essence, these first responses were about lowering the damage as much as possible so that things could go back to normal. Thus, the focus was on the past, not on change.

In this case, the role of alternative approaches in tourism development is mundane and limited. This could be marked as a micro-scale impact of alternative approaches, where the existing alternative initiative belongs to individual tourism providers or tourists. This scenario implies that only a small percentage of consumers are genuinely interested in alternative approaches in the tourism domain. These conditions replicate the pre-pandemic conditions – while recognising a certain shift in consumer preferences toward alternative agendas, the tourism offerings are still limited to specific programs or efforts that are tailored to this shift in demand, but not the mainstream market. For example, biodiesel has become a popular alternative fuel to petroleum products. While more hotels are converting to biodiesel as an eco-friendly alternative fuel, this has not yet become an industry standard, especially in the case of smaller and independently owned hotels. Furthermore, even though consumers are aware of the airline industry's carbon footprint, there is no evidence of a decrease in demand for air travel or a shift to other more sustainable modes of transportation (Kantenbacher et al., 2019). Moreover, many tourists will not pay extra for environmental activities unless they receive some sort of personal benefit in return for their investment (Pulido-Fernández & López-Sánchez, 2016).

In summary, this scenario assumes that the tourism industry will continue to operate as 'business as usual' after COVID-19, implying that alternative approaches to doing business will remain, in many cases, a marketing trend. For example, even during the pandemic, some Mediterranean countries forced reopening despite the existing unfavourable health crisis at that time. Despite the official measures in place, some countries were almost completely open and were welcoming tourists. Accordingly, tourists manifested the same behaviour as before the pandemic, which led to increased profit that 'saved the season', but at the cost of a new spike(s) in COVID-19 infections (Kajosevic, 2021). Furthermore, after looking at the possible influence of the 2020 vacation experience on future traveling, Tauber and Bausch's study (2022) could not find evidence for the pandemic to be a trigger for more sustainable tourism or a long-term game-changer for the future demand.

Adopting alternatives – a new normal and resilience narrative in tourism

Previously, the 9/11 attacks shocked the world, and they badly impacted the travel economy on a global scale. As a result, new safety ramifications were developed (Taylor & Toohey, 2006). These safety regulations were accepted as a new normal for international travel. In light of the significant harm that the prolonged COVID-19 pandemic has done to the tourism sector, businesses and entire destinations had to adapt by embracing and implementing non-traditional approaches in their search for the pandemic response or reset choices. Indeed, a growing number of researchers are now calling for more imaginative and innovative ways to improve the industry's long-term viability (Gössling et al., 2020; Nepal, 2020; Rowen, 2020) that could become a new normal for the entire tourism industry.

Within this scenario, alternative approaches are seen as necessary tools for recovery, healing and boosting resilience (Wen et al., 2021). This scenario implies that things will return to their usual state, or equilibrium, after a period of adversity. This is the underlying assumption of the concept of resilience (Novy, 2021). During the COVID-19 pandemic, the term 'resilience' has become a buzzword for industry insiders and policymakers. Resilience is seen as an ability to manage adversity and is seen as an essential quality for coping with uncertainty, change, stress and shock. However, it is not a new trend. As such, the concept of resilience is in danger of becoming as empty a notion as sustainability (Cretney, 2014;

Sharma et al., 2021). True resilience comes from integration and forming meaningful alliances, both vertical and horizontal (public-and private-community partnerships), since the tourism business could not overcome this global crisis relying on its own devices. Indeed, there is a need for interdisciplinary studies on COVID-19 in, but also beyond, tourism (Wen et al., 2020). For instance, with loosened travel restrictions, cruise ships have returned to Venice some weeks after the Italian government swore that they would not, prompting activist protests and widespread media coverage (Guiffrida, 2021). Finally, the Italian government decided to ban large cruise ships from entering Venice, to strike a balance between environmental and safety concerns and because the city is considered one of the world's most popular tourist destinations. This example may point to a new concept of post-COVID reality that is capable of overcoming long-term hurdles to tourism business viability.

This second scenario entails greater acceptance of alternative approaches in the tourism market, pinpointing the benefits of their use as sometimes more effective or at least most acceptable measures for dealing with post-pandemic turmoil. With the primary goal of coping with the post-pandemic repercussions, the tourism sector, by this scenario, recognises and even promotes the potential of certain alternative approaches and complements them with specialised services and experiences.

Following these instructions provides benefits to both tourists and the tourism industry. This scenario assumes a meso-level impact on tourism, and as such, it must be endorsed and governed by broader industry initiatives and ad hoc public policies. For instance, some successful destinations were quick to adapt to current situations. The best example is Dubai (Aburumman, 2020). Dubai has paved the way for a global tourism recovery due to timely and strict implementation of precautionary health protocol regimes, refocusing on domestic tourism (at the beginning of the pandemic), establishing tourism corridors and travel bubbles, and the use of innovative approaches to track infections, disinfect public spaces, etc. At the same time, several major events held in Dubai have proven to be success stories and beacons for upcoming events, such as the Dubai EXPO 2020 (held during 2021 and 2022). All these measures have been implemented to ensure consumers' and employees' well-being and to provide successful delivery of tourism services and experiences (Dubai Tourism, 2020).

As seen from the example of Dubai, COVID-19 further increased the dependency of the industry on technological solutions (Bas & Sivaprasad, 2021). Some other destinations, such as South Korea or Singapore, managed to rapidly 'flatten the curve' without shutting down their economy or its borders, with the help of smart technologies and alternative technology innovations (Choi et al., 2021; Radojević et al., 2020). Increased investment in alternative technological solutions due to pandemics could even create a competitive advantage for some destinations. For example, media coverage of the innovative use of robots or virtual reality in China created an image of the technological supremacy of the country, even though the first outbreak of the virus occurred in Wuhan (Chen et al., 2022).

An alternate future – embracing alternatives fully in everyday life and tourism

The first two scenarios are rooted in the assumption that things should go back to normal after a period of adversity caused by the pandemic (Cretney, 2014). These approaches bring the danger of bouncing back to old, unsustainable habits (Novy, 2021) that are rooted in the fabric of modern, largely unsustainable tourism (Fletcher et al., 2021; Ioannides & Gyimóthy, 2020). However, the current economic slump caused by the pandemic is unusual, as it affects everyone on every level and/or from every area (regulation, economic, social, physical and psychological) (Lichfield, 2020), thus creating a common challenge for all stakeholders. In other words, the gravity of the current situation allows for speculations that more structural changes would happen in the tourism industry, including in the everyday life of consumers.

The third scenario presents a somewhat utopian approach that implies an evolutionary leap forward in which the pandemic raises worldwide awareness (Galvani et al., 2020). As a natural continuation of customers' everyday life aims, the mass existence of different arising alternative lifestyles results in a spillover effect on tourism experiences (Lengyel, 2018; Lew, 2020; Stankov et al., 2020). In this case, the current alternative approaches become new prominent public discourses.

In this scenario, customers can see through the industry's key weaknesses (Dodds & Butler, 2019). Tourists, for example, might be tempted to avoid unnecessary travel in the aftermath of a pandemic (Cahyanto et al., 2016) not only out of concern for their safety but also out of a genuine desire to support long-term business models based on sustainability principles (Errmann et al., 2021). This viewpoint is consistent with the concept of 'compassionate tourism' (Stankov et al., 2020; Weaver & Jin, 2016) and supports voices inside the tourism industry calling for more conscious travel (Zannier, 2021). However, this scenario leaves an opportunity for the employment of so-called mastery marketing tactics (Stankov & Gretzel, 2021) in which alternative approaches are provided to those explicitly interested in them.

Thus, this approach appoints consumers as major agents of change. For instance, among numerous studies, Stankov et al. (2020) focused on (more) mindful tourists as a driver of mindful change for the tourism industry in the pandemic's aftermath. Mindfulness practices in tourism were portrayed as an opportunity for the industry to take advantage of the mindfulness trend in Western societies (Gotojones, 2013) that was amplified by COVID-19. In particular, Stankov et al. (2020) highlighted the significant potential of mindfulness to facilitate a short-term, but also a long-term transformational effect, on the tourism industry. A follow-up paper (Stankov & Filimonau, 2021) provided an in-depth discussion of the efficacy of mindfulness as an immediate coping strategy during the pandemic and elaborates on how the mindfulness movement could be positioned within the dynamics of tourism development in a post-pandemic future. This was possible for the authors, as the course of events facilitated prolific academic and industry research demonstrating the benefits of mindfulness-based approaches during the pandemic. For example, mindfulness practices were shown to be beneficial in providing mental relief, increasing subjective well-being during lockdowns, and improving resilience at work (Chapple, 2020; Roemer et al., 2021; Zhu et al., 2021). This vision identifies mindful consumer movement as a possibility to create a support network that nurtures the whole tourism ecosystem for the benefit of all, and it is complementary with the vision where alternative approaches of performing tourism business are in line with the rising momentum of alternative consumer lifestyle (Wen et al., 2020).

Concluding remarks

Many anti-COVID measures that were required to protect public health were, in many aspects, opposed to previous progress achieved in sustainability initiatives and the promotion of alternative solutions, such as reduced waste (e.g., increased use of single-use plastic, waste produced by personal protective equipment, and masks), rational water use (e.g., increased hygiene needs), or efficient business operation (e.g., decreased occupation rates to provide physical distance or the decrease in using public transport). At the same time, pandemic restrictions have induced some more favourable behaviours, such as responsible behaviour triggered and reinforced by the pandemic (for example, shifting preferences toward greener options) (Eichelberger et al., 2021).

Finally, a crisis like this requires wider advocacy for more knowledge and awareness. The pandemic, as a global phenomenon, has promoted the global consciousness that is essential for adopting alternative and more sustainable practices in the daily lives of individuals and cultures across the globe (Galvani et al., 2020; Wen et al., 2020)

References

Aburumman, A.A. (2020). COVID-19 Impact and Survival Strategy in Business Tourism Market: The Example of the UAE MICE Industry. *Humanities and Social Sciences Communications*, 7(1), 1–11. DOI: 10.1057/s41599-020-00630-8

Ateljevic, I. (2020). Transforming the (Tourism) World for Good and (re)generating the Potential 'New Normal.' *Tourism Geographies*, 1–9. DOI: 10.1080/14616688.2020.1759134

Bas, T., & Sivaprasad, S. (2021). COVID-19 and Implications for Future Trends in the UK Travel and Tourism Sector (SSRN Scholarly Paper ID 3623404). *Social Science Research Network*. DOI: 10.2139/ssrn.3623404

Becker, E. (2020). *How Hard will the Coronavirus Hit the Travel Industry?* www.nationalgeographic.com/travel/2020/04/how-coronavirus-is-impacting-the-travel-industry/

Cahyanto, I., Wiblishauser, M., Pennington-Gray, L., & Schroeder, A. (2016). The Dynamics of Travel Avoidance: The Case of Ebola in the U.S. *Tourism Management Perspectives*, 20, 195–203. DOI: 10.1016/j.tmp.2016.09.004

Chang, C.-L., McAleer, M., & Ramos, V. (2020). A Charter for Sustainable Tourism after COVID-19. *Sustainability*, 12(9), 3671–3671. DOI: 10.3390/su12093671

Chapple, C. (2020). *Downloads of Top English-Language Mental Wellness Apps Surged by 2 Million in April Amid COVID-19 Pandemic.* https://sensortower.com/blog/top-mental-wellness-apps-april-2020-downloads

Chen, H., Huang, X., & Li, Z. (2022). A Content Analysis of Chinese News Coverage on COVID-19 and Tourism. *Current Issues in Tourism, 25*(2), 198–205. DOI: 10.1080/13683500.2020.1763269

Choi, J., Lee, S., & Jamal, T. (2021). Smart Korea: Governance for Smart Justice during a Global Pandemic. *Journal of Sustainable Tourism, 29*(2–3), 541–550. DOI: 10.1080/09669582.2020.1777143

Cretney, R. (2014). Resilience for Whom? Emerging Critical Geographies of Socio-ecological Resilience. *Geography Compass, 8*(9), 627–640. DOI: 10.1111/gec3.12154

Dodds, R., & Butler, R. (2019). The Phenomena of Overtourism: A Review. *International Journal of Tourism Cities, 5*(4), 519–528. DOI: 10.1108/IJTC-06-2019-0090

Dragin, A., Mijatov, M., Majstorovic, N., Janicic, B., & Korovljev, D. (2022). COVID-19 Pandemic and Young Tourists' Travel Risk Perceptions: Impacts on Travel Restrictions (Local and International) and Tourism. In S.D. Brunn & D. Gilbreath (Eds.), *COVID-19 and a World of Ad Hoc Geographies.* Cham: Springer.

Dubai Tourism. (2020). *Dubai Tourism Annual Visitor Report 2020.* https://dubaitourism.getbynder.com/m/306b946f59b7d9ba/original/DTCM_Annual_Visitors_Report_2020.pdf

Dwyer, L., Peter, F., & Dwyer, W. (2010). *Tourism Economics and Policy.* Bristol: Channel View Publications.

Eichelberger, S., Heigl, M., Peters, M., & Pikkemaat, B. (2021). Exploring the Role of Tourists: Responsible Behavior Triggered by the COVID-19 Pandemic. *Sustainability, 13*(11), 5774. DOI: 10.3390/su13115774

Errmann, A., Kim, J., Lee, D.C., Seo, Y., Lee, J., & Kim, S.S. (2021). Mindfulness and Pro-Environmental Hotel Preference. *Annals of Tourism Research, 90*, 103263. DOI: 10.1016/j.annals.2021.103263

European Travel Commission. (2021). *European Tourism: Trends & Prospects (Q2/2021).* https://etc-corporate.org/uploads/2021/07/ETC_Quarterly_Report-Q2_2021.pdf

Fletcher, R., Blanco-Romero, A., Blázquez-Salom, M., Cañada, E., Murray Mas, I., & Sekulova, F. (2021). Pathways to Post-capitalist Tourism. *Tourism Geographies*, 1–22. DOI: 10.1080/14616688.2021.1965202

Galvani, A., Lew, A.A., & Perez, M.S. (2020). COVID-19 is Expanding Global Consciousness and the Sustainability of Travel and Tourism. *Tourism Geographies, 22*(3), 567–576. DOI: 10.1080/14616688.2020.1760924

Gössling, S., Scott, D., & Hall, C.M. (2020). Pandemics, Tourism and Global Change: A Rapid Assessment of COVID-19. *Journal of Sustainable Tourism*, 1–20. DOI: 10.1080/09669582.2020.1758708

Gotojones, C. (2013). Zombie Apocalypse as Mindfulness Manifesto (after Žižek). *Postmodern Culture, 24*(1). DOI: 10.1353/pmc.2013.0062

Guiffrida, A. (2021). *'We Were Deceived': Hundreds Protest in Venice at Return of Giant Cruise Ships.* www.theguardian.com/world/2021/jun/05/angry-protests-in-venice-at-shock-return-of-cruise-ships

Harris, J. (2020). Coronavirus Means We Really Are, Finally, All in This Together. *The Guardian.* www.theguardian.com/commentisfree/2020/mar/29/coronavirus-means-we-really-are-finally-all-in-this-together

Hideg, M. (2020). The Coronavirus Pandemic: A Post-Normal Crisis that Generates Possible Scenarios for Structural Changes of the Society: the Romania Case. *Revista de Asistență Socială, XIX*(4), 11–20.

Higgins-Desbiolles, F. (2021). The 'War Over Tourism': Challenges to Sustainable Tourism in the Tourism Academy after COVID-19. *Journal of Sustainable Tourism, 29*(4), 551–569. DOI: 10.1080/09669582.2020.1803334

Ioannides, D., & Gyimóthy, S. (2020). The COVID-19 Crisis as an Opportunity for Escaping the Unsustainable Global Tourism Path. *Tourism Geographies, 22*(3), 624–632. DOI: 10.1080/14616688.2020.1763445

Jahel, C., Bourgeois, R., Pesche, D., de Lattre-Gasquet, M., & Delay, E. (2021). Has the COVID-19 Crisis Changed Our Relationship to the Future? *Futures & Foresight Science, 3*(2), e75. DOI: 10.1002/ffo2.75

Kajosevic, S. (2021, July 29). Montenegro Marks Rise in COVID-19 Cases as Tourists Arrive. *Balkan Insight.* https://balkaninsight.com/2021/07/29/montenegro-marks-rise-in-covid-19-cases-as-tourists-arrive/

Kantenbacher, J., Hanna, P., Miller, G., Scarles, C., & Yang, J. (2019). Consumer Priorities: What Would People Sacrifice in Order to Fly on Holidays? *Journal of Sustainable Tourism, 27*(2), 207–222. DOI: 10.1080/09669582.2017.1409230

Kock, F., Nørfelt, A., Josiassen, A., Assaf, A.G., & Tsionas, M.G. (2020). Understanding the COVID-19 Tourist Psyche: The Evolutionary Tourism Paradigm. *Annals of Tourism Research, 85*, 103053. DOI: 10.1016/j.annals.2020.103053

Lengyel, A. (2018). *Spatial Aspects of Sustainablity Mindfulness and Tourism* (Ph. D. thesis, Szent Istvan University, 2018).

Lew, A.A. (2020). The Global Consciousness Path to Sustainable Tourism: A Perspective Paper. *Tourism Review, 75*(1), 69–75. DOI: 10.1108/TR-07-2019-0291

Lew, A.A., Cheer, J.M., Haywood, M., Brouder, P., & Salazar, N.B. (2020). Visions of Travel and Tourism after the Global COVID-19 Transformation of 2020. *Tourism Geographies, 22*(3), 455–466. DOI: 10.1080/14616688.2020.1770326

Lichfield, G. (2020). *We're Not Going Back to Normal.* www.technologyreview.com/2020/03/17/905264/coronavirus-pandemic-social-distancing-18-months/

Lyman, C. (2020). *Here's How Tourism Marketers Can Gear Up For Reopening.* www.forbes.com/sites/forbesagencycouncil/2020/05/07/heres-how-tourism-marketers-can-gear-up-for-reopening/#548dc4815175

Nepal, S.K. (2020). Travel and Tourism after COVID-19 – Business as Usual or Opportunity to Reset? DOI: 10.1080/14616688.2020.1760926

Novy, J. (2021). Amsterdam is Laying Down a Model for What Tourism Should Look Like after COVID. *The Conversation.* http://theconversation.com/amsterdam-is-laying-down-a-model-for-what-tourism-should-look-like-after-covid-162271

Pulido-Fernández, J., & López-Sánchez, Y. (2016). Are Tourists Really Willing to Pay More for Sustainable Destinations? *Sustainability, 8*(12), 1240–1240. DOI: 10.3390/su8121240

Radojević, B., Lazić, L., & Cimbaljević, M. (2020). Rescaling Smart Destinations: The Growing Importance of Smart Geospatial Services during and after COVID-19 Pandemic. *Geographica Pannonica, 24*, 221–228. DOI: 10.5937/gp24-28009

Roemer, A., Sutton, A., & Medvedev, O.N. (2021). The Role of Dispositional Mindfulness in Employee Readiness for Change during the COVID-19 Pandemic. *Journal of Organizational Change Management.* DOI: 10.1108/JOCM-10-2020-0323

Rowen, I. (2020). The Transformational Festival as a Subversive Toolbox for a Transformed Tourism: Lessons from Burning Man for a COVID-19 World. *Tourism Geographies,* 1–8. DOI: 10.1080/14616688.2020.1759132

Sharma, G.D., Thomas, A., & Paul, J. (2021). Reviving Tourism Industry Post-COVID-19: A Resilience-based Framework. *Tourism Management Perspectives, 37*, 100786. DOI: 10.1016/j.tmp.2020.100786

Sigala, M. (2020). Tourism and COVID-19: Impacts and Implications for Advancing and Resetting Industry and Research. *Journal of Business Research*, *117*, 312–321. DOI: 10.1016/j.jbusres.2020.06.015

Stankov, U., & Filimonau, V. (2021). Here and Now – The Role of Mindfulness in Post-pandemic Tourism. *Tourism Geographies*, 1–16. DOI: 10.1080/14616688.2021.2021978

Stankov, U., & Gretzel, U. (2021). Digital Well-being in the Tourism Domain: Mapping New Roles and Responsibilities. *Information Technology & Tourism*, *23*(1), 5–17. DOI: 10.1007/s40558-021-00197-3

Stankov, U., Filimonau, V., & Vujičić, M.D. (2020). A Mindful Shift: An Opportunity for Mindfulness-driven Tourism in a Post-pandemic World. *Tourism Geographies*, *22*(3), 703–712. DOI: 10.1080/14616688.2020.1768432

Tauber, V., & Bausch, T. (2022). Will COVID-19 Boost Sustainable Tourism: Wishful Thinking or Reality? *Sustainability (Switzerland)*, *14*(3). DOI: 10.3390/su14031686

Taylor, T., & Toohey, K. (2006). Impacts of Terrorism-related Safety and Security Measures at a Major Sport Event. *Event Management*, *9*(4), 199–209. DOI: 10.3727/152599506776771544

Vujičić, M.D., Kennell, J., Morrison, A., Filimonau, V., Štajner Papuga, I., Stankov, U., & Vasiljević, D.A. (2020). Fuzzy Modelling of Tourist Motivation: An Age-Related Model for Sustainable, Multi-Attraction, Urban Destinations. *Sustainability*, *12*(20), 8698. DOI: 10.3390/su12208698

Weaver, D.B., & Jin, X. (2016). Compassion as a Neglected Motivator for Sustainable Tourism. *Journal of Sustainable Tourism*, *24*(5), 657–672. DOI: 10.1080/09669582.2015.1101130

Wen, J., Kozak, M., Yang, S., & Liu, F. (2020). COVID-19: Potential Effects on Chinese Citizens' Lifestyle and Travel. *Tourism Review*, *76*(1), 74–87. DOI: 10.1108/TR-03-2020-0110

Wen, J., Wang, W., Kozak, M., Liu, X., & Hou, H. (2021). Many Brains are Better than One: The Importance of Interdisciplinary Studies on COVID-19 in and beyond Tourism. *Tourism Recreation Research*, *46*(2), 310–313. DOI: 10.1080/02508281.2020.1761120

Zannier, A. (2021, March 23). *How to Become a More Conscious Traveler.* https://csq.com/2021/03/arnaud-zannier-how-to-become-a-more-conscious-traveler/

Zhu, J.L., Schülke, R., Vatansever, D., Xi, D., Yan, J., Zhao, H., Xie, X., Feng, J., Chen, M.Y., Sahakian, B.J., & Wang, S. (2021). Mindfulness Practice for Protecting Mental Health during the COVID-19 Pandemic. *Translational Psychiatry*, *11*(1), 1–11. DOI: 10.1038/s41398-021-01459-8

2

CRISIS MANAGEMENT

Managing tourism in the face of adversity

Peter Vlachos

Introduction

Over three and a half thousand years ago, a devastating volcanic eruption occurred in the eastern Mediterranean ocean (Friedrich et al., 2006). At the time, it must have seemed unimaginable that centuries later the same location, the Aegean island of Santorini (Thera), would become one of the most popular tourist destinations in the world. Such is the long-standing complex relationship between disasters and tourism. Pforr and Hosie (2009) suggest a risk-based approach in which crisis is inevitable for tourism organisations; the question is when, where and how the crisis will occur.

Baggio and Baggio (2020) note that whilst modelling and simulations in the tourism and hospitality industries may be useful for projecting demand and planning supply, these management techniques have more limited application in disaster situations:

> Problems can be defined on a continuum from simple to complicated to complex or *wicked*, those that are difficult or impossible to solve because of incomplete, contradictory or changing requirements, or situations that are often difficult to recognise.
>
> *(Baggio & Baggio, 2020:14)*

Thus, at the core of crisis management in the tourism industry are the classic techniques of risk management, namely, risk identification, risk assessment, and risk mitigation. However, in recent years, up until the COVID-19 pandemic, the main emphasis in tourism research and tourism policy was on the consumption-side themes of sustainability and over-tourism.

Crisis management in the face of natural or human-made disasters in recent decades has received relatively little systemic analysis. The extended period of

DOI: 10.4324/9781003295839-4

global economic growth following the financial downturn of the late 2000s helped to unleash tourism demand in eastern Europe, China and other developing nations that pointed to an upward trajectory of profitable, environmentally sustainable, and socially responsible tourism management.

Natural or human-made crises?

The COVID-19 pandemic reminded us how natural phenomena and human interventions are closely intertwined. Global warming is a natural disaster when the causal factors are so closely related to human activity. Nonetheless, it is useful to identify some broad categories to help organise our analysis.

Human-made disasters and crisis situations can be driven by economic factors (domestic or international), political factors (domestic or international), or overlapping factors that can lead to, for example, terrorism. The terrorist attacks in Manchester, UK (Corbet et al., 2019), and Nice, France (Schmude et al., 2020), were detrimental, at least in the short term, to those cities' tourism reputations. We may also add here disasters that are the result of human error, for example, mechanical failure (e.g. Lim, 2017).

Meanwhile, natural disasters and crisis situations can arise from a variety of elements, including water disasters (e.g., floods, tsunamis), earthquakes, weather (e.g., hurricanes), or communicable diseases. Such natural phenomena are sometimes periodic, if not quite predictably cyclical. Greece, for example, is one of many tourism-reliant destinations that has learnt to live with the threat of earthquakes. The evolving relationship between disasters and tourism is similarly reflected elsewhere in the world: for example, the island of Hawaii is essentially the tip of a volcano in the midst of the Pacific Ocean that was formerly used as a leper colony. Pompeii, again, a volcano that caused notable disruption, is now part of the historic touristic aura of modern Italy. The debilitating impact of Hurricane Katrina on New Orleans, USA, in 2005 was devastating for the city's festival and jazz tourism (Chacko & Marcell, 2008). The recovery continues over a decade and a half later (Gotham & Irvin, 2018).

More recently, however, two strands of incidents have precipitated increased attention to disasters and crises in tourism and tourism management's specific and collective responses.

One phenomenon is that of widespread, communicable diseases such as SARS and avian flu (Kuo et al., 2008), Ebola (Maphanga & Henama, 2019), and most recently Coronavirus. The inherent nature of the globalised mass tourism industry creates contained environments like airplanes, hotels, cruise ships and large-scale events such as sports and music where serious, contagious diseases can spread.

'Over-tourism' is not a disaster or crisis in itself, but rather the human-made consequence of strategic marketing and infrastructure miscalculations that result in an excess of demand over supply. The circumstances of over-tourism, however, can in turn create disaster-prone conditions.

Economic downturns in the modern era have also affected the travel and tourism industries (Papatheodorou et al., 2010):

1960s – buoyant Baby Boomer era
Early 1970s – global oil crisis
Early 1980s – recession
Late 1980s – stock market crash, e.g., 1987 'Black Monday'
Early 1990s – recession, various national banking crises
1997 – Asian financial crisis
Late 2000s – global recession
2020 ongoing – COVID-instigated global recession

Other than short-lived declines in 2003 and 2009, the international tourism industry not only has weathered natural disasters and economic and political turmoil, but also demonstrated a consistently upward growth trajectory. In 1950, there were 25 million international tourism arrivals globally; by the end of 2019, this figure had reached nearly 1.5 billion, a growth of 57 times (UNWTO, 2021). Increases in global wealth, leisure time, and affordability, coupled with technological innovation, have enabled the tourism industry to expand and adapt despite these challenges.

Etymologies and definitions

The word 'disaster' has its origins in the Latin 'dis-' (out of place) and Greek 'astro' (star) (Merriam Webster, 2020a), in other words, a situation in which the stars have fallen out of place and thus the world in disarray. This etymology reflects the notion of being out of place or a situation that is ill-fated. The related word 'catastrophe' denotes a similar 'downward spiral' of fate. In the ancient world, there seems to have been little scope for crisis 'management' in the face of the twofold formidable forces of nature and fate. 'Disaster' implies disorder and upheaval in the face of our evolutionary presumption that order and continuity are the natural state of the world.

In modern times, we tend to use the terms 'disaster' and 'crisis' almost interchangeably; however, these two concepts are distinct and the nuanced differences in meaning are useful for the present discussion. 'Crisis' (from the Greek 'krisis', meaning 'turning point') marks the point where decisions and judgements are needed to respond to a sudden change (Merriam Webster, 2020b). The point in question may refer to a geographic, physical, temporal, economic or strategic node. An overlap of several of these parameters may result in more intense crisis situations. The main emphasis here is that the 'crisis' requires an urgent, directional decision in response to the new scenario conditions. The 'krisi' is like a fork in the road where the decision maker is forced to make a decision because the *status quo* is no longer tenable.

In short, the 'disaster' is the incident and the 'crisis' is the decision vacuum that tourism businesses, agencies and policy-makers need to fill.

Scale of crisis

The COVID-19 experience has forced us to think more closely about the scale, scope and intensity of crisis situations. In recent years, we have seen these various scales played out in the manner in which populations and governments responded to the COVID-19 challenge, for example, with the increased awareness of the distinctions regarding endemic, epidemic and pandemic health.

Ripple effects in society may be seen from diseases that are:

- Endemic (local, widespread, contained)
- Epidemic (regional, widespread, contained)
- Pandemic (exponential growth, international, out-of-control)

Whilst global agencies and the scientific community may try to establish universally understood definitions and measures, there are also significant political and legal implications for crisis management. Who gets to decide or declare when a 'disaster' has occurred and whether 'crisis' management protocols should now apply? Political leaders may have the legal authority and power to declare a *public* emergency, disaster or crisis based on established legislation at the local, regional or national level. Supra-national declarations (e.g., by the EU or WHO) rely on largely voluntary international agreements.

Crisis or calm? Is there a 'natural' state of the tourism industry?

Classical economics presumes market equilibrium, where there is an 'invisible hand of the market' (Smith, 1950). Rational strategic theory, such as Porter's (1980) 'five forces', treat disasters and the crises that emanate as externalities. On the other hand, theories of *continuous change* suggest that in the modern world, there can be no long-lasting equilibrium and that businesses and industries are subject to constantly evolving conditions, a state of turmoil where day-to-day management consists of responding to constantly changing circumstances, whether ongoing competitively or technologically driven challenges, or more overt emergencies and crises.

An alternative to these is presented by the 'punctuated equilibrium' model of change, which is an in-between concept described as when 'long periods of small, incremental change are interrupted by brief periods of discontinuous, radical change' (Brown & Eisenhardt, 1997:1). On the other hand, change can instead be Episodic (i.e., occasional, radical change) (Weick & Quinn, 1999).

Based on the escalating level of severity, we can now establish a more detailed and nuanced explication of disaster and crisis phases:

The temporal component is a significant one. Small tourism firms may be more entrepreneurial in their response to periods of crisis compared to larger firms (Dahles & Susilowati, 2015). The present author, for example, observed how

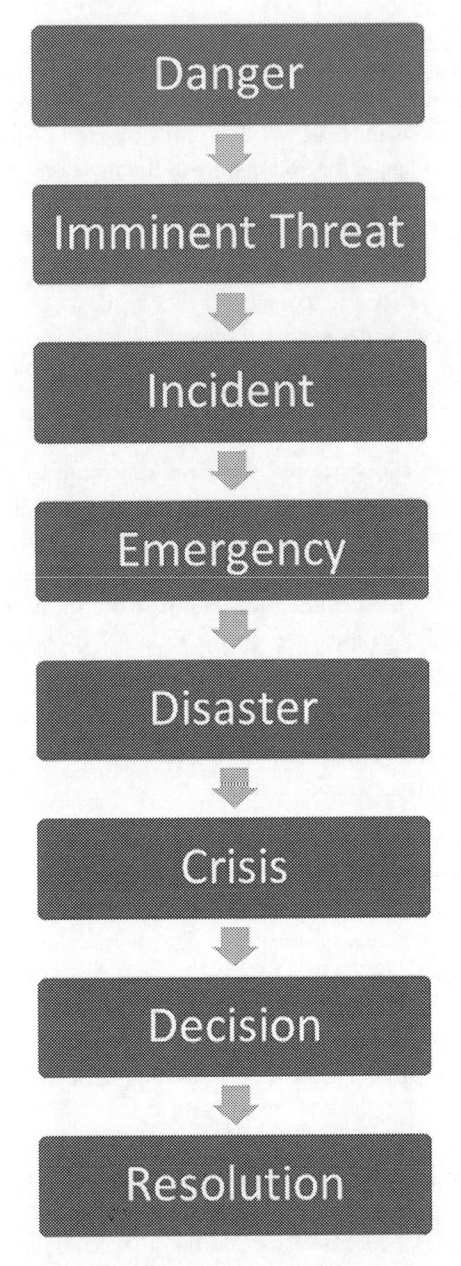

FIGURE 2.1 Eight phases of disaster and crisis management

smaller hotels in Brighton, England were able to re-orient themselves to accommodate quarantining people and key workers, whereas larger hotels in Penang, Malaysia and Singapore decided to shut entirely and use the periods of COVID travel restrictions to carry out refurbishment works.

Crisis management and risk management

'Crisis' relates to the decision-making point when previously assessed risk scenarios have been activated. Classical risk management strategy involves risk assessment (likelihood, severity) and risk response (proceed, mitigate, avoid). The sequence of risk management is well established in the literature (see e.g. AICST, 2006):

1 Prevention/Mitigation
2 Preparedness
3 Response
4 Recovery

'Resilience' refers to an organisation's capacity to withstand and work through a crisis situation. As we have noted during the COVID-19 lockdowns, different firms have demonstrated differing strategic responses and capacities to respond, some with more success than others.

The crisis response management literature paints a generally defensive picture of crisis situations with two main areas of focus. The first is inward-facing, aimed at internal business continuity. The second is outward facing, whereby much attention is given to organisational image and reputational damage containment.

'Disaster tourism'?

As we have noted earlier, the term 'disaster' in conjunction with tourism may take on multiple meanings. The 'disaster' in question may refer to unforeseen and threatening environmental or social conditions that threaten lives, well-being, or at least the normal activities of visitors, tourists and host communities. These disasters can have scales of:

- Temporal duration
- Geographic proximity
- Intensity and severity of impacts (e.g., economic, environmental, social)
- Political and legal reach
- Number of people affected

Meanwhile, the notion of danger that is typically associated with disasters in itself is, if in moderation, not necessarily a bad thing for the tourism industry. For example, niche tourism sectors, such as adventure tourism (Wang et al., 2019) and tourism in climatically extreme conditions, such as Nordic tourism (Vlachos, 2022) or desert tourism (Kohl, 2002) all incorporate an element of danger.

The morbid curiosity of attendees at some spectator sporting events, such as bullfighting or high-speed automobile racing, is an amplified expression of the apparently inherent human desire for a taste of the unknown or the perilous, albeit from a safe distance. Hurricane Katrina displaced music tourism with 'disaster landscape' tourism (Miller, 2008).

I am not suggesting here that human beings travel or seek touristic experiences with the intention of putting themselves at personal risk. To venture into foreign lands and thereby become a foreigner inevitably carries a certain degree of risk, if only due to being seen as a potentially threatening outsider or simply lacking local knowledge to deal with local circumstances.

Navigating a local rail or river crossing may be a minor inconvenience for a native person with local knowledge; the same situation may easily transform into an accident or disaster for the less-knowing tourist.

There is a further dimension to the concept of 'disaster' in relation to tourism. Here I wish to draw attention to 'disaster' not so much in relation to the aforementioned conditions but rather as a content (consumable product). There is a growing academic interest in the fascinating field of 'dark tourism'. (Stone et al., 2018). In dark tourism, the sites of previous disasters become in themselves sites of touristic interest or even tourist destinations in their own right. Examples include battlefield tourism, political tourism (e.g., Holocaust memorials, Communist monuments, ground zero of the 9/11 attacks), as well as visiting environmental disaster sites like those of hurricanes (e.g., Katrina), climate change (e.g., iceberg melting viewing expeditions), or human-made disasters (e.g., Grenfell tower apartment fire in London).

Conclusion

The aim of this chapter has been to unpack the conceptual complexities with regard to the notions of 'disaster' and 'crisis' as applied to tourism management. We noted that 'disaster' is a highly multi-faceted concept that incorporates a wide range of human-made and natural phenomena with varying kinds and scales of impacts. Crisis response similarly involves a variety of strategies and tactics. Disasters are generally considered to impart a negative influence on tourism; however, we have also demonstrated how, especially with the passage of time, disasters can be subverted, eventually even becoming drivers of tourism.

Our fragile ecosphere, however, is a constant reminder that neither the planet nor humanity has inexhaustible capacity or resources to deal with the seemingly ever-increasing number of serious disasters, catastrophes and crises, whether naturally triggered or human-made.

References

Albrecht, J.N. (Ed.). (2016). *Visitor Management in Tourist Destinations* (Vol. 3). Wallingford: CABI.

Ast, S.A. (2016). *Managing Crises Overseas*. Boca Raton: CRC Press.

Baggio, J.A., & Baggio, R. (2020). Modelling and Simulations for Tourism and Hospitality. In *Modelling and Simulations for Tourism and Hospitality*. Bristol: Channel View Publications.

Brown, S.L., & Eisenhardt, K.M. (1997). The Art of Continuous Change: Linking Complexity Theory and Time-Paced Evolution in Relentlessly Shifting Organizations. *Administrative Science Quarterly, 42*(1), 1–34. DOI: 10.2307/2393807

Chacko, H.E., & Marcell, M.H. (2008). Repositioning a Tourism Destination: The Case of New Orleans after Hurricane Katrina. *Journal of Travel & Tourism Marketing, 23*(2–4), 223–235.

Corbet, S., O'Connell, J.F., Efthymiou, M., Guiomard, C., & Lucey, B. (2019). The impact of terrorism on European tourism. *Annals of Tourism Research, 75*, 1–17.

Dahles, H., & Susilowati, T.P. (2015). Business Resilience in Times of Growth and Crisis. *Annals of Tourism Research, 51*, 34–50.

Friedrich, W.L., Kromer, B., Friedrich, M., Heinemeier, J., Pfeiffer, T., & Talamo, S. (2006). Santorini Eruption Radiocarbon Dated to 1627–1600 BC. *Science, 312*(5773), 548–548.

Gotham, K.F., & Irvin, C. (2018). Revitalizing the Damaged Brand. In M. Karavatzis, M. Giovanadri, & M. Lichrou (Eds.), *Inclusive Place Branding: Critical Perspectives on Theory and Practice*. London: Routledge.

Kohl, I. (2002). The Lure of the Sahara: Implications of Libya's Desert Tourism. *Journal of Libyan Studies, 3*(2), 56–69.

Kuo, H.I., Chen, C.C., Tseng, W.C., Ju, L.F., & Huang, B.W. (2008). Assessing Impacts of SARS and Avian Flu on International Tourism Demand to Asia. *Tourism Management, 29*(5), 917–928.

Lim, W.M. (2017). Restoring Tourist Confidence and Travel Intentions after Disasters: Some Insights from a Rejoinder to a Series of Unfortunate Events in Malaysian Tourism. *Current Issues in Tourism, 20*(1), 38–42.

Maphanga, P.M., & Henama, U.S. (2019). The Tourism Impact of Ebola in Africa: Lessons on Crisis Management. *African Journal of Hospitality, Tourism and Leisure, 8*(3), 1–13.

Merriam-Webster.com (2020a). Disaster. *Dictionary, Merriam-Webster*. www.merriam-webster. com/dictionary/disaster. Accessed 20 February 2022.

Merriam-Webster.com (2020b). Crisis. *Dictionary, Merriam-Webster*. www.merriam-webster. com/dictionary/crisis. Accessed 20 February 2022.

Miller, D. (2008). Disaster tourism and disaster landscape attractions after Hurricane Katrina: An auto-ethnographic journey. *International Journal of Culture, Tourism and Hospitality Research, 2*(2), 115–131.

Papatheodorou, A., Rosselló, J., & Xiao, H. (2010). Global Economic Crisis and Tourism: Consequences and Perspectives. *Journal of Travel Research, 49*(1), 39–45.

Pforr, C., & Hosie, P. (2009). *Beating the Odds: Crisis Management in the Tourism Industry*. London: Routledge.

Porter, M.E. (1980). *Competitive Strategy: Techniques for Analyzing Industries and Competitors*. New York: The Free Press.

Santana, G. (2004). Crisis Management and Tourism: Beyond the Rhetoric. *Journal of Travel & Tourism Marketing, 15*(4), 299–321.

Schmude, J., Karl, M., & Weber, F. (2020). Tourism and Terrorism: Economic Impact of Terrorist Attacks on the Tourism Industry. The Example of the Destination of Paris. *Zeitschrift für Wirtschaftsgeographie, 64*(2), 88–102.

Smith, A. (1950). *An Inquiry into the Nature and Causes of the Wealth of Nations*. London: Edwin Cannan, Methuen & Company.

Stone, P.R., Hartmann, R., Seaton, A.V., Sharpley, R., & White, L. (Eds.). (2018). *The Palgrave Handbook of Dark Tourism Studies* (pp. 335–354). London: Palgrave Macmillan.

United Nations World Tourism Organisation (2021). *The Economic Contribution of Tourism and the Impact of COVID-19*. Madrid: UNWTO.

Vlachos, P. (2022). Nordic Tourism. In D. Buhalis (Ed.), *Encyclopedia of Tourism Management and Marketing*. Cheltenham: Edward Elgar Publishing.

Wang, J., Liu-Lastres, B., Ritchie, B.W., & Pan, D.Z. (2019). Risk Reduction and Adventure Tourism Safety: An Extension of the Risk Perception Attitude Framework (RPAF). *Tourism Management, 74*, 247–257.

Weick, K.E., & Quinn, R.E. (1999). Organizational Change and Development. *Annual Review of Psychology, 50*(1), 361–386.

3

DESTINATION RECOVERY

Recovery of the post-pandemic tourism destination economy

Charles Bladen and Carol Callinan

Introduction

Much recent research has attempted to analyse the effects of the 2020–21 COVID-19 pandemic on the travel and tourism industries, with proposals to facilitate their recovery. It is proposed that tourism destination marketing should be viewed from the perspective of co-production between tourists, travellers and destination marketing agencies and other stakeholders. It is also suggested that particular attention is paid to destination marketing using semiotics, nudge theory and customer knowing.

Tourism effects of the COVID-19 pandemic

Researchers such as Yeh (2021) group the 2020–21 COVID-19 pandemic and its associated impacts on tourism together with disasters such as tsunamis, earthquakes and terrorism. However, there is wide consensus that the pandemic has possibly much further reaching, longer term and more substantial impacts on the global industry than these more local occurrences.

The effects of the pandemic in relation to tourism have been wide reaching, with tourism representing 10% of the global GDP and over 320 million jobs (Behsudi, 2020). It is proposed that following lockdowns and travel restrictions around the world, a return to tourism levels of 2019 is not expected until 2023 (Behsudi, 2020). Levels of job losses and other negative financial consequences depend on how much a country relies on tourism as a contributor to its GDP. Babii and Nadeem (2021) proposed that tourism remained one of the sectors to be hardest hit by the pandemic, particularly in the Asia-Pacific region and the Western hemisphere.

Travel restrictions were imposed by over 40 countries at some point following March 2020. There remains much local variation between countries regarding

DOI: 10.4324/9781003295839-5

approaches to control the spread of the coronavirus, both by tourists and in destination communities. There are several reasons for disparities, relating mainly to the once-in-a-lifetime occurrence of pandemics, the relative emphasis of governments to apply limited scientific data, to management controls such as travel bans and community lockdowns, as well as approaches such as 'zero-COVID' policies, versus attempts to achieve 'herd immunity'.

Pandemics do not occur often, and previous pandemic playbooks provide limited guidance to governments, as the last occurrence of similar magnitude was the 1918 influenza pandemic, which killed 50 million people worldwide. It is also tempting to compare the COVID-19 pandemic to the 2002–2003 SARS outbreak, an overreaction to which disrupted tourism, mainly in its South-East Asian catchment (McKercher & Chon, 2004). However, with little more than 8000 cases, 11% of which resulted in reported fatalities, the COVID-19 global infection rate of 521 million and a current death toll of 6.26 million suggest that any direct comparison is also largely inconsequential.

A range of different approaches have been adopted in countries around the world as a response to the pandemic. Some countries, such as the United Kingdom, introduced full lockdown measures as a response to increasing infection rates, whilst others recommended restrictions (e.g., Sweden). A reduction in travel was observed and tracked (Dunford et al., 2020). Many countries limited or completely prohibited visitors from other countries (Ritchie et al., 2020). Ritchie et al. presented a useful website that permits the tracking of restrictions by country, and this included data on infection rates, mask wearing and localised travel within counties.

With hindsight, it is generally agreed that the travel bans imposed to reduce COVID-19 infection rates in tourism destinations, mainly from inbound tourism, were met with limited success due to the lateness of their introduction, which generally occurred after local community infections were already established. However, their economic effect on tourism destinations was devastating, particularly in destinations with larger inbound rather than domestic tourism, estimated as high as a global loss of $2 trillion in 2021.

The effectiveness of the travel ban was also mixed due to variations in local measures, including social distancing, vaccination rollouts, and lockdowns. Travel bans worked most effectively in island destinations (Chinazzi et al., 2020). Summarised by the Oxford Martin School, travel ban effectiveness is considered as being 'most useful in the early and late phase of an epidemic,' and 'restrictions of travel from Wuhan unfortunately came too late,' (2020).

Other shocks to tourism included important factors which will continue to strongly hamper destination and wider industry recovery, also exacerbated by the impacts of the Russia-Ukraine war, which began in March 2022. Combining pandemic effects with the war, reports suggested that the effects for businesses, including those in the tourism and travel industries, are linked to increasing demand for oil and gas and shortages of goods, which impact increasing prices (Thomas, 2021).

According to reports released between February and May 2022, air travel is facing rising fuel prices. Reports suggest that between February 2021 and February 2022, jet fuel traded at over 75% higher price levels, with more detailed data drawn from the Amsterdam-Rotterdam-Antwerp areas suggesting an almost $400 increase per metric tonne between January 2021 and January 2022 (Luman, 2022). Samanta (2022) proposed that this surge in price represents a 14-year high, which significantly influences the recovery for air travel following the pandemic.

Daniel (2022) reported that although airlines had begun to recover between September 2021 and March 2022, as restrictions were eased, with estimates suggesting a return to 84% of January 2019's figures, the increasing fuel prices, particularly in response to the conflict in Ukraine, was resulting in longer periods of threat.

Saga, the over 50s travel and insurance specialists, were one of the first tour operating companies to enter into talks following reports of a £170 million debt package (Mayling, 2021). The company has been established for over 70 years and offers specialist packages that are designed for specific groups of travellers and tourists (Saga, 2022), but experienced such uncertainty during the pandemic because of the impact on the travel aspects of its company that it sought additional support so that it could return to its travel operations, post-pandemic. Saga was not the only travel company to feel the effects of the pandemic, with the TUI group reporting a three-billion-euro annual loss and increasing debts (Young, 2020). TUI was able to secure several bailout payments from the German government to support it through the crisis but did experience significant reductions in stock price, losing 55% of its value in 2020 (Young, 2020).

Virgin Atlantic also suffered financial difficulties due to travel restrictions and lockdowns, asking staff in 2020 to take unpaid leave and needing to secure £5–7.5 billion in emergency credit facilities to reduce the financial pressure on the aviation industry (Dawkins, 2020). Flybe, another company partly owned by Virgin Atlantic, collapsed and ceased trading due to the pandemic (Dawkins, 2020).

Hospitality venues were perhaps one of the first industries to feel the effects of the pandemic lockdowns and travel restrictions. Reports made in 2021 suggested that around 10% of Britain's restaurants closed (Hooker, 2021). Similar concerns were expressed about other hospitality venues, such as public houses and night-time entertainment (Russon & Smith, 2021).

Reports of consumer price inflation for the UK released in March 2022 and collecting data from the preceding 12 months stated that owner occupiers' housing costs rose by 6.2%, with the largest increases coming from electricity, gas and other fuels and transport costs (Gooding, 2022). Of note is that restaurants and hotels contributed to 0.53% of the increase. Furthermore, the consumer prices index rose by 7.0%, with a monthly basis increase of 1.1%, which, when compared to the 0.3% increase in March 2021, suggested substantial and sustained inflation rates in the UK and highest levels captured in the statistical series which began in 1997. Gooding (2022) reported that the last time the inflation rates were at this level was in February 1992.

Recent reports from May 2022 suggested that inflation rates are increasing on a worldwide scale, with the levels in the UK highlighted previously; however, it is significant to note that US inflation has remained at a 40-year high (Marko-vitz & Marchant, 2022). The UN's Food and Agriculture Organization, which tracks food prices, has reported its highest level since its inception at 12.6% and an increase of 17.9% was observed in the FAO's cereal price index. Whilst several factors have contributed to this increase, it is suggested that the increase in demand for goods in 2021, following lockdowns and restrictions, has significantly contrib-uted to this increase (Markovitz & Marchant, 2022). However, it is also important to consider the contribution that the war in Ukraine has made to local and global inflation rates.

Alongside the issues of inflation, some areas of the travel and tourism industries are facing significant difficulties in recruiting qualified and effective staff. A good example of these difficulties can be observed through a case study of British Air-ways. At the height of the pandemic, British Airways (BA) were controversially reported to have made 10,000 jobs redundant as a response to the lockdowns and travel restrictions. Many staff members were proposed to have taken voluntary redundancy (Davies, 2021), as BA restructured its business to survive mounting debts and uncertainty. However, in October 2021, the company was aiming to rehire 3,000 cabin crew. However, in February 2022, reports suggested that the airline was short staffed and that it was seeking to recruit internally using incentive schemes (Maszczynski, 2022).

Global food supply shortages, due to key areas of crisis, can include wheat, the production and distribution of which has been affected by the COVID pan-demic and the recent outbreak of conflict in Ukraine. World food prices were already surging and the war in the area, which typically supplies around 30% of the wheat throughout the world, has led to serious concerns over the availability of this resource, which is used in the production of pasta, breads and cereals. Canada, another major wheat producer, experienced crop failures due to drought and heat (Druisin et al., 2021). The International Grains Council reported that the export price has increased by 46%. Similar findings occurred with corn and cooking oil. In May 2021, it was reported that corn had a 50% increase in price (Dezember & Maltais, 2021) to an 8-year high (Daniel, 2021), continuing in 2022 (Wood, 2022). Concerns have also been raised about the availability of cooking oil (Wood, 2022), with reports suggesting that limited stocks remained due in part to the post pan-demic situation, environmental factors such as weather and the conflict in Ukraine (Singh, 2022). This access to staple foods was also matched with commodities such as aluminium with production being hampered in China (Barrera, 2022).

In tourism destinations, as the WTTC estimated global economic shrinkage at 73% (2021), a risk of 120 million tourism jobs, and tourism-dependent destina-tions such as Macao experiencing as much as a 69% drop in GDP, the COVID-19 pandemic may justifiably be considered the largest threat that modern global tour-ism has ever seen. However, organisations existing to support the tourism indus-try have provided little guidance to address tourism destinations' post-pandemic recovery strategies, other than repetition of broad, existing themes applied to the pandemic, such as collaboration, partnerships, focus on humanity, government, flexibility of systems, stakeholder trust, health and hygiene as the new normal, the impact of travel and tourism on societies, sustainability, mental health, reducing domestic abuse, digitisation and so on (WTTC, 2021). Kreiner and Ram (2021) commented that little adoption of the UNWTO's recommendations beyond tourism's containment of the pandemic was evident, along with the observation that most nations had not formulated plans for coherent pandemic exit strategies for their national tourism industries.

What is still required is the proposal of specific remedies by the leaders of global tourism. Whilst the WTTC (2021) observed that leisure tourists' desires to travel remain undiminished, business tourism has transformed, perhaps permanently, into a new and different normal, due to strategic pandemic adaptations such as virtual meetings and hybrid events. This new normal still needs to be better understood to be more effectively exploited, and to facilitate future tourism recovery in all markets. However, this also requires a departure from a rather tourist-centric view, which often neglects more focussed approaches from economy-based statistical analyses (e.g., Jaipuria et al., 2021) presented by the international, scholarly community.

The breadth and generality of responses to the pandemic from global tourism bodies are understandable considering its sudden emergence, rapid, far-reaching, and seemingly ever-changing implications. Lewis et al. (2021) remarked on a 'messiness' in multi-agency communications which lead to confusion caused by differing specialisms and interests. As far as 'Providing Stimulus and Accelerating Recovery' (UNWTO, 2022), proposals can be made for more effective, post-pandemic stakeholder actions.

We propose that planned stakeholder management strategies are combined with the strategic design of post-pandemic destination marketing messages, combined with nudge theory to shape behaviours and other destination stakeholder perceptions.

Nudge theory

Nudge theory is developed from research on behavioural insights which explore human decision making. Central to the premise is the idea that humans do not behave in a rational way and that they often make decisions that may contradict their beliefs and values and are unpredictable (Thaler & Sunstein, 2009). Nudge theory is coherent and congruent with insights which have been captured by Kahneman's (2011) influential work, which proposed that we have two thinking processes: one fast, automatic system, which is instinctive, intuitive and draws on routines; and one slow, reflective system, which requires significantly more processing effort and draws on rational decision making.

The ideas underpinning nudge theory suggest that we can use prompts, which include placing certain items in the line of view, or cues that direct behaviour, to influence behaviour. It is proposed that this allows behaviour to become much more predictable. Furthermore, nudges should not restrict or limit other choices, nor should they be financial incentives. Importantly, individuals should still be free to make choices that are guided in terms of what will make their lives easier and better (Thaler & Sunstein, 2009). Fundamentally, nudges can come in a wide variety of forms and these draw on the signs and symbols that are used in the environment to direct behaviour (Heijden & Kosters, 2015). In essence, these aim to influence decision making in subtle ways through hints that may change the heuristics and biases that people draw on. To date, the approach has been applied in terms of promoting organ donation (Johnson & Goldstein, 2003), energy consumption and reduction (Schultz et al., 2007) and retirement savings (Thaler & Sunstein, 2009).

The concept of nudge theory has been introduced to tourism and tourism research. Shaw et al. (2015) linked nudge to the use of social marketing with potential application to tourism marketing. A number of early studies (e.g. Dinan & Sargeant, 2010; Bright, 2000) highlighted the importance of willingness to change on the part of the consumer and what travel and tourism can add to experiences, with some tourists showing behaviour that drew on existing heuristics (i.e. making choices that are based on previous routines or biases). Shaw et al. (2015) proposed three phases to support this approach: 'identification', 'co-construction of materials', and 'experimental and evaluated marketing'. We suggest that tourist knowing combined with nudge theory has the potential to support destination marketing by stakeholders to better facilitate travel-purchase decision-making.

Sautter and Leisen's (1999) earlier analysis of tourism stakeholder roles assists our delineation of their various marketing communication objectives and messages, using nudge theory. Table 1 has potential for research development into an applicable model for tourism planning and policy applications for post-pandemic and wider disaster recovery, using nudge marketing.

These messages can be designed to establish a coherent destination branding strategy which can unite multi-agency perspectives, which include brand identity, image and personality, politics, heritage, communication/media, country-of origin and design and infrastructure (Hanna et al., 2021), required for the execution of a successful multi-media destination marketing communications campaign using nudge-messaging.

However, to depart from the complexities and potential confusions associated with such a managed, multi-agency approach, which generally disregards any sort of meaningful, tourist-centric perspective, a better understanding of the processes of tourist formation of destination image is proposed. This becomes even more relevant with the ever-increasing tourist adoption of digital marketing technologies, requiring a more customer-centric, two-way perspective on destination marketing. This accords with Oliveira and Panyik's earlier (2015) recommendation that destinations abandon top-down approaches to their marketing in favour of brand co-creation strategies, which incorporate traditional stakeholder inputs but are coupled with those of social media and other internet users.

Such departures from a Destination Management Organisation (DMO) solely formulating a destination's image put travellers and tourists, as well as professional online agencies, more in control. This approach would also provide advantages, including measurement of data-driven, online consumer behaviours and decision-making, whilst conversely releasing direct control from destination management stakeholders to consumers, which it could be argued is already taking place. Such a transfer of control could also be influenced by the application of nudge theory.

Such nudges apply semiotics as a 'formal doctrine of signs' (Peirce, 1931), and can be used to support post-pandemic tourist formation of their destination perceptions. This is an under-researched area and will likely prove important regarding tourist perceptions of destinations (Bladen and Callinan, 2022).

To use semiotics in nudge theory to help destinations recover, more knowledge is needed about how tourists come to understand and know the world, also known as Social Constructionism (Gergen, 1985). This knowledge and understanding are arrived at via social negotiation, which means that different social groups share collective ideas and these influence individual perceptions. Social groups may be defined by several different characteristics, which include, but are not limited to, age, gender, socio-economic status, political affiliations, job roles and geographic locations. Regardless of their characteristics, what is significant is the shared understanding of ideas that comes from group membership (Turner et al., 1979). In the context of tourism, this understanding will include background information on the location (including cultural considerations such as predominate religious beliefs, language spoken, openness of the culture), appreciation of the types of people who will travel there (e.g., gender, social groups that engage, etc.), and evaluations of what might be gained from visiting the destination (e.g., social activities, learning opportunities, explorations of sites of historical significance). It is possible for there to be multiple understandings and these will be dependent on the peer groups in which the individual interacts; some individuals may bond exclusively with one social group, thus meaning that their ideas may be bound to one social construction of the destination.

Post-pandemic, destinations which received negative media coverage may be the most vulnerable. These negative perceptions will influence the value judgements that are formed around the destination (Gergen, 1985) as key tourist decision-making attributes. Knowledge does not just lie within the individual; it is multi-dimensional and includes considerations from the broader context, including the stakeholder messages from Table 3.1. As society evolves, so too do tourist ideas, beliefs and explanations for the tourism experiences that they have (Gergen, 1985). It is proposed that nudge marketing can cause a significant renegotiation of tourism and tourist experiences to overcome the potential limitations of negative evaluations by marketing provision of a more positive destination image and the value of visiting.

Changes to social constructions can be facilitated using nudge messaging to change destination perceptions through renegotiation through cultural traditions and language and will directly relate to the tourist's own understanding of their experiences. Here, language not only relates to the native dialect spoken and the affordances that this has for the audience in terms of what it is possible

TABLE 3.1 Key factors related to tourists and stakeholders in relation to nudge-marketing messages

Tourist destination stakeholder group	Key destination brand marketing objectives	Main marketing communication audiences	Nudge-message examples
Local businesses	Generate profits.	Government, customers.	'Come and support'
Residents	Minimise community disruption.	Tourists, government, local and national businesses.	'Join our rich culture'
Activist groups	Promote wider ecological and social sustainability and well-being.	Government, tourists, local residents, national business chains.	'Global well-being'
Tourists	Derive optimum experiences.	Government, local and national businesses.	'New experience'
National Business Chains	Generate profits.	Government Local residents Employees Tourists Activists	'Here to serve, customers, employees, communities and the world'
Competitors	Promote own destination as a favourable alternative for tourists.	Tourists Government Employees Activists	'We provide value for all through differentiation and advantage'
Government	Economic recovery, societal well-being, employment, taxation.	Tourists Local businesses Residents Activists Employees	'Let us take care of you, let us take care of everyone.'
Employees	Maintain stable and rewarding employment.	Local and national businesses Government	'Welcome, let us serve you'.

to communicate but also the way that the destinations are described, discussed and understood. Language is fundamental to evaluations as this may include either negative or positive connotations that influence the evaluation of the destination.

Nudges can be enacted or communicated using multimodal resources (Kress, 2010), requiring an appreciation of a range of different communication strategies, which include language-based media, but also extend to the use of non-verbal communication, including the images portrayed. The central premise of the multimodal social semiotic approach is that different communication approaches have different affordances; therefore, taken together (e.g., a combination of language and image), these can be used to communicate complex ideas and concepts. For example, the types of words or images used to describe an experience can be used to cue specific emotional responses. For learning to take place, or for the full extent of knowledge to be understood, it is a combination of multimodal resources and responses that offers the highest level of efficacy (Callinan & Sharp, 2012, Callinan, 2015, 2016), to fully meet the needs (engagement) of the tourist.

This was demonstrated by Vojnovic (2020) who presented an analysis of tourism campaigns from three countries (North Macedonia, Serbia and Slovenia) which were aimed at English speakers. The data corpus included websites, short films, and slogans. Overall, the study aimed to explore how different communicative modes were used to present cultural values to potential tourists. The results suggested that the multimodal resources employed had the potential to trigger considerations of culture and identity and could be a useful resource for allowing professionals and students in the sector to appreciate how these techniques can be used to convey important messages to potential tourists. Work such as this begins to show the potential of this area to appreciate not only more fully what the messages contain but also appreciate how these may be interpreted by the audience. The latter has not yet received much attention in the literature from this domain and offers a fruitful and rich area for development.

Multimodal research also provides implications for the use of nudge theory, with concerns for the notion of congruency. Nudge communication approaches (visual/auditory) should convey a message that offers the tourist consistency and coherence, at the risk that the communication will be mixed and likely demonstrates instability or uncertainty. This does not mean that different communication strategies should have identical content, merely that they should not contradict each other. The spaces, virtual, print or media, and locations in which the communication occurs also play a role in the meaning that will be conveyed (Kress, 2010). Like the modes used, these offer their own affordances in terms of audience engagement and characteristics.

Post-pandemic, safety and health considerations at destinations remain an important part of communication; however, to fully engage target audiences, it is important that the characteristics of the destination are communicated. Tourists make decisions about visiting destinations and engaging in activities based on their identity (Stryker, 2008) and the affinity that they see between their self-concept (Rogers, 1959) and the value and characteristics of the location. Nudge communication messages should aim to draw on multimodal resources to communicate the social construction of the destination and to support a rich and detailed marketing approach.

Kress's work (2010) adopts a semiotics approach and links to the previous work of Peirce (1931) discussed in this chapter. It is fundamentally the way that the communications strategy is applied that will facilitate either a positive or a negative message that may engage the returning tourist. Furthermore, there is a strong link between the way that these communication strategies can elicit emotional responses, cue memory, and priming existing understanding regarding post-pandemic tourism management.

In Figure 3.1, our new model captures significant factors related to the destination and tourists, and we propose that it is through the interaction of these factors

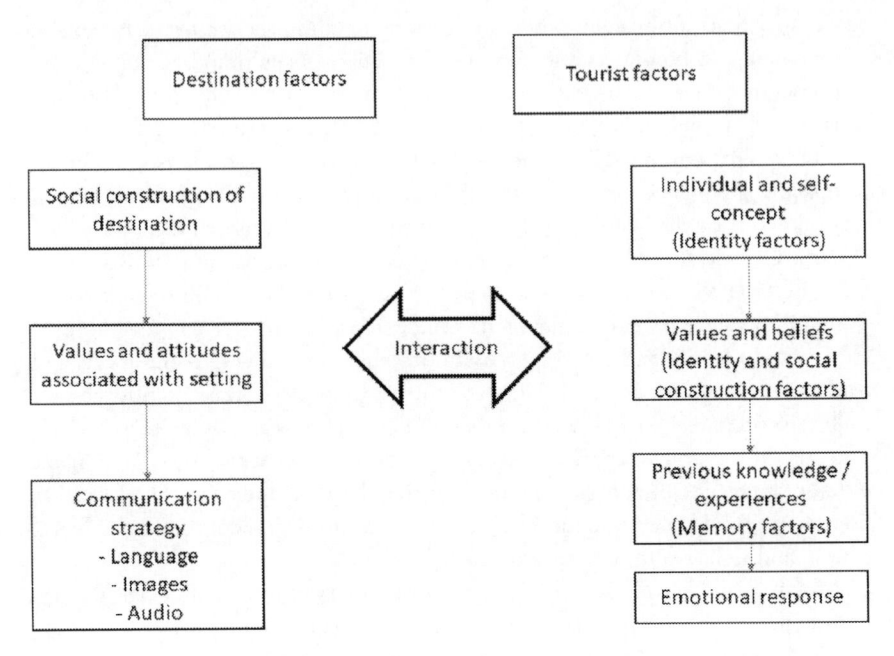

FIGURE 3.1 Interaction between destination and tourist factors

through nudge marketing that decisions about engagement with destinations are made. It is proposed that this model moves away from a destination focus and begins to consider the rich background of the tourist, which will enable researchers and practitioners in this area to appreciate the rich context more fully, in which tourism occurs, and stakeholders to design suitable nudge messaging more effectively. It is here that considerations of effective tourism recovery can be generated. Therefore, destinations that convey clear communication about the social construction of their destination through nudges which appeal to tourist-related factors should witness more effective engagement.

Furthermore, given the fluid nature of social construction, it is possible to use what is known about a destination to enhance or challenge the tourists' perceptions through nudges, thus on some level achieving re-construction at least at a basic level.

Implications for future academic and management research

Following the foregoing discussion, the authors propose that future academic and management research should:

- Further investigate the specific impacts of COVID-19 destination perceptions.
- Formulate a more tourist-centric understanding of travel motivations.

- Establish core stakeholder nudge messaging with respect to post pandemic destination marketing.
- Examine a more customer-centric and two-way perspective on destination brand marketing.
- Examine the formation of consideration and choice sets used by potential tourists when choosing a destination.
- More clearly examine the destination attributes selected and evaluated by tourists.
- Test the application of the Bladen-Callinan 'Interaction between destination and tourist factors' model to specific destinations.
- Evaluate the use of nudge theory and messaging by destinations.

References

Babii, A., & Nadeem, S. (2021). Tourism in a post-pandemic world. *International Monetary Fund.* [Online] www.imf.org/en/News/Articles/2021/02/24/na022521-how-to-save-travel-and-tourism-in-a-post-pandemic-world

Barrera, P. (2022). Aluminum Outlook 2022: Analysts Bullish on Prices, Deficit Ahead, *INN.* [Online] https://investingnews.com/aluminum-outlook-2022/

Behsudi, A. (2020). Wish You Were Here. *International Monetary Fund.* [Online] www.imf.org/external/pubs/ft/fandd/2020/12/impact-of-the-pandemic-on-tourism-behsudi.htm

Bladen, C., & Callinan, C. (2022). Post-Pandemic Destination Recovery: Social Constructionism and Understanding the Roles of Semiotic Representation of Customer Perception Through-knowing. In P. Mohanty, A. Sharma, J. Kennell & A. Hassan (Eds.), *The Emerald Handbook of Destination Recovery in Tourism and Hospitality Tourism.* London: Emerald.

Bright, A.D. (2000). The Role of Social Marketing in Leisure and Recreation Management. *Journal of Leisure Research, 32*(1), 12–17.

Callinan, C. (2015). Talking about Electricity: The Importance of Hearing Gestures as Well as Words. In C.P. Constantinou, N. Papadouris, & A. Hadjigeorgiou (Eds.), *Insights from Research in Science Teaching and Learning: Selected papers from the ESERA 2013 conference.* New York: Springer.

Callinan, C. (2016). Multimodal Science Learning: A Hybrid Model of Conceptual Change. In J. Lavonen, K. Juuti, J. Lampiselkä, A. Uitto, & K. Hahl (Eds.), *Electronic Proceedings of the ESERA 2015 Conference. Science Education Research: Engaging Learners for a Sustainable Future,* Part 1 (co-ed. O. Finlayson, & R. Pinto) (pp. 192–199). Helsinki: University of Helsinki.

Callinan, C., & Sharp, J. (2012). Constructing Scientific Knowledge in the Classroom: A Multimodal Perspective on Conceptual Change. In Bruguière, C., Tiberghein, A., & Clément, P. *E-Book Proceedings of the ESERA 2011 Conference, Lyon France* [online]. Available from: www.esera.org/media/ebook/ebook-esera2011____Strand1.pdf

Chinazzi, M., Davis, J. T., Ajelli, M., Gioannini, C., Litvinova, M., Merler, S; Pastore y Piontti, A., Mu, K., Rossi, L., Sun, K., Viboud, C., Xiong, X., Yu, H., Halloran, M.E., Longini, Jr., I., & Vespignani, A (2020). The Effect of Travel Restrictions on the Spread of the 2019 Novel Coronavirus (COVID-19) Outbreak. *Science, 368* (6489), 395–400.

Daniel, W. (2021). Corn Prices have Jumped 142% in the Past Year Amid Rising Demand from China, Drought in Brazil. *Insider Markets.* [Online] https://markets.businessinsider.

com/news/stocks/corn-prices-jumped-142-past-year-demand-china-drought-brazil-2021–5-1030386126

Daniel, W. (2022). Pandemic-weary Airlines Now Face a Fuel Crisis that Could Bring Even More Pain and Higher Airfares for Travellers, *Fortune*. [Online] https://fortune.com/2022/03/09/airlines-fuel-crisis-higher-airfares-russia-ukraine/

Davies, P. (2021). BA 'Set to Rehire 3,000 Cabin Crew' after Pandemic Job Cuts. *Travel Weekly*. [Online] https://travelweekly.co.uk/news/air/ba-set-to-rehire-3000-cabin-crew-after-pandemic-job-cuts

Dawkins, D. (2020). Bad Times For Billionaire Branson – Staff At Virgin Atlantic Asked to Take Unpaid Leave as Coronavirus Cripples Air Travel, *Forbes*. [Online] www.forbes.com/sites/daviddawkins/2020/03/16/bad-times-for-billionaire-bransonstaff-at-virgin-atlantic-asked-to-take-unpaid-leave-as-coronavirus-cripples-air-travel/?sh=629ebe9258ef

Dezember, R., & Maltais, K. (2021). Corn Is the Latest Commodity to Soar, *Wall Street Journal*. [Online] www.wsj.com/articles/corn-is-the-latest-commodity-to-pop-11620644400

Dinan, C., & Sargeant, A. (2010). Social Marketing and Sustainable Tourism: Is There a Match? *International Journal of Tourism Research, 2*, 2–14.

Druisin, M., Chipman, K., & Kothia, K. (2021). Wheat Supplies Are Shrinking and It's Bad News for Bread Prices. *Financial Post*. [Online] https://financialpost.com/pmn/business-pmn/wheat-supplies-are-shrinking-and-its-bad-news-for-bread-prices

Dunford, D., Dale, B., Stylianou, N., Lowther, Ahmed, M., & Torre Arenas, I. (2020). Coronavirus: The World in Lockdown in Maps and Charts. *BBC World News*. [Online] www.bbc.co.uk/news/world-52103747

Gergen, K. (1985). The Social Constructionist Movement in Modern Psychology. *American Psychologist, 40*(3), 266–275.

Gooding, P. (2022, March). Consumer Price Inflation. *Office for National Statistics*. www.ons.gov.uk/economy/inflationandpriceindices/bulletins/consumerpriceinflation/latest

Hanna, S, Rowley, J., & Keegan, B. (2021). Place and Destination Branding: A Review and Conceptual Mapping of the Domain. *European Management Review, 18*, 105–117.

Heijden, J., & Kosters, M. (2015). From Mechanisms to Virtue: Evaluating Nudge Theory. *Reg Net Research Papers*. [Online] https://openresearch-repository.anu.edu.au/bitstream/1885/71637/8/01_Kosters_From_Mechanism_to_Virtue_2015.pdf

Hooker, L. (2021). COVID: A Tenth of Britain's Restaurants Lost during Pandemic. *BBC Business News*. [Online] www.bbc.co.uk/news/business-57087070

Jaipuria, S., Parida, R., & Ray, P. (2021). The Impact of COVID-19 on Tourism Sector in India. *Tourism Recreation Research, 46*(2), 245–260.

Johnson, E., & Goldstein, D. (2003). Do Defaults Save Lives? *Science, 302*(5649), 1338–1339

Kahneman, D. (2011). *Thinking Fast and Slow*. New York: Farrar, Straus and Giroux.

Kreiner, N.C., & Ram, Y. (2021). National Tourism Strategies during the Covid-19 Pandemic. *Annals of Tourism Research*, 103076.

Kress, G. (2010). *Multimodality: A Social Semiotics Approach to Contemporary Communication*. London: Routledge.

Lewis, M., Holland, K., & Govender, E. (2021). The Interdisciplinary Communication Dynamics of the COVID-19 Pandemic. In M. Lewis, E. Govender, & K. Holland (Eds.), *Communicating COVID-19: Interdisciplinary Perspectives*. London: Palgrave Macmillan. https://ssrn.com/abstract=3890630 or DOI: 10.2139/ssrn.3890630

Luman, R. (2022). Soaring Fuel Prices Complicate Aviation Sector's Recovery from the Pandemic. *Think Economic and Financial Analysis*. [Online] https://think.ing.com/articles/soaring-fuel-prices-complicate-aviation-sectors-recovery-from-pandemic/

Markovitz, G., & Marchant, N. (2022). Why is Inflation So High and Will it Stay That Way? An Economist Explains. *World Economic Forum*. [Online] www.weforum.org/agenda/2022/05/inflation-rising-economist-explains/

Maszczynski, M. (2022). Exclusive: British Airways is So Short Staffed its Asking Pilots and Office Staff to be Cabin Crew. *Paddleyourownkanoo*. [Online] www.paddleyourown-kanoo.com/2022/02/14/exclusive-british-airways-is-so-short-staffed-its-asking-pilots-and-office-staff-to-be-cabin-crew/

Mayling, S. (2021). Saga in Talks about £170m Debt Package. *Travel Weekly*. [Online] https://travelweekly.co.uk/news/tour-operators/saga-group-in-talks-about-170m-debt-package

McKercher, B., & Chon, K. (2004). The Over-reaction to SARS and the Collapse of Asian Tourism. *Annals of Tourism Research, 31*(3), 716–719. DOI: 10.1016/j.annals.2003.11.002

Oliveira, E., & Panyik, E. (2015). Content, Context and Co-creation: Digital Challenges in Destination Branding with References to Portugal as a Tourist Destination. *Journal of Vacation Marketing, 21*, 53–74.

Oxford Martin School (2020, March 25). COVID-19: Study Shows that Travel Restrictions are Most Useful in the Early and Late Phase of an Epidemic. *Oxford Martin School, University of Oxford*.

Peirce, C.S. (1931). *The Collected Papers*, Vols. 1–6. Eds. Charles Hartshorne and Paul Weiss. Cambridge, MA: Harvard University Press.

Ritchie, H., Mathieu, E., Rodés-Guirao, L., Appel, C., Giattino, C., Ortiz-Ospina, E., Hasell, J., Macdonald, B., Beltekian, D., & Roser, M. (2020). Coronavirus Pandemic (COVID-19). *Our World in Data*. [Online] https://ourworldindata.org/policy-responses-covid

Rogers, C. (1959). A Theory of Therapy, Personality and Interpersonal Relationships as Developed in the Client-centered Framework. In S. Koch (Ed.), *Psychology: A Study of a Science*. Vol. 3: Formulations of the Person and the Social Context. London: McGraw Hill.

Russon, M.A., & Smith, O. (2021). We're in Serious Trouble, Says Hospitality Industry. *BBC Business News*. [Online] www.bbc.co.uk/news/business-57476419

Saga (2022). Saga Homepage. [Online] *Saga Holidays & Cruises 2022/23 – UK*. London: Worldwide l Saga Travel

Samanta, K. (2022). Jet Fuel Price Surge Deals Heavy Blow to Fragile Air Travel Recovery. *Reuters*. [Online] www.reuters.com/markets/europe/jet-fuel-price-surge-deals-heavy-blow-fragile-air-travel-recovery-2022–03–08/

Sautter, E.T., & Leisen, B. (1999). Managing Stakeholders a Tourism Planning Model. *Annals of Tourism Research, 26*(2), 312–328.

Schultz, P.W., Nolan, J.M., Cialdini, R.B., Goldstein, N.J., & Griskevicius, V. (2007). The Constructive, Destructive, and Reconstructive Power of Social Norms. *Psychological Science, 18*(5), 429–434. DOI: 10.1111/j.1467-9280.2007.01917.x

Shaw, G., Barr, S., & Wooler, J. (2015). The Application of Social Marketing to Tourism. In S. McCabe (Ed.), *The Routledge Handbook of Tourism Marketing*. London: Routledge.

Singh, D. (2022). Why Edible Oil Prices are Set to Surge Again. *Money Control*. [Online] www.moneycontrol.com/news/business/companies/why-edible-oil-prices-are-set-to-surge-again-8158711.html

Stryker, S. (2008). From Mead to Structural Interactionism and Beyond. *Annual Review of Sociology, 34*, 15–31. DOI: 10.1146/annurev.soc.34.040507.134649

Thaler, R., & Sunstein, C. (2009). *Nudge* (revised edition). London: Penguin

Thomas, D, (2021). Inflation: UK Prices Soar at Fastest Rate for Almost Ten Years. *BBC Business*. [Online] www.bbc.co.uk/news/business-59316544

Turner, J.C., Brown, R.J., & Tajfel, H. (1979). Social Comparison and Group Interest in Ingroup Favouritism. *European Journal of Social Psychology, 9*(2), 187–204.

UNWTO (2022). Coronavirus Pandemic Could Cost Global Tourism $2 Trillion this Year, [Online] https://news.un.org/en/story/2021/11/1106712

Vojnovic, D.Y. (2020). Multimodal Discourse Analysis of Tourism Websites – The Promotion of Cultural Values Through the Language of Tourism. *Conference: International*

Conference to Mark the 90th Anniversary of the English Department. Faculty of Philology, University of Belgrade, BELLS90 Proceedings, 1. DOI: 10.18485/bells90.2020.1.ch27

Wood, J. (2022). 2 Charts that Show the Sharp Rise in Food Prices. *World Economic Forum.* [Online] www.weforum.org/agenda/2022/04/food-prices-fao-index-cereals-commodities-exports/

WTTC (2021). *Lessons Learnt* [Online]. https://wttc.org/Portals/0/Documents/Reports/2021/Lessons-Learnt-%20COVID-19.pdf?ver=2021-08-19–095731–037. Accessed 4 September 2021.

Yeh, S.S. (2021). Tourism Recovery Strategy against COVID-19 Pandemic. *Tourism Recreation Research*, 46(2), 188–194.

Young, S. (2020). Travel Group TUI Looks to Cut Debt after Pandemic Pushes It to $3.6 Billion Loss. *Reuters.* [Online] www.reuters.com/article/us-tui-results-idUSKBN28K0IS

4

SUSTAINABILITY AND DESTINATION RECOVERY

Alternatives to overcome the crossroads of the pandemic crisis

Francisco Antônio dos Anjos, Sara Joana Gadotti dos Anjos and Vitor Roslindo Kuhn

Introduction

The context of change that has presented itself to tourism worldwide since 2020 has brought a set of opportunities that allow universities, the tourism industry and public institutions to investigate alternatives to the often disorganised, unsustainable and unmanaged advance of tourism activity. The global crisis generated by the pandemic caused by COVID-19 in its several variations has revealed a crisis in tourism activity that has developed intensely and quickly to a global scale, but which almost always presents a multiplicity of strategies in destinations that do not concur with the principles of sustainability.

Tourism is an economic activity that possibly best portrays the economic amalgam of the twenty-first century, to the extent that it integrates mobility, connectivity, technology, management and sustainability, not only positively, but also in a paradoxical way. Before the crisis generated by the pandemic, themes such as overtourism, environmental degradation, the homogenisation of places, concentration of income, conflict between residents and tourists, low quality of tourist services, and decharacterisation of local cultures, among others, were presented as the central scope of much academic research in tourism across several continents.

In this sense, the significant mobility of people – 1.466 billion international tourist arrivals according to the WTO (UNWTO, 2020) – that allowed tourism to present itself as an activity that generates and distributes capital, enables encounters between cultures, and promotes greater integration between places and regions, also presents a framework of negative factors, perceived with greater clarity during the pandemic. The pandemic context has created a situation of contrasts, such as isolation tourism, the intensification of domestic tourism (involving intra-regional and national displacement) and the reduction of contact between people (restricted

DOI: 10.4324/9781003295839-6

almost always to the same social or family group). Perhaps the most emblematic issue is the much-vaunted Smart Tourism, which is based on intense connectivity between territories, people and services, providing a personalised tourism of few contacts between people or with people with similar characteristics and interests.

This greater connectivity, however, suggests that physical displacements are not always accompanied by psychosocial displacements. Associated with connectivity, technological development, which once provided great advances in the field of tourism, such as commercial air connections and online services, has recently been associated with the robotisation of service in a scenario that values less contact between people. If the conditions of connectivity, mobility, and technology that dominated the expansion of tourism in the first two decades of the 21st century are put in check during the pandemic, then these same conditions can sometimes be an obstacle, and sometimes as an opportunity for safer tourism.

In this context, two issues linked to the current crisis that relate to the safety of destinations are highlighted and will be dealt with in specific sections of this chapter. First, we address previous discussions in the tourism literature on governance and sustainability. The issue of health security is treated in the literature as a factor in the social dimension, allowing sustainability issues to be placed at the centre of academic and commercial discussions. Almost always associated with the ability of destinations to manage risks, many of which are not new, the pandemic has brought to the attention public and private managers, the key factors for the principles of good governance that need to be reaffirmed for a sustainable recovery of destinations strongly impacted by the COVID pandemic.

In the second section, based on the tourism literature, we address the challenges that the pandemic has brought to the management of tourism services, not only affecting the tourist experience, but the conditions and risks facing the entire structure of tourism in the current context, presenting challenges to destinations that need to recover in the context of sustainable tourism. Orîndaru et al. (2021) reinforces the importance of developing effective marketing strategies for this, based on a solid knowledge of consumer behaviour.

This chapter presents a synthesis of discussions in the tourism literature relating to sustainability and destination recovery. Beyond this systematic review, it also seeks to present critical reflections on this context, seeking to indicate possibilities for the theoretical and managerial fields of tourism.

Sustainability and destination management

During the years of the COVID-19 pandemic, empirical research and theoretical reflections sought to illuminate moments of severe crisis in tourism that, with different intensities, impacted places and nations that have in tourism activities a main or simply significant source of their income.

It is noticeable that a significant part of the literature in the field of tourism has treated destination governance as its main focus. In fact, the current crisis that impacts the economy and society has created the need to review or at least reflect on the principles that guide these management processes. Based on a study of the tourism system in Catalonia, Spain, Bono i Gispert and Anton Clavé (2020) identified dimensions of good governance, which, even though it was developed in a pre-crisis period, presents a broad perspective, appropriate to the management of a complex system such as tourism.

Participation, the first dimension that is considered in this model, recognises that good governance is based on an effective participation of the actors, based on a process that strengthens responsibility, understood as the ability to ensure sustainable development. The coherence dimension concerns management focused on a certain purpose that allows the capacity to project future scenarios based on effectiveness and the efficient use of resources under criteria that allow the control of procedures and results. The Know-how/Quality dimension is directed towards excellence, based on quality and continuous improvement, which allows for simplification, understood as the ability to act in a simple, flexible and effective way. Finally, good governance should be centered on the principle of openness, allowing public access to updated information in an understandable and simple way, which is important because the governance of a destination is a complex system (Bono i Gispert & Anton Clavé, 2020).

The indications of the UNWTO (2020) on the recovery of destinations reinforce the need for broad, permanent and detailed monitoring, supported by reliable data, which should guide decision-making and new strategies that allow a quick and consistent recovery. The European Union's Tourism Recovery Program (NextGenerationEU[1]) for the bloc's countries requires members to invest heavily in projects that strengthen the conditions for government decisions based on reliable information. The principles of the NextGeneration program are based on Green, Digital, Healthy, Strong and Equitable Tourism.

The governance model adopted in this scenario of conflict and risk management seems to be close to what has been recognised in the literature as network management, emphasising the strengthening of resilience and balance between competition and cooperation. The concerns of the actors in network governance focus on the partnership, transparency, representativeness and communicability of the process. Articulation and leadership are fundamental characteristics of these governance actors.

McCartney et al. (2021) show that destination resilience is strongly centered on the collaboration and diversification of the tourism system. The conflicts and crises that characterise tourism require management to focus on planning its activities, considering various scenarios. Gallego and Font (2021: 17) contend that using reliable, fast and dynamic information allows tourism governance to have the capacity to acquire knowledge in order to reduce risk, in situations of uncertainty, and to improve organisational effectiveness, and reinforce this by indicating the need for managers to 'understand market behaviour and act quickly to restore confidence and stimulate demand'. The joint action of the public spheres of government at different scales (from local to supranational) in the collection, use and monitoring of data needs to involve official statistical agencies and sectors of the tourism market, as in the case of the creation of Eurostat, an agreement between the European Commission and Airbnb, Booking, Expedia Group and TripAdvisor.

Novel contemporary challenges reinforce the need for an approach to tourism governance that should, at the very least, integrate the perspective of the business ecosystem, the complexity of the tourism system and the vision of creative and smart tourism. In this direction, Vargas (2020) argues that the elements that make up the tourism destination are interdependent and evolve as a complex adaptive system, influenced by the creative and smart economy perspective.

To better respond to the crisis, destinations that have understood tourism as a complex system have been making decisions in a cooperative manner between the public and private sectors. Contemporary trends in tourism governance originate from the pressures of the private sector, focus on the creation of a legal structure that guarantees a favourable business environment, as well as for providing lines of financial support to the companies that were most impacted by the crisis and also on promotional campaigns, with an emphasis on those that reinforce security at the destination in order to generate more confidence in tourist markets.

Despite these changes in the focus of governance, the current crisis requires that the focus on demand management needs to be rethought in view of the need to understand the new behaviour patterns of tourists. The ambiguities of this uncertainty have raised awareness about investing in data-driven technologies and smart solutions (Vargas, 2020).

The great challenge facing sustainable governance in a time of crisis is to minimise the negative impacts of tourism and support a sustainable recovery of the destination. The pillars of this process are the strengthening of management structures, the introduction of financial support measures for the tourism industry, investment in large, dynamic and reliable databases, and the development of advertising campaigns focused on safety and new patterns of tourist behaviour.

Sustainability and tourist confidence

Moments of crisis or rupture are opportunities for great transformations, and for the tourism industry this is no different. The pandemic is a unique moment to rethink tourism, reinvent and innovate, not only to recover the economy, but to establish new directions. The pandemic scenario caused by COVID-19 has brought about a crisis that can lead to profound and long-term structural and transformational changes for tourism as a socio-economic activity and industry (Sigala, 2020).

One of the aspects to be rethought concerns the reestablishment of the tourist's trust. Trust in this context can involve providing reliable information on how to avoid crowds and on local health strategies that promote tourist safety. Destinations as a whole, or companies in the sector such as hotels and restaurants, must communicate and convey a sense of security in the actions they have taken (Matiza, 2020; Orîndaru et al., 2021). Trust is understood as an essential element for the creation of a strategy to attract tourists (Villacé-Molinero et al., 2021). In this direction, some aspects should be taken into consideration when understanding travel decisions: culture, family, gender, health, income, information and education, regulated holidays, location, political rights, protection and safety, time and work (Cooper & Hall, 2011).

Consumer behaviour and buying decisions are the foundation of strategies for tourism and consumer habits are responsible for the growth of the tourism industry. Maintaining contact with customers or potential customers and developing lasting relationships with them is an even more significant challenge with the advent of the pandemic (Assaf & Scuderi, 2020; Orîndaru et al., 2021).

The recovery from the crisis in the Spanish tourism market in 2021, for example, was analysed from the point of view of the perception of the sector's entrepreneurs in a study by Sánchez-Rivero et al. (2021) demonstrating how the region behaved during the crisis. The results show how a series of measures based on benchmarking with other destinations enabled the region to overcome the crisis in the sector. On the economic front, direct help to companies to withstand the loss of income and recover business liquidity had a significant impact. Additionally, reductions or cancellation of taxes in fiscal measures compensated for the drop in revenue and helped to maintain employment.

Domestic destinations have become the top travel destinations in the post-pandemic period, as these are seen as safer. This shift is suggested by psychological risk and how it affects travel-related consumption attitudes (Han et al., 2020). Due to the specific characteristic of the Extremadura region researched by Sánchez-Rivero et al. (2021) as a hinterland destination and not very busy, there was the reinforcement of the promotion of its diversified offer of rural and nature tourism, which was further strengthened by the aspect of a low local contagion rate compared to destinations with large tourist flows. Thus, it is convenient to increase the promotion of the destination aligned with the image of a safe area.

Orîndaru et al. (2021) study focused on providing guidance to entrepreneurs in the sector for their recovery and sustainable guarantees for the business models developed in the tourist destination, in particular for lodging enterprises. The study concluded with recommendations for strategies to modify and build new services that address the concerns caused by the pandemic crisis, thus leading to a change from a psychological state of fear to a feeling of relaxation.

The use of creativity, innovation and a strong sense of empathy are cornerstones for these resolutions. Complementing this, radical experiments in formulating and implementing innovations bring conditions to broaden the base of the tourism industry and provide new prospects for its expansion (Sharma et al., 2021; Sigala, 2020).

In this context, key findings related to inter-organisational trust, collaboration, communication and openness to merger and resource sharing indicate that unity and support among businesses can be more effective than intra-destination competition during a prolonged crisis (Mirehie & Cho, 2021).

Understanding the feelings and social conditions of tourists, as well as quality in tourism services, present themselves as pillars for reinforcement in recovery when destinations are experiencing the pandemic crisis to ensure the sustainability of business models in a sector that was heavily shaken (Orîndaru et al., 2021). Nair and Sinha's (2020) study looked at the differences and similarities between groups of individuals with distinct travel characteristics. The research looked at the behaviour of people who have undergone prolonged quarantine, individuals who had no previous travel experiences, and tourists with a history of international travel. Its findings showed that concerns about accessibility (proximity) and discounts, as well as health and hygiene, are highly motivating for future destination choices.

Post-crisis marketing has focused on increasing perceptions of destination safety, including safe travel guarantees, cut-off rates, and collaboration with medical and health certifications (Nair & Sinha, 2020), which came with the reinvention of communication systems, themselves becoming a source of reassurance and comfort for concerned tourists. Customer emotions are more important than ever in marketing tourism businesses, regardless of external effects; customer perceptions prove to be the most important indicator of their intentions, decisions and actions (Orîndaru et al., 2021).

This sense of security is reinforced in studies showing that customers in the tourism sector highly value security issues, such as hygiene and privacy standards in hotels (Jiang & Wen, 2020; Kourgiantakis et al., 2021). It has also been noted that natural-based and adventure tourism are products with less inter-human contact, thus becoming the preference of many customers during and after the pandemic crisis (Baba & Dinu, 2020).

Trust in a brand's health and safety policies will continue to be critical in the future. Backing away from this aspect will not be an option for companies involved in the tourism industry. Rather, to restore traveller confidence and stimulate demand, the health and safety of guests and employees must be prioritised. Thus, it reinforces the importance of a communication strategy to keep tourists and potential new consumers informed (Orîndaru et al., 2021).

In this general scenario, we can visualise a distinction between the impacts and repercussions that the COVID-19 pandemic crisis caused in the tourism sector according to the type of destination and service offered. New businesses could see increased tourism development, such as in rural regions, destinations with natural attractions, and activities in open spaces or with smaller flows of people (Sánchez-Rivero et al., 2021). These characteristics have become a favourable factor for resilience in this context of crisis, as public health actions to mitigate the contagion are carried out with greater confidence by authorities.

Orîndaru et al. (2021) reinforces this by indicating tactical priorities to maintain the sustainability of the destination with attitudes of increased sanitary control and safety, in addition to the encouragement of new services, such as leveraging people's interest in local and domestic tourism and the elaboration of cheaper services for low-income or even middle-income consumers. Mirehie and Cho (2021) emphasise that most of the transformations stimulated by the pandemic were considered improvements, so organising post-crisis campaigns to sustain the positive changes will certainly help in the long-term success of destinations.

The changing preferences of tourists, presented in the study of Chebli and Ben Said (2020), are demonstrated in a behaviour of predilection for destinations not massified and closer to home, with an expanding awareness about environmentally responsible practices and intensification of the demand for knowing the situation of health security of the intended destination. In this same direction, Orîndaru et al. (2021) emphasise that the sense of uncertainty about well-being was induced by the COVID-19 global crisis, as well as caused by reductions in household income, leading to new travel choice habits.

Conclusion and theoretical and practical implications

Destination recovery based on sustainability necessarily requires changes in the context of tourism studies, as well as in the managerial and commercial practices in the tourism industry. Alternatives that support overcoming the crossroads generated by the pandemic crisis are based on governance that involves social actors who take ownership of a tourist destination as a broad, complex and dynamic system. Based on this assumption, the sectors involved in the tourism industry need to strengthen the resilience of the destination by developing strategies that increase tourist confidence.

The generation of tourist confidence in this pandemic crisis framework can be seen from a reductionist perspective as a strategy solely focused on health security. However, academic debates during the pandemic and data from the first more consistent studies refer to a broader perspective on the achievement of tourist safety. The psychosocial dimensions related to trust challenge destinations to offer, in addition to safety, products, services and tourism experiences that allow visitors to take their time for emotional restoration.

The transmission of a safe destination image is a collective process involving the tourism industry and the local/regional/national government to create an enabling environment for the development of tourism activity. An attractive destination for tourists includes a business environment that allows the tourism industry to fully provide its services with excellence. New motivations for tourists to visit less crowded places, increasing the demand for alternative destinations, in particular nature-based destinations, reinforce the need for consolidated destinations to expand their catalogue of experiences and get to know their tourists in a deeper way.

In the search for a better understanding of tourists' profiles and motivations, it has been revealed that the literature in the area has reinforced the need for governments to invest in broad and reliable data. Knowing the customer better allows for greater effectiveness in marketing strategies, particularly those focused on customisation, diversification and flexibility in promotional actions.

New partnerships between tourism companies, and between them and governments, must be the basis of governance, which involves the effective participation and shared responsibility of the different actors. This should be seen in the simplification and openness of the communication processes in the network and in the principles of coherence and effectiveness in the development of strategies. The context of the pandemic crisis reinforces, requalifies and values the principles of good governance in the sustainability context of tourism destinations and allows each destination to design its own alternative for coping and recovery. Good governance contributes to a resilient destination, while a good business environment allows tourism providers to offer excellent services and experiences.

Note

1 NextGenerationEU (europa.eu)

References

Assaf, A., & Scuderi, R. (2020). COVID-19 and the Recovery of the Tourism Industry. *Tourism Economics*, *26*(5), 731–733. DOI: 10.1177/1354816620933712

Baba, C., & Dinu, A.C. (2020). Considerations Regarding the Effects of COVID-19 on the Tourism Market. *Theoretical and Applied Economics*, *XXVII*(3), 271–284.

Bono i Gispert, O., & Anton Clavé, S. (2020). Dimensions and Models of Tourism Governance in a Tourism System: The Experience of Catalonia. *Journal of Destination Marketing & Management*, *17*, 100465. DOI: 10.1016/j.jdmm.2020.100465

Chebli, A., & Ben Said, F. (2020). The Impact of COVID-19 on Tourist Consumption Behaviour: A Perspective Article. *Journal of Tourism Management Research*, *7*(2), 196–207. DOI: 10.18488/journal.31.2020.72.196.207

Cooper, C.P., & Hall, C.M. (2011). *Turismo Contemporâneo: Uma Abordagem Internacional* (1st ed.). Londres, Reino Unido: Routledge.

Gallego, I., & Font, X. (2021). Changes in Air Passenger Demand as a Result of the COVID-19 Crisis: Using Big Data to Inform Tourism Policy. *Journal of Sustainable Tourism*, *29*(9), 1470–1489. DOI: 10.1080/09669582.2020.1773476

Han, H., Al-Ansi, A., Chua, B.L., Tariq, B., Radic, A., & Park, S.H. (2020). The Post-coronavirus World in the International Tourism Industry: Application of the Theory of Planned Behavior to Safer Destination Choices in the Case of US Outbound Tourism. *International Journal of Environmental Research and Public Health*, *17*(18), 1–15. DOI: 10.3390/ijerph17186485

Jiang, Y., & Wen, J. (2020). Effects of COVID-19 on Hotel Marketing and Management: A Perspective Article. *International Journal of Contemporary Hospitality Management*, *32*(8), 2563–2573. DOI: 10.1108/IJCHM-03-2020-0237

Kourgiantakis, M., Apostolakis, A., & Dimou, I. (2021). COVID-19 and Holiday Intentions: The Case of Crete, Greece. *Anatolia*, *32*(1), 148–151. DOI: 10.1080/13032917.2020.1781221

Matiza, T. (2020). Post-COVID-19 Crisis Travel Behaviour: Towards Mitigating the Effects of Perceived Risk. *Journal of Tourism Futures*, *2012*. DOI: 10.1108/JTF-04-2020-0063

McCartney, G., Pinto, J., & Liu, M. (2021). City Resilience and Recovery from COVID-19: The case of Macao. *Cities*, *112*, 103130. DOI: 10.1016/j.cities.2021.103130

Mirehie, M., & Cho, I. (2021). Exploring the Effects of the COVID-19 Pandemic on Sport Tourism. *International Journal of Sports Marketing and Sponsorship*. DOI: 10.1108/IJSMS-04-2021-0081

Nair, B.B., & Sinha, S. (2020). COVID-19 and Future Travel Decisions: How Do the Destination-Choice-based Motivators Redefine Tourist's Choices? *Enlightening Tourism*, *10*(2), 306–322. DOI: 10.33776/et.v10i2.4919

Orîndaru, A., Popescu, M.F., Alexoaei, A.P., Căescu, Ştefan C., Florescu, M.S., & Orzan, A.O. (2021). Tourism in a Post-COVID-19 Era: Sustainable Strategies for Industry's Recovery. *Sustainability (Switzerland), 13*(12), 1–22. DOI: 10.3390/su13126781

Sánchez-Rivero, M., Rodríguez-Rangel, M.C., & Ricci-Risquete, A. (2021). Percepción empresarial de la pandemia por COVID-19 y su impacto en el turismo: un análisis cualitativo del destino Extremadura, España. *Estudios Gerenciales, 37*(159), 265–279. DOI: 10.18046/j.estger.2021.159.4427

Sharma, G.D., Thomas, A., & Paul, J. (2021). Reviving Tourism Industry Post-COVID-19: A Resilience-based Framework. *Tourism Management Perspectives, 37*, 100786. DOI: 10.1016/j.tmp.2020.100786

Sigala, M. (2020). Tourism and COVID-19: Impacts and Implications for Advancing and Resetting Industry and Research. *Journal of Business Research, 117*, 312–321. DOI: 10.1016/j.jbusres.2020.06.015

UNWTO, W.T.O. (2020). Supporting Jobs and Economies through Travel and Tourism – A Call for Action to Mitigate the Socio-Economic Impact of COVID-19 and Accelerate Recovery. *World Tourism Organization.* https://webunwto.s3.eu-west-1.amazonaws.com/s3fs-public/2020-04/COVID19_Recommendations_English_1.pdf

Vargas, A. (2020). COVID-19 Crisis: A New Model of Tourism Governance for a New Time. *Worldwide Hospitality and Tourism Themes, 12*(6), 691–699. DOI: 10.1108/WHATT-07-2020-0066

Villacé-Molinero, T., Fernández-Muñoz, J.J., Orea-Giner, A., & Fuentes-Moraleda, L. (2021). Understanding the New Post-COVID-19 Risk Scenario: Outlooks and Challenges for a New Era of Tourism. *Tourism Management, 86*. DOI: 10.1016/j.tourman.2021.104324

SECTION 2
Case studies

5

INDUCING DOMESTIC TOURISM THROUGH *STOKVELS* IN SOUTH AFRICA

Post-COVID-19 tourism recovery in the global South

*Unathi Sonwabile Henama, Lwazi Apleni,
Madiseng Messiah Phori, Petrus Mfanampela
Maphanga, Simiso Lindokuhle Mabaso
and Xolile Dlamini-Mnisi*

Introduction

The structural challenges facing South Africa include poverty, unemployment and inequality. Creating jobs and growing the economy are major challenges facing South Africa. The economy of South Africa has always been dominated by mining, and the decline in the fortunes of mining has caused economic havoc for many cities and towns in South Africa. Golubski (2020) noted that before the pandemic hit, the unemployment rate in the first quarter of 2020 was 30%, and South Africa was in its second recession in two years. Even before the COVID-19 pandemic, the economy of South Africa had been in trouble, finding itself in a growth trap. Tourism had emerged as a reliable partner in growing the economy of South Africa, creating employment opportunities as a catalyst for the development of small businesses and spreading wealth, along with opportunities for entrepreneurship.

The interconnectivity of the world, especially through aviation, has led to the spread of the COVID-19 pandemic to all countries. The COVID-19 pandemic has been a health and economic crisis for the world economy and this impacted profoundly on tourism due to limits on travel and border closures. A pandemic can be classified as one type of the major categories of disasters, next to political events, natural disasters, financial events and man-made events, and the travel and tourism sectors have suffered the hardest thus far from the series of pandemics and epidemics like avian flu and swine flu.

DOI: 10.4324/9781003295839-8

Tourism in South Africa

Saunders (2019) noted that tourism contributed 2.9% of GDP, supports 726 000 jobs, and 9.2% of all employment in South Africa. South Africa's total tourism arrivals remain stagnant at 10 million visitors, dominated by regional tourists. Phillips (2020) noted that the tourism industry is valued at R270 billion in South Africa. Tourism is often developed due to its positive economic impacts on a destination.

On 5 March 2020, the Minister of Health made an official announcement of a local confirmed COVID-19 case in South Africa: a 38-year-old man from KwaZulu-Natal who had recently returned from a trip to Italy. To stop the spread of COVID-19, South Africa announced a national lockdown on 26 March 2020 (Rogerson & Rogerson, 2020). Bama and Nyikana (2021) noted that tourism in South Africa is not considered an essential service and therefore fell within the category of services that had to remain closed down. The lockdown, the curfew, stay-at-home orders and limits to both domestic and international travel negatively affected the tourism industry. The decline of international tourism has had a detrimental impact on developing countries, especially on the African continent. Tourism is disproportionately important for African countries, seeking especially to attract foreign exchange through tourism expenditure.

Impact of COVID-19 on tourism

Woyo (2021) noted that COVID-19 is a global health pandemic that has triggered an unprecedented crisis in the tourism industry globally. Tourism continues to be one of the sectors hardest hit by the coronavirus pandemic and the outlook remains highly uncertain (OECD, 2020). Sigala (2020) explained that there was an estimated global loss of $US 1.2 trillion in export revenues from tourism and 120 million job cuts.

The tourism industry is very sensitive to crises and the COVID-19 pandemic had a detrimental impact on tourism. The tourism industry is travel intensive and it requires simultaneous production and consumption for tourism consumption, which is led through human interactions. Kampel (2020) noted that several features of the tourism sector make it very vulnerable to the COVID-19 pandemic, namely:

- First, unlike other services (e.g., insurance, finance and telecoms), tourism and its related activities require physical proximity for the service to be delivered and utilised.
- Second, unlike goods, which can still be produced, stored and consumed at a later stage, a halt to services trade means that lost revenues and income cannot be recouped later on.
- Third, tourism is a critical sector for many countries because it generates employment and foreign exchange. It is also one of the most dynamic

economic sectors, with important backward and forward linkages and multiplier effects across many productive sectors and activities in the tourism value chain.

- The tourism industry is impacted by unique characteristics, which includes the high concentration of small businesses that do not have the deep financial pockets of established big businesses, which makes small businesses less resilient to economic shocks. The tourism industry is seasonal in nature, which means that economic fortunes are dependent on high and/or low seasons, and this means that a sizeable number of jobs are seasonal in nature, which offer poor job security.

As the world has learnt to co-exist with the COVID-19 pandemic, millions of people continue to work from home, and this has important implications for the tourism industry. This led to an increase in leisure time, as time to commute to and from work was no longer exercised. This led to an opportunity to use that increased leisure time and to promote domestic tourism. The continued infections and death from COVID-19 and the now universal requirement that one must be vaccinated to travel have limited the recovery of the tourism industry. Countries see domestic tourism as a panacea for tourism recovery, as the recovery of international arrivals was not certain. On the African continent, as noted by the United Nations World Trade Organisation (2021), travel and tourism GDP in Africa dropped by 49.2% in 2020, domestic spending declined by 42.8% and international spending saw a steeper contraction at 66.8%.

One of the immediate impacts of the COVID-19 pandemic has been the exodus of South Africans from major cities for coastal holiday destinations and the rural hinterlands. Muller (2020) noted that the working-from-home trend, the rise of remote meetings via online platforms such as Zoom and Microsoft Teams, has led to the growth of Zoom towns in smaller coastal and popular rural villages. In the case of South Africa, Rogerson and Rogerson (2020) noted that there it is evident that in South Africa's risk-adjusted strategy, the tourism sector was the last sector to re-open fully. By the time South Africa was reopened for international arrivals, the holiday season was already in full swing, and domestic tourism was the only solution for the tourism value chain.

Theoretical framework: Butler's Tourism Area Life Cycle (TALC)

A theoretical framework grounds research on a particular body of knowledge and centres any study on theory and concepts. The theoretical framework used here is the Tourism Area Lifecycle Model (TALC). The TALC is used to reflect that domestic tourism was used as an available panacea for the tourism recovery phase. Kruczek and Szromek (2011) show that in the past 30 years, Butler's concept of the TALC has been widely applied to research on the development of tourist sites and areas. Bojanic (2006) noted that according to the TALC concept, a tourist destination progresses through five stages: exploration, involvement, development, consolidation, stagnation and post-stagnation.

- Exploration: the destination is still relatively unknown, attracting a small number of tourists due to the area's unique natural and cultural attractions. Adventurers are drawn to such a destination.
- Involvement: this marks the beginning of tourism development for a tourism destination. According to Bojanic (2006) as the destination moves into the involvement stage, there is limited interaction between tourists and the local community, resulting in only basic services. 'Contact between visitors and locals can be expected to remain high and, in fact, increase for those locals involved in catering for visitors' Butler (1980: 7).
- Development: outsiders begin to control the tourism industry, through their investments that change the character of the destination. Marketing attracts more tourists, and tourists outnumber locals during the peak tourism season. Butler (1980) noted that changes in the physical appearance of the area will be noticeable and it can be expected that not all of them will be welcomed or approved by all of the local population.
- Consolidation: the destination is known, but the rate of increase in visiting tourists has plateaued. Tourism is a major component of the local economy, and tourists exceed local residents in terms of numbers.
- Stagnation: the stagnation stage represents the beginning of the decline in tourism numbers. Growth continues until it reaches its peak and becomes more mature and even saturated in the fifth stage (Nordin & Wastlund, 2009). 'The destination has a well-established image, but it is no longer popular' (Bojanic, 2006: 141). According to Uysal et al. (2012) at this stage, the peak numbers of visitors will have been reached, and most are repeat visitors.
- Decline: Butler (1980) noted that during the decline stage, the area will not be able to compete with newer attractions and so will face a declining market, both spatially and numerically. Nordin and Wastlund (2009) argue that in the sixth stage, two things happen: the number of tourists can begin to decrease and revenues stagnate or fall or the destination is able to reinvent and move into the seventh stage.
- Rejuvenation: 'Rejuvenation may occur, although it is almost certain that this stage will never be reached without a complete change in the attractions on which tourism is based' (Butler, 1980: 8). According to Uysal et al. (2012) the rejuvenation stage corresponds to the renovation phase or the reintroduction of the product with new features in the product life cycle.

The TALC model can be used to reflect on the trajectory of tourism in South Africa during the COVID-19 pandemic. According to Matiza and Kruger (2021), the impact of health crises such as SARS, H1N1 and Ebola was not on the scale of the disaster brought by the COVID-19 pandemic Jungwei (2021). COVID-19 has triggered a global economic crisis that may last for years and has also brought some changes to people's consumption and travel preferences. The outbreak of the COVID-19 pandemic can be regarded as the sharpest decline in the tourism industry globally. World tourism can be regarded as being on a recovery path, reflected by the rejuvenation phase of the TALC. However, the recovery path located on the rejuvenation phase of the TALC would differ from continent to continent and country to country. The analysis of the rejuvenation of the tourism industry will now focus on South Africa, located in the Global South.

Domestic tourism

Domestic tourism is defined as all trips that take place over 40 kilometres outside of one's usual habitat, which can be a day trip or an overnight trip (Kabote et al., 2017). Statistics South Africa (2019) show that the volume of Visiting Friends and Relatives tourism (VFR) was estimated at 24.0 million trips with a total expenditure of R2.5 billion. Rogerson and Hoogendoorn (2014) explain that domestic tourism dominates VFR trips, expenditure and geographic spread in South Africa. Black South Africa represents 78% of VFR trips, using communal transport such as buses, minibus taxis and trains, reflecting the working-class nature of this niche market. The decline in the economic fortunes of South Africa led to fewer jobs being created, less wealth creation, and less tourism consumption. This means that, even before the pandemic, domestic tourism had been declining.

The outbreak of the COVID-19 pandemic also had a negative impact on domestic tourism, due to stay-at-home orders, the closure of internal borders and the implementation of the curfew. With the announcement that there were community infections due to the COVID-19 pandemic in South Africa, a lockdown was announced. Total income from tourist accommodation fell by 81.2% in August 2020 when compared to August 2019 (Dludla, 2020). According to Dube-Xaba (2021) South Africa's Minister of Transport announced interprovincial travel, which is responsible for most Visiting Friends and Relatives (VFR) tourism. Domestic tourism was also negatively affected by the COVID-19 pandemic, which means that the tourism industry in South Africa has suffered more profoundly, as domestic tourism was already declining. The Department of Tourism (2018) noted that VFR represents the largest percentage of domestic trips and in the year 2015, there was a 15% drop in domestic tourism trips. The drop in domestic tourism had a negative impact on the tourism value chain in South Africa, reflected in a loss of revenue, fewer bed nights and a reduction in the geographical spread of tourism.

Domestic tourism was seen as the primary means to restart tourism recovery in many destinations, including South Africa. According to Masihleho (2020) industry leaders believe domestic tourism will be the focus for the South African tourism industry in the short to medium term in the post-COVID-19 future. In many countries, the vaccine rollout has lagged behind, and international arrivals have not recovered due to several reasons, such as the host country being 'red listed' and slow vaccination, leading to poor visitor sentiment. Domestic tourism has emerged as a lifeline for the tourism industry, considering that international tourism will take some time to recover. Panashe (2020) noted that tourism is one of the low-hanging fruits that South Africa could exploit to rejuvenate the economy post-COVID-19. The initial focus of tourism recovery was domestic tourism. According to the Department of Tourism (2016) the three major reasons that depressed travel within South Africa included affordability, time constraints and no reason for travelling. This decline in domestic tourism has occurred, despite there being a billion-rand stokvel economy, which is essentially a savings vehicle. The stokvel savings economy is dominated by the demographic groups that constitute the majority of VFR tourists, which make up the majority of domestic tourism trips and tourism spending in South Africa.

The sustainability of South Africa as a tourism destination generally, and domestic tourism specifically, is dependent on stimulating domestic tourism. The inability of the tourism value chain, especially from the supply side, to cater to the majority of VFR tourists can be associated with the lack of its ability to tap into the needs of the VFR market through packages for members of *stokvels*. This mismatch means that the domestic tourism supply chain has been unable to tap into the cash-laden *stokvel* economy generally and growing domestic tourism. The economic might of the *stokvel* economy has been acknowledged by tourism authorities in South Africa. The Department of Tourism (2018), in a study titled 'Domestic Tourism Strategy Review – Theory of Change Approach', argued that there *is a need* to develop an in-depth understanding of Stokvel group travel and to measure this properly. *Stokvels* are critical for tourism recovery in South Africa, especially when domestic tourism is regarded as the primary means of achieving tourism recovery. Tourism recovery in South Africa will be slower because several countries, which are major source markets, have placed South Africa on their travel red lists. With reference to the TALC, tourism rejuvenation could depend on convincing the plethora of *stokvel* members to either save extra for tourism consumption or channel their existing savings towards tourism consumption. This would, over time, achieve two things: grow the number of domestic tourists, and institutionalise tourism consumption and the habit of holidays amongst members of *stokvels*.

Stokvels

South Africa has a billion-rand informal savings industry called *stokvels*. Traditionally, *stokvel* are pooled savings and investment schemes (Enterprise Development Property Fund, 2007). They organise themselves into groups and they meet on a monthly basis to exchange money (National Stokvel Association of South Africa, 2020; Enterprise Development Property Fund, 2007). *Stokvels* have historically operated mostly outside the realm of the traditional banking systems. The *stokvel* sector in South Africa is massive and controls huge financial resources. Stokvels in South Africa generate around R49.5 billion in member savings and have 11.6 million participants (University of Cape Town, 2020). In the South African context, these informal financial structures have been developed due to barriers to accessing formal banking structures. The Old Mutual Savings and Investment Monitor survey in 2017 confirmed that 74% of black middle-class people also use informal savings such as *stokvels*, saving clubs or unbanked cash (Orange, 2017). The study further indicated that stokvels continue to grow, with 42% of black metropolitan South Africans who earn R40k+ per month belonging to more than one *stokvel*. The integration of *stokvels* into the tourism value chain is imperative to grow domestic tourism and to support the VFR market, which dominates domestic tourism.

The long-term sustainability of the tourism value chain depends on growing domestic tourism, so that South Africa's tourism industry can be robust and resilient based on the bulk of its tourism transactions, which are dominated by locals. The tourism industry has begun some initial engagement with the National Stokvel Association of South Africa (NASASA). According to Phakathi (2016), NASASA entered into partnership with South African Tourism (SAT) to boost domestic leisure tourism and make domestic tourism available to millions of *stokvel* members. However, 'despite the wide use of *stokvels* and lay-by payment systems in a variety of economic fields, their use in tourism has been rather recent and has flown under the research radar. Travel stokvels are a relatively new phenomenon on the commercial market' (Adinolfi et al., 2021: 309). The government agency that manages the national parks in South Africa, the South African National Parks (SANParks) have launched a Stokvel & Travel Club programme. According to Experience Northern Cape (2021) SANParks created this new product as part of the marketing strategy of growing non-traditional markets and positioning SANParks as the primary holiday destination amongst the domestic market. The Government Communication and Information Service (2021) noted that to qualify for the adapted payment terms, stokvels would have to register with the reservation staff at SANParks as a stokvel, which would be allocated a client code that could be used for making bookings, showing how these relationships are starting to become more institutionalised.

Several established tourism companies have jumped on the *stokvel* tourism bandwagon, coming up with products and *stokvel* packages. One such company had been Flight Centre, which began a *stokvel* for travel, and the initial trends show that South African love islands such as Mauritius and Thailand, in addition to local destinations, when redeeming travel benefits through the *stokvel* for travel. According to Stokveldeals (2020) the *stokvel* market has proven too lucrative to be ignored and these deals are made to entice *stokvels* to spend some of that R44 billion on travel. Their packages for travel begin from a minimum of R100 per month to R500 per month. These *stokvel* packages would not only make travelling easier, but would also address the affordability challenge that has depressed domestic tourism. The growth of tourism *stokvels* that are created for the sole purpose of tourism consumption are welcomed to ignite tourism recovery. Tourism recovery in South Africa is dependent on domestic tourism and a declining domestic tourism market cannot lead to recovery. *Stokvels* can be a panacea for tourism recovery in South Africa by stimulating the billion-rand *stokvel* economy to participate in tourism consumption.

Conclusions and recommendations

In the case of South Africa, tourism has been an economic messiah since the end of apartheid in 1994. The decline of tourism has detrimental impacts on South Africa's economy, and tourism recovery is paramount. Tourism is not only included in the economic development policies of the state, but tourism was regarded as a low-hanging fruit to achieve economic recovery from the COVID-19 pandemic. The snail's pace return of international tourism due to restrictions in source countries meant that stimulating greater domestic tourism is a matter of life and death for the tourism value chain in South Africa. Unfortunately, there were not enough domestic tourists to promote sustained growth. One of the major lessons of the COVID-19 pandemic for South Africa is that the tourism industry can be resilient only if the majority of its tourism transactions are dominated by the locals. Domestic tourism is very important in making the tourism value chain robust and resilient. In the case of the People's Republic of China, the tourism value chain was able to recover almost immediately after the COVID-19 pandemic because the country had a sizeable domestic tourism market.

The recovery of the tourism industry will not be the same across destinations, considering that the vast majority of transactions are dominated by countries in the Global North. Developing countries in the Global South depend on tourism to diversify their economy, but may lack the existence of a substantial domestic market because of domestic challenges. A small domestic tourism market is not sufficient for developing impacts from tourism, but it must be borne in mind that not all destinations are the same. Small island destinations and developing countries may have small domestic tourism markets when compared to developed countries. This makes many small islands and developing countries vulnerable to shocks, and the COVID-19 pandemic was a major shock. Countries in the Global North sustained their tourism industries under lockdown through domestic tourism, but the experience of the Global South was divergent. There were insufficient domestic tourists to sustain the tourism value chain. To make the situation more in South Africa, domestic tourism had already been experiencing a decline, which meant that fewer domestic tourists could be depended on to stimulate rejuvenation. Domestic tourism is a function of the economy, and the South African economy has not been doing well in terms of job creation, attracting new investments and economic growth, and this has meant fewer people are employed, leading to a decline in domestic tourism. South African society is very much mobile in nature, helping to explain the predominance of VFR trips in the domestic tourism market. The majority of those who are VFR tourists are members of *stokvels* and it makes perfect sense to convert them into leisure tourists. The *stokvel* economy has the potential to grow domestic tourism, introduce new markets to tourism consumption and institutionalise the habit of holidays.

The use of *stokvels* for tourism consumption is still in its infancy, and *stokvels* for tourism consumption are yet to be exploited fully. This depends on a greater collaborative effort between the private sector, destination marketing agencies and representative bodies in the *stokvel* economy. With the assistance of the *stokvel* economy, tourism will recover and continue on its trajectory as the second largest employer and second contributor to gross domestic product.

References

Adinolfi, M.C., Harilal, V., & Giddy, J.K. (2021). Travel Stokvels, Leisure on Lay-by, and Pay at Your Pace Options: The Post COVID-19 Domestic Tourism Landscape in South Africa. *African Journal of Hospitality, Tourism and Leisure, 10*(1), 302–317.

Bama, H.K.N., & Nyikana, S. (2021). The Effects of COVID-19 on Future Domestic Travel Intentions in South Africa: A stakeholder Perspective. *African Journal of Hospitality, Tourism and Leisure, 10*(1), 179–193.

Bojanic, D. (2006). Tourism Area Life Cycle Stage and the Impact of a Crisis. *ASEAN Journal of Hospitality and Tourism, 4*, 139–150.

Butler, R.W. (1980). The Concept of a Tourism Area Cycle of Evolution: Implications for Management of Resources. *Canadian Geographer*, XXIV(1), 5–12.

Department of Tourism. (2016). *State of Tourism Report 2015/16*. Pretoria: GCIS.

Department of Tourism. (2018). *Domestic Tourism Strategy Review - Theory of Change Approach*. Pretoria: GCIS.

Dludla, S. (2020, October 20). *Tourism in SA Battling to Recover with New COVID-19 Surge Overseas*. IOL. https://www.iol.co.za/business-report/economy/tourism-in-sa-battling-to-recover-with-new-covid-19-surge-overseas-c07b1393-2e1e-4233-9e6d-0fdefe8d9e33

Dube-Xaba, Z. (2021). COVID-19 Lockdown and Visitor Friends and Relatives Travellers: Impact and Opportunities. *African Journal of Hospitality, Tourism and Leisure, 18*(3), 856–862.

Enterprise Development Property Fund. (2007). *Changing the LANDscape of South*. www.edpf.co.za/wp/. Accessed 14 March 2021.

Experience Northern Cape. (2021). *SANParks Launches Stokvel & Travel Club Programme*. www.experiencenortherncape.com/visitor/blog

Golubski, C. (2020, July 18). *South African Economy Struggles under the Weight of the Pandemic*. https://www.brookings.edu/blog/africa-in-focus/2020/07/18/africa-in-the-news-south-africas-economy-tensions-in-mali-and-mozambiques-liquified-natural-gas-project/

Government Communication and Information Service. (2021). *Travel Discounts for Stokvels and Travel Clubs*. Pretoria: GCIS.

Jungwei, S. (2021). China's Domestic Tourism in Speedy Recovery as Spring Arrives. *CGTN*. https://news.cgtn.com/news. Accessed 8 September 2021.

Kabote, F., Mamimine, P.W., & Muranda, Z. (2017). Domestic Tourism for Sustainable Development in Developing Countries. *African Journal of Hospitality, Tourism and Leisure, 6*(2), 1–12.

Kampel, K. (2020). *COVID-19 and Tourism. Charting a Sustainable, Resilient Recovery for Small States. Trade Hot Topics*. London. The Commonwealth Library.

Kruczek, Z., & Szromek, A.R. (2011). Using R.W. Butler's Model to Interpret the Development of Tourists Attractions, Based on the Example of the Salt Mine in Wieliczka. *Folia Turistica, 25*(1), 250–263.

Masihleho, B. (2020). Domestic Tourism the Answer Post COVID19? *Tourism Update*. www.tourismupdate.co.za/article/domestictourism. Accessed 8 September 2021.

Matiza, T., & Kruger, M. (2021). Ceding to Their Fears: A Taxonomic Analysis of the Heterogeneity in COVID-19 Associated Perceived Risk and Intended Travel Behaviour. *Tourism Recreation Research, 46*(2), 158–174.

Muller, J. (2020). 'Zoom boom' Spark City Exodus. *Business Live*. www.businesslive.co.za/fm/features/. Accessed 1 February 2021.

National Stokvel Association of South Africa. (2020). *Statement on Measures to Prevent COVID-19 Coronavirus Transmission*. https://nasasa.co.za/. Accessed 14 March 2021.

Nordin, S., & Wastlund, H. (2009). Social Capital and the Life Cycle Model: The Transformation of the Destination of Are. *Tourism, 57*(3), 259–284.

OECD. (2020). *Rebuilding Tourism for the Future: COVID-19 Policy Responses and Recovery*. https://www.oecd.org. Accessed 1 February 2021.

Orange, S. (2017, August 1). A Modern Approach to Stokvels. *Risk Africa Magazine*.

Panashe, P. (2020). Domestic Tourism to the Rescue. *Mail & Guardian*. https://mg.co.za/opinion/. Accessed 1 February 2021.

Phakathi, B. (2016). Tourism Body in Stokvel Tie-up. www.businesslive.co.za/bd/companies/transport-and-tourism/. Accessed 1 February 2021.

Phillips, X. (2020). South Africa vs Coronavirus: Billions Already Lost in Tourism. *Under Pressure*. www.theafricareport.com/30653/. Accessed 1 February 2021

Rogerson, C.M., & Hoogendoorn, G. (2014). VFR travel and second home tourism: The missing link? The case of South Africa. *Tourism Review International, 18*(3), 167–178

Rogerson, C.M., & Rogerson, J.M. (2020). COVID-19 tourism impacts in South Africa: Government and Industry Responses. *GeoJournal of Tourism and Geosites, 31*(3), 1083–1091.

Saunders, G. (2019). *A Foundation for South African Tourism Growth*. www.tourismupdate.co.za/news/column. Accessed 1 February 2021.

Sigala, M. (2020). Tourism and COVID-19: Impacts and Implications for Advancing and Resetting Industry and Research. *Journal of Business Research, 117*, 312–321.

Statistics South Africa. (2019). *Domestic Tourism*. Pretoria: StatsSA.

Stokveldeals. (2020). *Stokvel Travel: The Ultimate Guide to Making Travelling Affordable*. www.stokveldeals.com/article/stokvel-travel-the-ultimate-guide-to-making-travelling-affordable.php. Accessed 1 February 2021.

United Nations World Trade Organisation. (2021). *Tourism Recovery Tracker*. www.unwto.org/unwto-tourism. Accessed 4 September 2021.

University Cape Town (2020). *Customary Saving Scheme Seldom Resort to the Law*. www.law.uct.ac.za/news/customary-savings-and-law. Accessed 22 February 2021.

Uysal, M., Woo, E., & Singal, M. (2012). The Tourism Area Life Cycle (TALC) and its Effects on the Quality-of-Life (QOL) of Destination Community. In M. Uysal, R.R. Purdue & M.J. Sirgy (Eds.), *Handbook of Tourism and Quality-of-Life Research: Enhancing the Lives of Tourists and Residents of Host Communities*. Cham: Springer.

Woyo, E. (2021). The Sustainability of Using Domestic Tourism as a Post-COVID-19 Recovery Strategy in a Distressed Destination. *Information and Communication Technologies in Tourism*, 476–489.

6

INNOVATIVE MARKETING STRATEGIES DURING TOURISM RECOVERY IN THE POST-COVID-19 PERIOD IN NIGERIA

Shuaibu Chiroma Hassan

Introduction

For the past three decades, tourism has been among the fastest sectors in terms of economic growth and the most dynamic in the promotion of national economic development, product development, cultural heritage, and has been a significant driver for job creation (International Labour Organization, 2020). Many countries depend on tourism as the main supporter of livelihoods and economic growth – this makes the 'tourism re-start' pivotal (UNWTO, 2020). Tourism comprises two main industries – travel and hospitality. Therefore, there is a need for successful marketing in hospitality, which is highly dependent on the travel industry (Harrington et al., 2014).

The COVID-19 pandemic has forced the world to an unprecedented halt, and tourism is one of the sectors that was hit the worst (China Global Television Network, 2020). The impact of the COVID-19 pandemic crisis on the travel and tourism industry is the worst compared to other sectors – it was one of the first sectors to be impacted deeply, due to the measures introduced for containing the virus around the globe (China Daily, 2020). The African Development Bank (AfDB) forecasts that countries or regions which depend on tourism and oil as their main exports for revenue will be facing an external economic imbalance, which will lead to huge public debt (Obioha, 2020).

The COVID-19 pandemic presents a change catalyst to hospitality, tourism and food service industries, leading to a tough future trend in the industry (Future Food, 2020). During the COVID-19 pandemic, the tourism industry was forced to a halt due to the closure of airports, other public transportation, event centres and public services as a result of the global lockdown (Suleiman, 2020). History reveals that organisations that invest more in innovation during crisis periods outperform their competitors during recovery (Haas et al., 2020). Due to these challenges,

DOI: 10.4324/9781003295839-9

the tourism industry, more than ever, needs more innovative marketing strategies for recovery. During the current restart of tourism and hospitality businesses, there are good responses from various governments and stakeholders to counter the COVID-19 challenges, which are resulting in an easing of travel restrictions, as revealed by the World Tourism Organization (UNWTO, 2020).

It has been observed that:

> The immediate imperative is to ensure the survival of tourism enterprises through large-scale support, without which they will disappear before the virus does. And that support must extend to the workers concerned who would otherwise have no income or social protection.
> Guy Ryder, ILO Director General, Extraordinary G20 Tourism Ministers Meeting, 24 April 2020.
> *(International Labour Organization, 2020)*

More emphasis is required on services and other tourist offerings by organisations to give customers a sense of safety and security. This chapter will present and analyse the role of existing and innovative marketing strategies that can support tourism and hospitality organisations during this period.

Model to be applied

The study employs the Strengths, Weaknesses, Opportunities and Threats (SWOT) analysis technique to analyse the internal and external environments of tourism that influence marketing. SWOT analysis has been used as a tool in tourism and hospitality organisations to identify, develop and exploit their potentials and opportunities on one hand, and to strive to improve on their areas of weaknesses and protect from the threats facing them, on the other. For example, Hel Kafi (2019) applied SWOT analysis to analyse strategy development in Bangladesh tourism and SWOT analysis was employed by Ayodele et al. (2013) for situational analysis of the *Thomas Cook Group*.

Trends and megatrends in tourism

Hassan (2016b) identifies trends as the main driving force in the tourism and hospitality industries. The trends before the year 2020 saw significant changes to many tourists' behaviours, such as in Chinese outbound markets, with increasing numbers losing interest in package tours (China Daily, 2020). Entire tourist destinations and hospitality industries must be conscious of trends for developing new products due to the need for new products and services (Kotler et al., 2006). Meanwhile, megatrends affect tourism as well as its future (Milano et al., 2019). The growth of Information and Communication Technologies (ICT), an example of a mega-trend, has brought a global network that today is becoming an integral part of today's society and penetrated deeply in our day-to-day activities, more importantly among tourists (Karpova et al., 2019). Therefore, technology should be embraced in the hotel and tourism sectors. 'Digitalisation' is therefore needed for tourism destinations for effective advertisements and marketing. The emergence of new social media platforms as well as technology are part of important trends in travel that need to be considered among tourism and hospitality consumers (Curran, 2020).

Another trend that emerges in tourism and hospitality industries – consciousness about hygiene, health and safety to protect visitors from COVID-19 infections; these necessitate creativity and innovation, customer communication, harnessing technology, and locally oriented practices (Future Food, 2020). The following sections of this chapter identify examples of innovative strategies in tourism and hospitality that have been prompted by these new contexts.

Innovative strategies implemented in tourism and hospitality

Innovative new tourism products were developed by students of NHL Stenden for Dutch tourism entrepreneurs during the COVID pandemic. The strategies include:

- Cooking workshop – by children using local ingredients; includes cycling to a play park;
- Treasure hunt – a children's activity;
- Animation of a tour guide (Folmer, 2020).

Benchmarking is another strategy employed in this context. It is not new, but its application by tourism management and marketing organisations will help boost business recovery in the post-COVID-19 era. Obioha (2020) identifies the copying of strategies by tourism destinations from other competitors to develop and improve on their models during competition. Jovicic and Ivanovic (2006) emphasise benchmarking as a strategy, particularly in marketing, which will give tourism businesses and destination marketing organisations (DMOs) leverage against competitors.

Thailand's strategy to boost its tourism market during COVID included the introduction of discounts for air travel with a concessionary travel package for up to 1.2 million health workers. Similarly, China's local governments employ the same strategy in order to boost its domestic tourism by suspending ferry fees for vehicles (China Global Television Network, 2020). Chinese tourism businesses launched free and discounted tourism offers in order to attract more tourists, which in turn led to more spending by the tourists, particularly on food, transport, shopping and accommodation (Xingyu, 2021). According to Suleiman (2020), some African destinations are leveraging on the existing rapport with their clients, mostly the U.S. and E.U., offering them affordable packages in advance that encourage them to book during the lockdown.

Clustering is a strategy involving the collection of industries or businesses in a geographical region to inter-connect their market, products and suppliers to get synergy as the main purpose (Soteriades et al., 2009). Jovicic and Gajic (2016) see clustering in both tourism and hospitality as a tool that promotes strategic partnership, cooperation and horizontal relationships and enables innovations and competitiveness.

Franchising is employed by small and medium tourism enterprises that do not have the capital strength to operate, expand and sustain competitions and promote entrepreneurship and innovations (Lewandowska, 2014). It is affordable and provides them with a competitive advantage in the market. It is a marketing strategy that enables the franchisee to gain the technical knowhow, training, brand (trademark), management support, fairs and advertisements of the franchisor (Lewandowska, 2014). During the recovery period, tourism enterprises need innovation more than ever to avoid business collapse. In the next sections of this chapter, innovations in marketing more specifically, will be the focus.

Marketing and marketing concepts

According to Kotler et al. (2006) marketing is seen as a managerial and social process whereby individuals as well as groups obtain satisfaction they want or need by exchanging and creating service/produce and values with others. Harrington et al. (2014) further describe marketing as a business task for providing real value to targeted and identified customers to elicit purchase of the product or services as well as the fulfilment of the customers' needs. Marketing to create customer satisfaction and value is the heart of the tourism and hospitality sectors.

Meanwhile, marketing management involves the analyses, controlling, planning and implementation of business programs that are designed to build, create and maintain beneficial exchanges between the target customers for achieving the set organisational objectives or goals. Therefore, market and marketing concepts show that the achievement of organisational goals depends on determining and satisfying the wants and needs of the target markets as well as delivering the desired customer satisfaction (Harrington et al., 2014).

The next sections of this chapter present short case studies of how different national tourism organisations have developed their marketing strategies during and following the COVID-19 pandemic.

The United Arab Emirates

The UAE has recently launched a new strategy to boost its domestic tourism by developing a comprehensive scheme to develop and regulate its local tourism through a strong collaboration with the federal and local tourism entities and other stakeholders. The strategy presents the UAE as a New Unified Tourism Identity to position the UAE as an ideal tourism destination globally and domestically through sharing inspirational stories with the outside world. A federal tourism campaign was launched as 'World's Coolest Winter'. The aim is to emphasise the main attractions and landmarks. This promotes all the individual destinations with their diverse experiences and attractions (Alfaham, 2020).

Thailand

Thailand has employed new techniques for boosting the hotel and tourism sector by injecting up to 72 million US dollars for domestic tourism as their borders remain closed to international tourists. Under the plan, guests booking into hotels will only pay 60% of the accommodation bills for up to five nights, while the government will pay the remaining 40%. In addition, there are discounts for air travel with concessionary travel packages for up to 1.2 million health workers as well as volunteers (Bond, 2020). The strategy aims to boost domestic tourism for a restart for the local economy, which will make it easy for international tourists to visit the country.

China

The first strategy China employed for quick recovery was its ability to contain the virus and become a winner in tourism (China Daily, 2020; China Global Television Network, 2020). China – being a major tourism source market, used an online exhibition to boost hospitality and tourism and help re-start tourism. The intangible cultural heritage food festival of 2020 was kick-started in Beijing on the 13th of June, showcasing various foods and drinks brands of more than 1300 companies, to mark China's cultural and National Heritage Day. The exhibition was hosted by innovative means employing technology to convey the message to the target audience. Classic delicacies were offered online through red envelopes, vouchers and consumer coupons. Cooking skills were displayed via popular reviews and rating platforms on live stream on Meituan's Dianping app. Consumers were able to order cuisine on the Meituan app. The strategies to employ in marketing tourism should first and foremost ensure that tourists will feel safe and have their needs satisfied.

Rwanda

Strategies and measures taken by the government in revitalising their tourism sector to bounce back during the COVID-19 crisis have included:

- Tourism promotions for domestic and international travellers, with credit incentive negotiations for the private sectors. Tourism operations are being supported through a scheme for special funds to support the affected businesses – as recovery funds for small and medium enterprises;
- More innovative initiatives for supporting the lives of the affective employees and tourism businesses to help their businesses through capacity building in the country;

- Involving the Green Global Institute, who initiated a one-year project plan for $10 million to support Rwanda's tourism industry (Ndicunga, 2020).

Following these short examples, this chapter will now turn to a more detailed examination of the strategies and innovations developed in Nigeria's tourism industry in the wake of the crises prompted by the COVID-19 pandemic.

Strategy and marketing innovations in Nigeria's tourism industry

Marketing strategies and their implementation are important for capturing the target customers of a particular business operation. A strategy for effective marketing is needed to promote tourism and its products and services at the destination (Hel Kafi, 2019). Before designing marketing strategies, certain factors need to be considered: trends in consumer markets, consumer behaviour, and segmentation of the consumer market. Looking at the current tourism markets, China has become the major tourism source market due to the huge population and the growth in their disposable incomes in recent years (Bloomberg, 2020). For these reasons, Chinese tourists need to be considered to tap into their potential markets. In addition, factors that shape or influence consumers, such as trends, mega-trends and behaviour, need to be considered. These can include technology, travel mobility, sustainability, urbanisation, economic inter-connectedness of nations, and changes in the nature of visitor demand (Organisation for Economic Co-operation and Development, 2018). New marketing strategies are needed in tourism organisations to attract more tourists and maintain their loyalties in competitive tourism markets locally or globally.

In Nigeria, marketing tourism takes advantage of the huge convergence of information superhighways. Therefore, hotels will need to aggressively invest in digital futures and improve their marketing strategies to embrace innovation (Proshare Confidential, 2021). The Nigerian Tourism Development Corporation (NTDC) supports the promotion of the tourism industry through engagements with technical giants such as Google and Wikipedia for creating tourist experiences through the leading offerings of 'Tour Nigeria' (Coker, 2021). The NTDC use 'Tour Nigeria' as a brand to drive domestic tourism consumption in the country in order to generate sales and employment. The essence of this approach is to identify, develop and market key tourism sites like Kurra Falls in Plateau state as national treasures (Agency Report, 2021). Meanwhile, Plateau state, in Nigeria, which largely depends on tourism as a source of revenue, encourages digitisation in the tourism and hospitality sectors as a strategy to market its product offerings against the pandemic shocks (Jungu et al., 2021).

Strategy is the entire uniting 'theme', which suggests actions and decisions within the group or organisation in order to succeed in its market. It is generally the plan of how an organisation should achieve its own set goals in addition to how it survives and prospers against its competition (Bryson, 1988). The first strategy for marketing tourism is to set a vision and goal and establish marketing promotions to achieve them (Hel Kafi, 2019). After identifying the objectives of the business, strategic planning is needed to get the right marketing strategies to enter competitive markets.

Innovation is an important factor for boosting the competitiveness of firms in the tourism and hospitality sectors. It can be seen as any method used for translating ideas or inventions into services or products that gives value for money to customers. Innovation is a deliberate utilisation of initiatives, information and imagination in obtaining a different value from the available resource in the form of new processes, products or services (Olimovich & Alinovich, 2019). Innovation has to satisfy the customer in terms of quality product or service for the money paid, satisfy the needs of the customers and improve the brand on one hand, and provide the organisation with convenience, low cost, efficiency and quality of service or product on the other. Ungerman and Dědková (2019) identify four groups of innovations for tourism and hospitality: (i) organisational innovations, (ii) marketing innovations, (iii) process innovations, and (iv) product innovations. Innovation serves as leverage that improves the positioning of tourism organisations in competitive tourism markets.

Transcorp Hotel (Nigeria) applied various innovations in its strategies, which are pivotal for its remarkable business recovery recorded in Q3 and Q4 of 2020, raising their room occupancy to 55% in December compared to that of June (10.90%) (Proshare Confidential, 2021). Transcorp Hotel, a leading hospitality company in Nigeria with more than 30 years' experience, which has more than 800 rooms between Calabar and FCT – Abuja, applied various innovations for their recovery during the Pandemic period. Innovation in presenting entertainment ('in-room entertainment') has evolved due to developments in technology. It is employed for tourists based on their expected preferences in entertainment in order to meet their needs.

Embracing technology has taken on a more important strategic role than before the pandemic and is moving the tourism and hospitality industries forward (Coker, 2021). These include social network tools such as Instagram, Facebook and Vkontakte; and internet sites such as TripAdvisor, map sites, navigation engines, wikitravel.org, Skyscanner, budgetyourtrip.com, Avisales, etc., which catch large audiences without any border restrictions (Karpova et al., 2019). Many subjects are being covered in a podcast on e-marketing and e-campaigning, attracting millions of listeners (Xingyu, 2021). Nigeria's Transcorp Hotel used social media to launch 'Top of Mind Awareness' to market its products and services during the recovery period (Proshare Confidential, 2021). Events and activities were used as a marketing strategy by Transcorp to boost sales and attract more customers. Staycations, festivities and social and leisure activities attracted couples, families and singles during the coronavirus pandemic (Proshare Confidential, 2021). Transcorp applied a strategy to market its services by providing virtual technology to enable its guests to be involved in both virtual and physical meetings using hybrid events for conferencing facilities to leverage technology (Proshare Confidential, 2021).

Customer information and data is critical for tourism businesses for the provision of unique, inspirational and authentic travel experiences for hospitality and tourism customers' convenience. It is not a marketing strategy; however, it will enhance any marketing strategy to be employed. Data is crucial in meeting the needs and requirements of current and future tourists. Big Data, Artificial Intelligence and Data Analytics are used to give hospitality and tourism organisations a competitive advantage in the markets. For example, Airbnb has successfully employed a big data strategy to gain competitive advantage and change the tourism market (Yallop & Seraphin, 2020).

The main strategy for a recovery in tourism and hospitality sectors for reaching the new normal is to ensure that the virus is curbed and health and safety practices are enforced with effective testing upon arrival, along with COVID-19 passport. This will give the 'new tourists' a sense of confidence to visit the destination. With the discovery of vaccines by countries like China, Russia and the USA, many countries like the UK, Germany, France and the USA began using them in early 2021. This was followed by the progressive lifting of travel restrictions worldwide.

Conclusion and recommendations

Tourism needs marketing to sell its attractions and product offerings to potential tourists. As the pandemic is being contained, with China as the only country to have contained the menace so far, and many countries are vaccinating their populations, there is optimism that the pandemic will be addressed and tourism will recover gradually. China's tourism has been on the recovery track for the past ten months at least. It is likely that Chinese tourists will be ready for outbound tourism more quickly than any other country. The study employed a SWOT analysis model to evaluate tourism businesses and organisations vis-à-vis strengths, weaknesses, threats and opportunities, examining whether tourism organisations have employed suitable post-pandemic marketing strategies, with a focus on Nigeria.

Effective marketing strategies are needed more than ever by various tourism destinations, DMOs, travel agencies, and the hospitality sector globally for quick and competitive recovery. The future of tourism will continue to be impacted for some years to come in terms of economic and tourism recovery and COVID-19 precautions. Some destinations will have a quick recovery, like China, while others will face slow recovery. Meanwhile, in Nigeria, some hospitality and tourism firms have been highlighted in this chapter. The 'new tourist' will emerge who will prioritise hygiene, health and safety, while many tourism destinations will shift from being numbers-focused to more of an emphasis on quality with increased price. As a result, Nigeria's tourism and hospitality organisations, as well as the federal government, should position themselves through a strategic marketing approach.

References

Agency Report (2021, March 31). *Reviving Nigeria's Tourism Fortunes After COVID-19. Premium Times.*

Alfaham, M.R. (2020). *Mohammed bin Rashid Approves UAE Strategy for Domestic Tourism.* https:wam.ae/en/details/1395302894569. Accessed 12 December 2020

Ayodele, A., Ojo, P., Kamara, H., & Alli, M. (2013). *Situational Analysis of Thomas Cook Group.* Technical Report.

Bloomberg (2020). *China Bolster its Dominance of Global Trade*, Bloomberg News. Bloomberg. com.

Bond (2020, Jun 17). *Thailand Government Grants $720 Million Aid to Boost Domestic Tourism*. https:// www.hotelierindia.com/business/11228-thailand-government-grants-720-million-aid-to-boost-domestic-tourism

Bryson, J.M. (1988) A Strategic Planning Process for Public and Non – Profit Organisations. *Long Range Planning, 21*(1), 73–81

China Global Television Network (CGTN) (2020). *The New Normal: Tourism*. https:// newseu.cgtn.com/news/2020-07-26/The-New-Normal-Tourism-RQYCNFq5Fu/ index.html

China Daily (2020, June 15). *China Offers Hope to the Global Tourism Industry*. https://www. chinadaily.com.cn/a/202009/15/WS5f602ecea3101ccd0bee0759.html

Fife, R., & Atkins, E. (2021, January 5). Air Canada Hires Influencers to Promote Vacation Travels Even as Federal Guidelines Urge People to Stay Home. *The Globe and Mail*.

Folmer, A. (2020). Home >Blog>4 Post-COVID-19 Innovations in the Tourism Industry. *European Tourism Futures*. www.etfi.nl/en/blo.

Future Food (2020). *Food and Hospitality Trends – Five Food and Hospitality Trends for the Post – Lockdown World*. https://linkd.in/gNCC7XYMay

Haas, S., McClain, J., McInerny, P., & Timelin, B. (2020). *Reimagining Consumer – Goods Innovation for the Next Normal*. London: McKinsey & Company.

Harrington, R.J., Chalhoth, P.K., Ottenbacher, M., & Altinay, L. (2014). Strategic Management Research in Hospitality and Tourism: Past and Future. *International Journal of Contemporary Hospitality Management, 26*(5), 778–808. DOI: 10.1108/IJCHM – 12.2013–0576

Hassan, S.C. (2016a). *Event Management – The Case of London 2012 Olympic Games Legacy Report, Submitted to the Department of Marketing, Tourism and Hospitality Management*. Bedfordshire: University of Bedfordshire.

Hassan, S.C. (2016b). *International Tourism Marketing: A Marketing Plan for Katsina Hotel into a New Venture, Assignment Submitted to the Department of Marketing, Tourism and Hospitality Management*. Bedfordshire: University of Bedfordshire.

Hel Kafi, M.A. (2019). Strategy Development in Tourism: A Case Study on Bangladesh. Masters Report Submitted to the Department of Tourism and Hospitality, University of Dhaka in Partial Fulfillment for the Requirements for the Award of Master of Business Administration in Hospitality and Tourism.

ILO (2020). *Sectoral Brief – The Impact of COVID-19 on the Tourism Sector (Revised May)*. Geneva: International Labour Organisation.

Jovicic, A., & Gajic, S. (2016). Hotel Innovation and Inter-Cluster Differences. In *Thematic Proceedings II, 1st International Scientific Conference. Tourism in Function of Development of the Federal Republic of Serbia*. Kragujevac: University of Kragujevac, Faculty of Hotel Management and Tourism in Vrnjacka Banja.

Jovicic, D., & Ivanovic, V. (2006). Benchmarking and Quality Managing of Tourist Destinations. *Tourism and Hospitality Management, 12*(2), 123–134.

Jungu, Y.G., Ogenyi, M.A., Bodunde, T.D., & Saidu, A. (2021). Effects of COVID-19 Pandemic and Its Attendant Lockdown Policy on the Economy of Plateau State. *International Journal of Engineering & Management Research, 11*(2). DOI: 10.31033/ijemr.11.2.21

Karpova, G.A., Kuchumova, A.V., Voloshinova, M.V., & Testina, Y.S. (2019, October 24–25). Digitalisation of a Tourist Destination. *SPBPU IDE' 19*, Saint – Petersburg, Russia.

Kotler, P., Bowen, J.T., & Makens J.C. (2006). *Marketing for Hospitality and Tourism*. 4th ed. London: Pearson Prentice Hall.

Lewandowska, L. (2014). Franchising as a Way of Creating Entrepreneurship and Innovation. *Comparative Economic Research, 17*(3). DOI: 10.2478/cer-2014–0028.

Milano, C., Novelli, M., & Cheer, J.M. (2019). Overtourism and Tourismphobia: A Journey Through Four Decades of Tourism Development, Planning and Local Concerns. *Tourism Planning & Development, 16*(4), 353–357.

Ndicunga, R. (2020). *Reducing Operation Costs and Creating Green Jobs for COVID-19 Affected Tourism Industry in Rwanda*. A Technical Report, April.

Obioha, V. (2020, July 15). This Day. 'Mapping A Post – COVID-19 Landscape for Tourism, Creative Industries.' *Editorial Column.*

OECD (2018). Megatrends Shaping the Future of Tourism. In *OECD Tourism and Policies*. Paris: OECD Publishing.

Olimovich, D.I., & Alinovich, F.E. (2019). The Impact of Innovations in Tourism and Hospitality. *International Multi – Lingual Journal of Science and Technology (IMJST), 4*(9).

Proshare Confidential (2021). Hospitality Post COVID-19; Marketing the Future Count, (April), 1602–8842. *Proshare Economy, 1,* 260.

Soteriades, M., Tyrogala, E., & Varvaressos, S. (2009). Contribution of Networking and Clustering in Rural Tourism Business. *Tourismos, 4*(4), 35–56.

Suleiman, M.A.B. (2020, December 12). Mohammad bin Rashid Approves UAE Strategy for Domestic Tourism – WAM/Tariq Alfaham. https://wam.ae/en/details/1395302894569).

The Guardian (2020, January 14). *Readers' Travel Trips – 10 of the Best Virtual Travel Experiences: Readers' Trip.*

Ungerman, O., & Dědková, J. (2019). Marketing Innovations in Industry 4.0 and Their Impacts on Current Enterprises. *Applied Sciences, 9*(18), 3685.

UNWTO. (2020, June 19) 'Strong and Rapid' Governments' Response to COVID – Challenge. *As Tourism Restart, UNWTO Notes.*

Xingyu, C. (2021, January 1). 2020 China's Tourism in Review: Rising from the Ashes of COVID-19. *Travel.*

Yallop, A., & Seraphin, H. (2020). Big Data and Analytics in Tourism and Hospitality: Opportunities and Risks. *Journal of Tourism Futures.* DOI: 10.1108/JTF – 10–2019–0108.

7

THE COVID-19 PANDEMIC AND RISK ANALYSIS IN TOURISM DESTINATIONS

Insights from Queen of Hills 'Mussoorie'

Neha Mishra and Anindya J. Mishra

Introduction

> *We have to make our lives in a more active way than was true of previous generations, and we need more actively to accept responsibilities for the consequences of what we do and the lifestyle habits we adopt.*
>
> (Giddens, 1984).

This statement from Anthony Giddens seems more relevant in today's COVID-19 pandemic era than at any other time, which has entailed the need to amend one's lifestyles and choices and to become more responsible for saving oneself from the infectious virus. The COVID-19 pandemic has unleashed various threats and risks in every sector across the world, including the tourism and hospitality sectors. The World Tourism Organization (WTO) has explained that, due to the COVID-19 pandemic, the entire world is undergoing an unprecedented economic, social and health crisis (WTO, 2020). It has also been highlighted by UNWTO (2020) that the tourism sector has lost around US \$13.5 trillion. The pandemic has affected various sectors of tourism (Gössling et al., 2020), which has impacted the tourism industry at both macro and micro levels. It has impacted the lives and livelihoods of many, especially those who derive their source of livelihood from the tourism sector. In the case of developing countries, the impact on vulnerable communities is more intense than in developed nations, as many workers are involved in the informal sectors of the tourism industry in the countries of Asia and East Asia. The International Labour Organisation (ILO, 2020: 2) has stated that 'in low and middle-income countries, hard hit sectors have a high proportion of workers in informal employment and workers with limited access to health services and social protection'.

DOI: 10.4324/9781003295839-10

Understanding 'risk society' and the current COVID-19 pandemic

The concept of 'risk society' was given by Ulrich Beck, highlighting that today's society is confronted with various side-effects produced due to the modernisation process, and its social impact is global, as modern society is no longer a closed system. For Beck, risk society is 'an inescapable structural condition of advanced industrialization' (Beck, 1992: 31). Thus, global risks are not restricted to any geographical boundaries. The current coronavirus crisis reflects the same reality. WHO has declared the current cataclysmic crisis as a pandemic that has spread all over the globe. Further, Beck's theory states that the risk, and an individual's position to it, are important to understanding how an individual resides in the world. Beck discusses *'positions of risk'* and also highlights that social positions and risks overlap increasingly frequently, which is clearly evident in COVID-19 pandemic times. COVID-19 has aggravated the existing inequities in society in terms of socioeconomic status. For example, coronavirus does not discriminate against people; however, the key thing to protect oneself from the virus is to maintain physical distancing, which is not possible for all. Vulnerable sections of society, such as slum dwellers, domestic workers, and migrant workers, could not afford to maintain physical distancing. Thus, one's position in society matters, as it determines whether we are at risk and to what degree risk is not universal and even for everyone; instead, it is quite complex and wide-ranging (Aiken, 2000).

Literature review

The COVID-19 pandemic has unleashed various social, economic, psychological and cultural influences on tourism sector stakeholders and the adverse effects will last for a long time (Abbas et al., 2021). Therefore, the literature has acknowledged that the COVID-19 crisis has to be viewed as an opportunity to review tourism's growth approach, emphasising that COVID-19 research needs a careful and conscious study of workers' physical, psychological and mental conditions (Horaira, 2021). Since the COVID-19-induced lockdown was imposed, hotels have opted to stop their operations, and prices dropped considerably for those hotels that decided to continue. In such situations, managerial decisions are highly dependent on travel restrictions (Arabadzhyan et al., 2021).

For example, in a study conducted in Hong Kong, it was found that the government of Hong Kong adopted international travel restrictions so as to prevent the spread of the COVID-19 virus, due to which that inbound tourism came to a standstill (Tsui et al., 2021). Studies have also emphasised organisational resilience to overcome the impact of COVID-19 on tourism businesses (Bhaskara & Filimonau, 2021). In their research, Bhaskara and Filimonau (2021) have conducted a study on tourism businesses in Bali. They conclude that poor organisational learning related to past disasters and crises has restricted their preparedness and may also delay the recovery from COVID-19. Similarly, another study conducted in the

Savannah region found that the impact of the pandemic was quite severe, which is due to overreliance on tourism in the Savannah region (Soliku et al., 2021). The study's findings also showed that the over-reliance of local communities on tourism and its related activities could have dire consequences on the livelihood of the local people and the local economy.

In the case of India, the COVID-19 pandemic has had a disastrous impact on the tourism sector. The tourism and hospitality industry employs approximately 87.5 million people in India, who are directly or indirectly dependent on tourism. However, due to the pandemic, it is estimated that 40–50 million people could have lost their jobs. Considering the socio-cultural impacts of this, a study done in the Kashmir region found that the current pandemic had devastating consequences in all spheres of socio-cultural systems and paved the way for unemployment and poverty (Singh et al., 2021). Similarly, in a study conducted in Rajasthan, it was found that the current pandemic has affected tourism at a large scale, and there is a need to develop a proper monitoring system. The literature has also stressed that well-being has also been affected by the stakeholders involved in the tourism sector due to the COVID-19 pandemic (McCartney et al., 2021).

From the previously mentioned studies conducted at the global level and at the Indian level, the need to refocus on sustainable tourism has also emerged. Previous studies conducted on sustainable tourism can guide us, even in today's pandemic times. For example, Soriya Yin (2016), in her work *Sustainable City Tourism in Developing Countries: Malaysia Experience* analysed how different stakeholders like government, industry and civil society organisations have conceptualised sustainable tourism. She also stated that balance does not exist between sustainable tourism's economic, environmental and social dimensions. Using a snowball sampling technique, the study sheds light on how our knowledge and understanding of how policymakers and practitioners perceive sustainable tourism in developing countries and what challenges they face in implementing them. They identify challenges such as poor maintenance, poor transportation connectivity, water pollution, and limited collaborative governance. Residents felt that their concerns are not incorporated in decision-making by policy-makers. At the same time, they also face walkability problems, parking problems, and waste disposal problems in their life.

Methodology

This chapter is based on primary data collection to identify the myriad risks in the lives of the local population dependent on the tourism sector for sustenance and survival. A total of 50 semi-structured interviews were conducted with diverse local population categories comprising the migrant population, local inhabitants, the Tibetan and the Nepali population during the period of May to November 2020. In line with the work of Earl Babbie (2015), who argued that observation is involved in field research, it is employed in this research to gain additional insights. The sampling strategy used in the study was non-probability purposive sampling, as the study was dependent on the respondents' availability.

Semi-structured interviews were conducted in the Hindi language, and responses were recorded. Thereafter, the responses were translated into English and categorised accordingly. All interviewees were offered anonymity and, where names are reported, full consent was given for this. Data were collected during the first phase of COVID-19 in India from May 2020 to November 2021. A six-month time span was undertaken to analyse the impact of COVID-19 on the lives of local communities over the phase of time.

Area of study

Mussoorie is a hill station situated in the foothills of the Himalayas in the state of Uttarakhand. Mussoorie is popularly known as the 'Queen of Hills'. It is popularly known for its beautiful natural places, such as Mall Road, Company Garden, Gun Hill, Kempty Fall, and Buddha Temple. Mussoorie became a hill station in 1823 during the colonial era when the British ruled over India. The colonial upper-middle class visited the place to escape from the heat of the Indian plains. However, after independence in 1947, tourism started growing by catering to upper-class Indians. Gradually, mass tourism started developing. After 2000, tourism in the place has grown to a level where the number of visitors has surpassed the local population.

Assessing the risks to the lives of marginalised communities during COVID-19 pandemic

The sudden lockdown in the country announced in March 2022 created an atmosphere of fear, anguish and uncertainty among all the tourism stakeholders. While interviewing Sandeep Sahni, Uttarakhand Hotel Association's President in Mussoorie, he stated that around a 70 percent loss has occurred in revenues. Thus, the government has to take immediate and long-term measures in order to revive tourism in the area as the sudden emergence of new COVID variants is hitting the hospitality sector again and again. Similarly, when interviewing Mr. Mohan Rayal, the resort owner near Kasmanda Temple, he stated that Mussoorie badly needs a fully-fledged tourism season to recover from the losses and become more sustainable.

Although everyone involved in the tourism industry in Mussoorie was affected, vulnerable communities comprising workers employed in restaurants and hotels, rickshaw pullers, and taxi drivers, Tibetans and the migrant population suffered in greater intensity in the hill station. First, considering the impact on the lives of local communities, it was found that those who were exclusively dependent on tourism for their survival were affected to a more considerable extent. Most of them ran small stalls of edible items such as Maggie, boiled eggs, momos or fruit salad. Some of them were sharing lanes consisting of small shops selling items such as knitted clothes, warm caps and shawls. The sudden lockdown, which lasted for more than six months, hit their lives very hard. For example, married couples who shifted to Mussoorie way back in the 1990s from the Almora region for employment opportunities had increasing concerns due to the current pandemic crisis. Currently, there is an existing risk of getting hospitalised, and the risk of getting infected, the biggest fear amongst all is how to sustain over this challenging time. One of the couples stated that:

> I have to look after seven members of their family. However, there is not enough ration left at home to sustain for more than two months. Also, no government support is being provided to them for the reason that they are registered neither under the tourism department nor they have enrolled under any scheme. The only support that they are dependent upon is relying on their relatives and close friends for survival.

There are two things that are reflected in her reply. Firstly, the question of absence of support from the government side and secondly, the solidarity among the family members and friends amongst the lower class in times of crisis. In the case of the first question, it has been examined separately in another section as to why government intervention remained ineffective during the COVID-19 pandemic, which made their families face additional risks that otherwise could have been avoided. The second part, solidarity, is significant to analyse, as it is the basis through which food security issues along with socio-economic issues can be addressed in times of pandemics. It again becomes significant, as during pandemics when physical distancing increasingly becomes common among the majority of people, it has affected the social fabric of society.

Another type of risk that was revealed by the respondents was social and psychological stress, which was mainly due to reduced social interaction amid pandemic times. Stress was also due to the dismal condition of primary healthcare, which led to distress and anxiety among the public. For example, a woman who used to work in a hotel as a caretaking staff member explained that:

> While working in the Hotel Himalayan Club, Mussoorie, I regularly interacted with my colleagues over there where we used to express each other issues, concerns, grievances and life happenings, etc. However, due to lockdowns imposed everywhere, we cannot meet our colleagues, which has led to psychological stress and emotional unwellness.'

One critical thing that was found while conducting interviews was that, in most of the cases, people who belonged to the lower caste and class suffered a loss of income due to which they fell into the trap of poverty. However, others were working in grocery shops and as vegetable and fruit sellers and found themselves at significant risk due to their physical proximity with the general public daily. Regular sanitising and handwashing were not possible for many. Looking at such cases, it can be stated that everyone is situated in different risk positions when it comes to averting risks induced by the COVID-19 pandemic, as in most cases, such people do not have the option of working from home. The social marginalisation of such lower caste communities and lack of access to services increases their vulnerability.

It also reflects that the nature of a job becomes more significant in these times, as argued by Williams (2020), who shows that the kind of job that one does was never so crucial as in today's times, as it determines life chances and safety against the virus. Those who have a stable income and are at home are privileged. Others who have no income or employment left and live in overcrowded areas have to deal with the challenges posed by the pandemic. One's gender, class and the nature of a job determine one's capability to limit the pandemic's negative impacts. Similarly, the position of risk describes individuals in different situations while acting and responding to the repercussions caused by the pandemic. This analysis provides a comprehensive and more precise picture, which would otherwise be impossible.

Similar to this was the situation of many women, especially those who were informal workers who suffered from a loss of livelihood and an increased burden of work at home. In the patriarchal society of India and due to poor social positioning in society, domestic violence and physical abuse were also high. For example, while interviewing a woman who used to work as a helper in a shop, she shared that:

> Earlier, I worked as a helper in a garment shop on Mall Road and earned around Rs.7000/- per month. However, after the lockdown, I have lost my job. Added to that there is constant pressure at home to do all house chores and look after aged grandparents. Sometimes my husband starts physically abusing me. It has become hard to survive in such a situation.

This burden on women has increased exponentially with the closure of schools for their children, and in most cases, husbands are also at home. As caregiving is traditionally considered part of women's jobs, they are called upon to give care to the sick, either at home or outside, with little or no preventive support. Due to the patriarchal mindset, men rarely share household work with wives in India. This overburden on women worsens their physical and mental health.

During the pandemic, many women lost the status of being independent. This has reduced women's status again to being 'dependent' on their male partner, leading to male domination at home. Even if the woman's husband's job status remains unemployed, the psychological mindset of males being the dictator of the family remains intact. And this has strengthened in such a cataclysmic event. Thus, the patriarchy and the overwhelming gaps in healthcare and social security systems have left these women more vulnerable in today's environment.

One significant aspect that emerges here is that it is intersectionality that determines one's capability amid the pandemic. The previous quotation reflects the experience that, as well as being a low-status woman, now financially dependent on the family for survival, she has to bear her husband's physical abuse too at home. She suffered along gender, caste and class lines.

One aspect of the impact of the COVID pandemic on the migrant people living in Mussoorie is that many of them have become homeless. While interviewing, it was found that, as most of them lost their job, they could not pay the rent for their rented flat. Just a few of them managed to live by opting for alternative options of survival, such as working in construction sites or selling fruits and vegetables door to door. One migrant worker, who was found working in a hotel site that was undergoing renovation, stated that:

> Earlier, I was working in a restaurant as a waiter, but I lost my job after lockdown. As I cannot afford to go to my native village in Bihar, I have started working in a construction site where I usually earn approximately Rs.700/- per day. This is how we are sustaining in these challenging situations.

This situation depicts how poor migrant people sustain themselves by choosing whatever means to support them in pandemic times. While interviewing Mr. Kukreja, Mussoorie Traders Association's secretary, he stated that local traders had witnessed a severe dip in their sales. Added to that, these local traders fear that the items may get damaged or lose their shine if they remain unsold for more than one tourist season, which mainly comes from April to June.

Why do government interventions remain ineffective?

Although the lockdown was essential to stop the spread of coronavirus, its implementation was problematic. The sudden announcement of lockdown came with many blind spots, which created disproportionate risk in the lives of vulnerable communities. The government did not consider the fact that the informal sector in India makes up to eighty percent of India's workforce, and they may be affected. The current lockdown situation has revealed the underlying problems of deficiencies and lacunae in our social security system. It has highlighted the unequal nature of society and poverty. It is quite astonishing that these vulnerable informal workers largely remain absent from government policies. For example, the government did not consider that women's hygiene products and sanitary napkins should be listed on the essential items amid the lockdown.

Women were treated as second-class citizens, and as a result, they suffered more in the crisis. However, the government came up with a scheme, namely, Prime Minister Garib Kalyan Yojana, under which 1.7 trillion dollars would be distributed among women, migrants and other vulnerable sections. However, it is still questionable how effective it is, as experts believe that the sanctioned amount is insufficient and India at current times needs at least two times that amount. Moreover, there is less awareness of public benefits and social security systems among these vulnerable communities. The government has also tried to combat domestic violence through running women's helpline numbers, but it is not enough, as very few women workers have access to phones and the internet. Thus, it is a matter of social urgency. The government needs to galvanise the social welfare system because COVID-19 has acted as a poverty multiplier. This limbo-like situation and the debacle have exposed the nature of how deep poverty is entrenched and how destitution has been visited in a manifold way by the most vulnerable people in India.

Conclusion

The current coronavirus pandemic has deepened the divide between privileged and underprivileged communities. Without an inclusive strategy, it would be difficult for vulnerable communities to overcome the crisis. A potential implication of the COVID-19 crisis is that it may intensify these multi-layered vulnerabilities. Now, it is important to focus more on social security measures, especially on capacity building, to deal with the health and existential crisis that vulnerable women workers face, in particular. The government and tourism industry should focus on capacity building of the workforce and engage local workers in hospitality services (Arshad et al., 2021). Recovery has to be carried out in a sustainable manner, which will require the coordination of all the agencies involved, such as tourism operators, travel agencies, central and state governments, and voluntary organisations, in order to ensure a smooth transition in the post-pandemic phase of the tourism industry (Pandey et al., 2021). In this direction, the research contributes in terms of practical implications for policymakers and decision-makers of local government, in particular, to focus on social sustainability that can positively impact local communities by improving their overall well-being. If policies are made without taking into account the dimension of social sustainability, then the benefits that are derived from such policies may be inequitably distributed, leading to greater social exclusion and inequality in society.

References

Abbas, J., Mubeen, R., Iorember, P.T., Raza, S., & Mamirkulova, G. (2021). Exploring the Impact of COVID-19 on Tourism: Transformational Potential and Implications for a Sustainable Recovery of the Travel and Leisure Industry. *Current Research in Behavioral Sciences*, 2, 100033. DOI: 10.1016/j.crbeha.2021.100033.

Aiken, M. (2000). Reflexive Modernisation and the Social Economy. *Studies in Social and Political Thought*, 2(3), 21.

Arabadzhyan, A., Figini, P., & Zirulia, L. (2021). Hotels, Prices and Risk Premium in Exceptional Times: The Case of Milan Hotels during the First COVID-19 Outbreak. *Annals of Tourism Research Empirical Insights*, 2(2), 100023. DOI: 10.1016/j.annale.2021.100023.

Arshad, M.O., Khan, S., Haleem, A., Mansoor, H., Arshad, M.O., & Arshad, M.E. (2021). Understanding the Impact of COVID-19 on Indian Tourism Sector through Time Series Modelling. *Journal of Tourism Futures*, 1–15. DOI: 10.1108/JTF-06-2020-0100.

Babbie, E. (2015). *Observing Ourselves: Essays in Social Research*. Long Grove, IL: Waveland Press.

Beck, U. (1992). *Risk Society: Towards a New Modernity*. London. Sage.

Bhaskara, G.I., & Filimonau, V. (2021). The COVID-19 Pandemic and Organisational Learning for Disaster Planning and Management: A Perspective of Tourism Businesses from a Destination Prone to Consecutive Disasters. *Journal of Hospitality and Tourism Management, 46*, 364–375. DOI: 10.1016/j.jhtm.2021.01.011.

Giddens, A. (1984). *The Constitution of Society: Outline of the Theory of Structuration*. Cornwall: Polity Press.

Gössling, S., Scott, D., & Hall, C.M. (2020). Pandemics, Tourism and Global Change: A Rapid Assessment of COVID-19. *Journal of Sustainable Tourism, 29*(1), 1–20.

Horaira, M.A. (2021). Impact of COVID-19 Pandemic on Tourism Industry: Possible Reconciliation Strategy for Bangladeshi Tourism Industry. *International Tourism and Hospitality Journal*. DOI: 10.37227/ithj-2021-03-108.

ILO (2020). Sectoral Brief – The Impact of COVID-19 on the Tourism Sector (Revised May). Geneva: International Labour Organisation.

McCartney, G., Ung, C.O.L., & Ferreira Pinto, J. (2021). *Creating Tourism Situational Awareness during COVID-19: A Collaborative Approach between Community Pharmacists and the Tourism Industry*. Available at SSRN 3913054.

Pandey, K., Mahadevan, K., & Joshi, S. (2021). Indian Tourism Industry and COVID-19: A5Sustainable Recovery Framework in a Post-Pandemic Era. *Vision, 3*, 1–15.

Singh, A.L., Jamal, S., & Ahmad, W.S. (2021). Impact Assessment of Lockdown Amid COVID-19 Pandemic on Tourism Industry of Kashmir Valley, India Research in Globalization Impact Assessment of Lockdown amid COVID-19 Pandemic on Tourism Industry of Kashmir Valley, India. *Research in Globalization, 3*, 100053. DOI: 10.1016/j.resglo.2021.100053.

Soliku, O., Kyiire, B., Mahama, A., & Kubio, C. (2021). Tourism Amid COVID-19 Pandemic: Impacts and Implications for Building Resilience in the Eco-tourism Sector in Ghana's Savannah Region. *Heliyon, 7*(9), e07892. DOI: 10.1016/j.heliyon.2021.e07892.

Tsui, K.W.H., Fu, X., Chen, T., Lei, Z., & Wu, H. (2021). Analyzing Hong Kong's Inbound Tourism: The Impact of the COVID-19 Pandemic. *IATSS Research, 45*(4), 440–450. DOI: 10.1016/j.iatssr.2021.11.003.

UNWTO. (2020). *Impact Assessment of the COVID-19 Outbreak on International Tourism UNWTO*. www.unwto.org/impact-assessment-of-the-covid-19-outbreak-on-international-tourism

Williams, M. (2020, May 19). Coronavirus Class Divide- the Jobs Most at Risk of Contracting and Dying from COVID-19. *The Conversation*. https://theconversation.com/coronavirus-class-divide-the-jobs-most-at-risk-of-contracting-and-dying-from-covid-19–138857

WTO (2020). www.unwto.org/impact-assessment-of-the-covid-19-outbreak-on-international-tourism

Yin, S. (2016). *Sustainable City Tourism in Developing Countries: Malaysia Experience*. Malaysia Sustainable Cities Program, Working Paper Series. Massachusetts Institute of Technology.

8

SEARCHING FOR A BREAK FROM THE DRUDGERY OF DAILY DIN

Analysing millennials' quest for spirituality and well-being during the COVID-19 pandemic

Manpreet Arora and Roshan Lal Sharma

Introduction

The United Nations World Tourism Organization (UNWTO) observes that by 2030, 'there could be 1.8 billion tourists – just over one in five persons in the world – travelling around the globe' (UNWTO, 2011). This indicated how huge an industry tourism is in view of its global appeal and the sheer magnitude of the tourist population keen on travelling the world. Millennial travellers have an altogether different approach to travel as they are aware, conscious, educated, truly adventurous, sharp and savvy travellers committed to exploring and experiencing the world in a way that adds to their inner growth and spiritual well-being (Ketter, 2020; Aceron et al., 2018; Agustina, 2018; Richards & Morrill, 2020). The mandate of UNWTO provides for the 'promotion of responsible, sustainable and universally accessible tourism' (UNWTO, 2022). However, restrictions on international travel due to COVID-19 rendered all efforts to promote international tourism meaningless (Irimiás & Mitev, 2020; McCartney, 2020). International flights were suspended during 2020 even though some countries resumed flights at the end of the year, but again due to the second wave of coronavirus the world over, many countries have been restricting international flights affecting the tourism industry immensely (Cheer, 2020; Gössling et al., 2020).

WHO declared COVID-19 to be a 'Public Health Emergency of International Concern' in January 2020, which later was termed 'pandemic'. It came as an uncouth and unexpected shock for people across the world (Kamata, 2021; Withers et al., 2021). Several economies where tourism was a major source of revenue were shattered, and consequently, many sectors of the economy dependent on the tourism industry were crippled (Lim & To, 2021; Qin et al., 2020). Millions of jobs all over the world in various service sectors were badly hit and people became unemployed.

DOI: 10.4324/9781003295839-11

According to a UN policy brief on 'COVID-19 and Transforming Tourism', 'Tourism is one of the sectors most affected by the COVID-19 pandemic, impacting economies, livelihoods, public services and opportunities on all continents' (UNSDG, 2020). Amidst such an abysmal and gloomy situation caused by the pandemic, millennial tourists' dreams and aspirations to travel were abruptly throttled (Baniamin et al., 2020). Nevertheless, as millennials are a generation that remains intrinsically motivated to look forward despite all odds, the pandemic, rather than curbing their aspirations, resulted in propelling their urge several-fold to move out, not necessarily because of their desire for adventure, but merely to seek change, to search for solace, to find spiritual gratification and a lasting sense of inner contentment with the help of spiritual or religious-mystical experiences.

Millennials, being tech-savvy, believe in sharing their real-time experiences with their friends and followers, which results in reshaping and rebuilding of a millennial psyche in the face of the coronavirus pandemic. A millennial's goal is to experience the world afresh from his/her perspective. Millennials exist in almost every socio-cultural clime of the world; their aspirations may differ owing to their cultural specificity. Likewise, their modus operandi as millennial travellers may change because of the socio-cultural and economic contexts from which they hail, and they are ecologically conscious, socio-culturally adaptable, politically aware and financially self-reliant. Therefore, millennials would remain on the cusp of transformation, as there is always a goal to transition their lives from drudgery and dullness to spiritual well-being and religious-mystical experiences.

There is evidence to suggest that the COVID-19 pandemic has tremendously increased millennials' unfulfilled desires to travel, whether it is domestic or international (Ivanova et al., 2020; Qiao et al., 2021). Religion and spirituality have been considered coping resources/mechanisms in terms of using them as a therapy (Molteni et al., 2021). Millennial travellers often get bored and feel stressed out due to the mechanical routine of daily life, and therefore, to rejuvenate themselves and to seek solace and peace of mind, they often travel to places that have spiritual and religious significance. There is a continuous increase in the percentage of the population that travels not to enjoy or to seek fun but to search for peace and solitude from the din and drudgery of life. Short breaks and smaller trips/visits with the sole objective of rejuvenation can have various forms, such as visits to religious places and meditation centres in the lap of nature, which help them to attain spiritual or mystical experiences. This chapter aims at examining various modes in which millennials try to search for peace, joy and inner contentment in view of the larger goal of spiritual well-being during the pandemic.

Research questions and methodology

This paper is qualitative in nature and uses content analysis. It presents an investigation of how, during the COVID-19 crisis, millennials have been craving deeply for spirituality and spiritual well-being, which was adversely affected due to millions of deaths across the globe. Such unprecedented gloom and an unendurable sense of despair has given birth to millennials' quest to realise spirituality and experience well-being.

This qualitative research uses data from secondary sources like websites and publication reports of international repute. We have also employed the qualitative software NVivo to extract and analyse public sentiments in the form of written tweets on key terms such as '#millennials,' 'travel and spirituality' and 'travel and COVID-19'. With the help of word clouds, the terms shared/posted by the public will help us understand their thoughts and excitement about travel. The research questions that this paper seeks to examine are as follows:

1   Can a crisis like the COVID-19 pandemic blunt/incapacitate millennials' quest for spirituality and spiritual well-being?
2   Are millennials intrinsically averse to drudgery and dullness in life, and why do they crave for a permanent sense of well-being through spiritual/religious/ mystical experiences?
3   What are the biggest takeaways based on our understanding of millennials' quest for well-being that may pave the way for humanity at large to endure as well as cope with the COVID-19 crisis?

Millennials' quest for spirituality

Millennials' search for spirituality and well-being has been the hallmark of their spirit of adventure and their commitment to exploring the inscrutable aspects of human existence (Berger, 2013). In fact, they break the conventional frame of notions concerning travelling with specific purposes. They are short-term planners who aim at attaining long-term benefits resorting to excessively intense experiences and believe in exploring the world around them to seek inner solace and transformation on psychological and spiritual planes (Sehlikoglu & Karakas, 2016). Millennials are intrinsically inclined toward adventure with a view to explore nature/the world around particularly when they are bogged down either by the drudgery of day-to-day routine activities or by the din/noise of city life/urban spaces (Dwivedi & Lewis, 2020).

As global citizens, millennials cannot afford to remain unconcerned about the psychological and spiritual distress caused by the pandemic. Spiritual and religious tourism thus becomes a ploy to understand the meaning of life, especially during such trying times. The whole idea of spirituality is to be able to understand the spirit behind this universe (Moran, 2017), while religion connects us with a Supreme Being and/or divine godhead, thereby evoking divinity in us (Cox & DeVeaux, 2019). For some people, getting close to nature and experiencing its beautiful offerings also have spiritual implications.

Social media has become an important platform for millennials to express their experiences in the form of tweets, posts, videos and pictures/photographs (Parra-López et al., 2012). They depend heavily on technology to decide about their plans for spiritual, religious and mystical tourism, and also for nature-based tourism

FIGURE 8.1   Word cloud 1: Keyword searched, '#millennials'

FIGURE 8.2   Word cloud 2: Keywords searched, 'travel and spirituality'

(Chu et al., 2020). To understand what they share as their sentiments about spirituality and travel, a Twitter search was conducted using NCapture and the cloud charts were prepared using NVivo software used as a qualitative research analytical tool. The Twitter search on the keywords '#millennials' and 'travel and spirituality' was done on 18 April 2021 and through NCapture 1448 and 47 tweets were captured, respectively. Thereafter, the following word clouds were prepared:

Figure 8.1 shows that 'Gen Z', 'pandemic', 'spirituality', 'India', 'corona-virus', 'conservative', 'experiences', and 'Changing times' are the prominent words used by millennials and these clearly indicate their inclination towards gaining newer experiences through travel during the pandemic, and also highlight the fact that for 'Gen Z' varied experiences matter the most.

Figure 8.2 clearly highlights words such as 'travel', 'physical activity', 'mental health', 'soul', 'mind', 'harmony', 'healthy lifestyle', 'wellness', and 'well-being', indicating that for those who express their views on travel and spirituality, connection between mind and body is critically crucial and becomes evident through important expressions such as wellness, well-being, and mental health.

As a matter of fact, millennial tourism implies tourist activities undertaken by people with a view to travel, see and experience the world around them (Gilli & Palmisano, 2021) to maximum possible extent and thus enrich mind and ennoble their spirit, which social media has become an indispensable part of (Miguéns et al.,

2008; Chung et al., 2015; Dillette et al., 2019; Sigala et al., 2012). To seek specific experiences, they travel within a relatively shorter span of time (McDonald, 2015). It can be a short adventure trip, travel plan, or an off-road excursion to experience something that breaks the monotony and tedium of life. At times, they may want to experience something about a particular culture or lifestyle (Ahn et al., 2020). The main goal of the younger generation today remains to become richer by watching, observing and experiencing whatever nature has to offer and whatever places having religious and spiritual significance have to offer to them (Fox & Xu, 2017; Pfeiffer et al.,2019).

Destinations such as Vatican City, Jerusalem, Mecca and in India *Haridwar, Kashi, Badrinath, Kedarnath and Rameswaram* are places that not only have religious significance but also form the cores of Christian, Jewish, Muslim and Indian psyches and ways of life. Therefore, a millennial traveller coming from overseas would connect with these places at symbolic as well as socio-cultural, psychological and anthropological levels (Montgomery et al., 2016). Thus, a millennial traveller's experience of India can be viewed in terms of awe, surprise, shock, elation, wonderment and disgust. S/he however would surely benefit from it in multifarious ways. Likewise, places such as *Sarnath*, MacLeod Ganj in Dharamshala, and several meditation centres at places such as *Rishikesh* and homes of spirituality such as Ojai in California where L. Krishnamurti attained enlightenment attract millennials from the viewpoint of spiritual quests which are concerned with matters of the human spirit/soul as opposed to worldly and material considerations. Millennials, by and large, prioritise embracing spirituality in a profounder and more rational manner owing to their innate proclivity toward scientific temperament (Sperry, 2016; Percy, 2019; Cabreja, 2017; Frederick, 2018).

Another aspect of millennial travel is an innate urge to find an inner self, which is their truer self. The chaos in our daily life makes us anxious, bitter and negative, but despite that, our materialistic desires do not stop. The more we desire, the deeper the inner void becomes. There comes a time when we do not even know exactly as to what is happening to us and why we are so insipid, dull and lifeless. The sense of enjoyment simply bids adieu and we lose the basic vitality in us. Living for the sake of living in a mechanical manner becomes the sole purpose of our lives. The true sense of being happy remains missing and we try to find happiness in the attention, care and love of people around us.

However, at a deeper level, many individuals feel a sense of vacuity and hollowness alongside the existential angst and start questioning the pointlessness of life. When such an irresolvable sense of meaninglessness creeps into our lives, we start asking fundamental questions related to human existence and life in general. Some millennial travellers thus remain engaged with such bewildering riddles of life and decide to live it as creatively and innovatively as possible. Movement/mobility of course remains at the core of a millennial's psyche. Millennials, through their quest for meaning in life, peace and spiritual well-being, often desire to get closer to nature, or centres/organisations that propagate spirituality and teach ways and methods of meditating and achieving spiritual well-being. They plan their travels to places that either have spiritual significance or are important from the viewpoint of religion. It may take the form of merely joining a meditation camp or just trekking to the countryside (Fotis, 2015). But what makes this travel important is the experience that is spiritually satisfying and thus heals the scars of our consciousness.

Millennials and religious tourism

Millennials claim to be more spiritual than religious owing to the dogmatic, ritualistic and orthodox dimensions attached to the latter. A religious person is theistic, as s/he believes in God as an omnipresent and omnipotent reality and who could be best served via following certain established practices and rituals. Spirituality is concerned with life at an inner level, at the level of spirit/soul. In religion, God may have an external as well as inner character, but spirituality points toward an inner life that helps one find her/his own truth (Watts, 2016). In spirituality, truth is discovered by the quester who follows his heart to unravel the mystery of life, but a religious person follows the well-established path of rituals, ceremonies and rigorous code of moral conduct to realise God. Religious practices may differ from culture to culture and in that sense, one religion is different from the other even though their basic tenets may be similar. Spiritual quest initiates and follows its own path and some people call it a 'pathless' pursuit of truth (Krishnamurti, 1929).

Even though spiritual tourism appeals more to millennials, it would be erroneous to say that they totally ignore the exploration of places of religious importance. There are millennial travellers who are theistic and believe in God in a religious sense. For them, undertaking pilgrimages to places of religious importance would form an intrinsic part of their travel plans/motives. The sole purpose of religious tourism is to provide solace and inner peace. However, travelling to seek pleasure and undertaking pilgrimage are totally different activities – the former aims at exploring nature, whereas the latter is centred on visiting a holy place which offers solace, peace and heals our soul. Authors such as Victor Turner (Turner & Turner, 1978) have argued that pilgrimage generally has to do with the special aspects of a particular place where the spatial experiences are related to the personal dimensions of a visitor and are achieved at a particular level, which can be mystical in nature.

Millennial tourism at times dovetails with pilgrim tourism, which in fact implies an endeavour to establish an indirect union with the Almighty as it is attained through rituals, teachings, etc., whereas a mystic establishes a direct union with God as the supreme being. It is possible that a millennial tourist as a pilgrim does not experience spirituality simply because his/her intentions can be purely religious and may give importance to certain rituals and ceremonies before experiencing divinity. Therefore, the concept of pilgrimage tourism cannot always be equated with spiritual tourism. Visiting a particular place of sacred nature to perform certain rituals in any religion can be easier to imagine, but the same can be difficult to describe theoretically. To demarcate between religious experiences and spiritual experiences to a great extent depends upon the intentions, feelings, emotions and sentiments of a tourist. This varies from person to person. Millennial tourists follow an eclectic approach in their selection of religious tourism destinations. For them, religious and spiritual tourism are not separate, sacrosanct categories as one may lead to the other and vice versa.

Millennials and their quest for well-being

Millennials are forced to face the challenges caused by pandemics like COVID-19 on a day-to-day basis. Whereas at one level, they have to sustain themselves financially, at another, they are forced to take care of those in the family who depend on them for their livelihood. As a result, millennials are left with no choice but to adapt to their changing circumstances. They are aware of the stress they undergo, the depression they cope with, and the angst that they experience owing to newer challenges thrown by the pandemic-caused crisis. Therefore, they remain conscious of their well-being under all circumstances. To see what they shared on social media in relation to travel during COVID-19 pandemic, a Twitter search was conducted using the keywords 'travel and spirituality'. The following cloud chart appeared by analysing 13706 tweets using NVivo software:

The major concerns of people are evident in Figure 8.3, as the words that prominently come out are 'health risk', 'well-being', 'restrictions', 'essential activities' and 'people'. Travel during the COVID-19 pandemic is making the general public think about risks, as they are seriously concerned about their health and well-being (Suar et al., 2019), and that is the reason that they have been talking about outdoor activities that lead to overall well-being.

'Well-being' signifies happiness, good health and contentment and a sense of purposefulness in one's life from perspectives such as financial, psychological, spiritual, educational, interpersonal, etc. Well-being is a concept which involves more than 'satisfaction' and 'happiness' and has multiple dimensions (Ruggeri et al., 2020). Well-being emanates from an inner sense of contentment and feelings of goodness, positivity and purposefulness (Huppert, 2009). The WHO equates it with 'mental health' and describes that 'in this state one realises his/her abilities and potential to the utmost and also has the capacity to endure stress and work productively to benefit community, can cope with the normal stresses of life, and

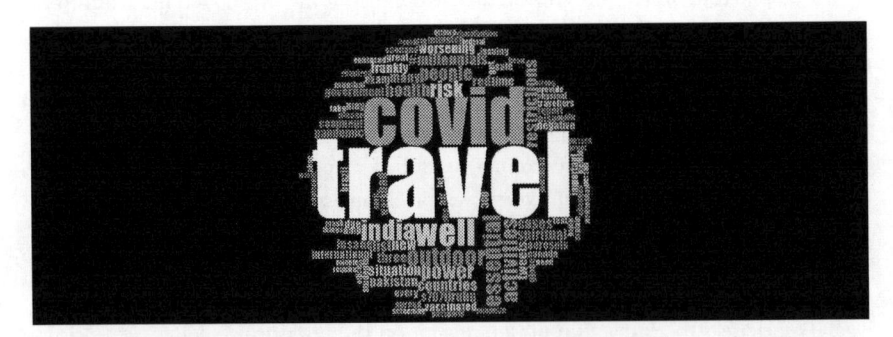

FIGURE 8.3 Word cloud 3: Keywords searched, 'travel and COVID-19'

can work productively and fruitfully, and to be able to make a contribution to his or her community' (World Health Organization, 2001).

Well-being for a millennial traveller has various dimensions, such as physical, mental/psychological, socio-cultural, economic, political, religious as well as spiritual. Millennials can differentiate between religion and spirituality, owing to their scientific temperament. Above all, millennials represent that portion of the world population who are affluent in the sense of financial self-reliance and who are passionate about the pursuits in their lives, such as exploration of nature, adventure in the lap of nature, exploration of various spiritual hubs in their immediate surroundings and around the world, visiting national and international destinations for their spiritual and psychological well-being.

Conclusions

We can say that millennials' activities and travels around the world cannot be underestimated because of the fact that they play a substantial role in generating billions of dollars in tourism through travel. Amidst the different kinds of activities/adventures that millennials undertake, spiritual well-being has shot into prominence due to the distress caused by the COVID-19 pandemic. When the scale of devastation rises to unimaginable heights, it is natural that humans tend to take recourse to either some god/deity, some kind of spiritual belief, or mystical quest/journey to realise the essence of being or to unravel the inscrutable mystery called life. Could anyone ever imagine that coronavirus would cause the death of millions of people across the globe, irrespective of their age, financial status, social position, and their geopolitical location? Could anyone ever think that this deeply polarised world would be reduced to a sheer passive bystander? Who would believe that the richest nations in the world would be the greater sufferers in terms of the loss of human lives? The gloomy and despondent situation has caused so much hopelessness and despair that it has started to appear as if the world will never be able to get over the shock given by the COVID-19 pandemic.

However, an interesting trend has been seen among millennials towards spiritual and religious tourism. If one takes a serious view of various Twitter trends, social media shares, stories and newspaper articles along with blogs, Facebook and Instagram posts, we may observe that millennials have shown a remarkable change in their attitude towards spiritual and religious tourism. Not that the millennials remained unaware of such developments. They could sense the fact that it's a call, either from nature or from the spirit behind this universe that regulates everything. They became unusually conscious of the spiritual aspect of this material world. They wanted to know about it; they wanted to experience it; they wanted to realise how important spiritual realisation was in the face of every single wrong that has taken place in the world inhabited by greedy, ambitious, inhuman and unfeeling human beings. For millennials, spirituality and spiritual well-being thus became newer goals to achieve. Likewise, well-being became germane to their understanding of life. Therefore, millennials, in a world devastated by the coronavirus pandemic, have been rising to the occasion by re-planning and rescheduling their travel visits in terms of destination selection and budgeting.

References

Aceron, R.M., Del Mundo, L.C., Restar, A.S.N., & Villanueva, D.M. (2018). Travel and Tour Preferences of Millenials. *Journal of Economics and Management Sciences, 1*(2), 141.

Agustina, N.K.W. (2018). Analysis of Preferences and Patterns of Millennial Travelers to Bali. *Jurnal Kepariwisataan, 17*(3), 1–4.

Ahn, Y.J., Lee, B.C., & Lee, S.K. (2020). Analysis of Korean millennials' Travel Expenditure Patterns: An Almost Ideal Demand System Approach. *Asia Pacific Journal of Tourism Research, 25*(1), 3–14.

Baniamin, H.M., Rahman, M., & Hasan, M.T. (2020). The COVID-19 Pandemic: Why are Some Countries Coping More Successfully Than Others?. *Asia Pacific Journal of Public Administration, 42*(3), 153–169.

Berger, D.O. (2013). On Means, Ends, and Millennials. *MissioApostolica, 12.*

Cabreja, K.M. (2017). *Meet the Millennials: On the Spirituality Fence* (Doctoral dissertation, University of Southern California).

Cheer, J.M. (2020). Human Flourishing, Tourism Transformation and COVID-19: A Conceptual Touchstone. *Tourism Geographies, 22*(3), 514–524.

Chu, S., Deng, T., & Cheng, H. (2020). The Role of Social Media Advertising in Hospitality, Tourism and Travel: A Literature Review and Research Agenda. *International Journal of Contemporary Hospitality Management, 32*(11), 3419–3438.

Chung, N., Han, H., & Koo, C. (2015). Adoption of Travel Information in User-generated Content on Social Media: The Moderating Effect of Social Presence. *Behaviour& Information Technology, 34*(9), 902–919.

Cox, D., & DeVeaux, A.T. (2019, December 12). Millennials are Leaving Religion and Not Coming Back. *Five Thirty Eight.*

Dillette, A.K., Benjamin, S., & Carpenter, C. (2019). Tweeting the Black Travel Experience: Social Media Counternarrative Stories as Innovative Insight on #TravelingWhileBlack. *Journal of Travel Research, 58*(8), 1357–1372.

Dwivedi, A., & Lewis, C. (2020). How Millennials' Life Concerns Shape Social Media Behaviour. *Behaviour& Information Technology,* 1–18.

Fotis, J.N. (2015). *The Use of Social Media and its Impacts on Consumer Behaviour: The Context of Holiday Travel* (Doctoral dissertation, Bournemouth University).

Fox, D., & Xu, F. (2017). Evolutionary and Socio-cultural Influences on Feelings and Attitudes Towards Nature: A Cross-cultural Study. *Asia Pacific Journal of Tourism Research, 22*(2), 187–199.

Frederick, W.C. (2018). Corporate Social Responsibility: From Founders to Millennials. In *Corporate Social Responsibility.* Bingley: Emerald Publishing Limited.

Gilli, M., & Palmisano, S. (2021). Spiritual Seekers in Esoteric Tourism Contexts. The Damanhur Community in Italy. *Journal of Tourism and Cultural Change,* 1–13.

Gössling, S., Scott, D., & Hall, C.M. (2020). Pandemics, Tourism and Global Change: A Rapid Assessment of COVID-19. *Journal of Sustainable Tourism, 29*(1), 1–20.

Huppert, F.A. (2009). Psychological Well-being: Evidence Regarding its Causes and Consequences. *Applied Psychology: Health and Well-Being, 1*(2), 137–164.

Irimiás, A.R., &Mitev, A.Z. (2020). Lockdown Captivity: The Wish to Break Out and Travel. *Current Issues in Tourism,* 1–4.

Ivanova, M., Ivanov, I.K., & Ivanov, S. (2020). Travel Behaviour after the Pandemic: The Case of Bulgaria. *Anatolia,* 1–11.

Kamata, H. (2021). Tourist Destination Residents' Attitudes towards Tourism during and after the COVID-19 Pandemic. *Current Issues in Tourism*, 1–16.

Ketter, E. (2020). Millennial Travel: Tourism Micro-trends of European Generation Y. *Journal of Tourism Futures*, 7(2), 192–196.

Krishnamurti, J. (1929). *Truth is a Pathless Land*. https://jkrishnamurti.org/about-dissolution-speech

Lim, W.M., & To, W.M. (2021). The Economic Impact of a Global Pandemic on the Tourism Economy: The Case of COVID-19 and Macao's Destination-and-Gambling-dependent Economy. *Current Issues in Tourism*, 1–12.

McCartney, G. (2020). The Impact of the Coronavirus Outbreak on Macao. From Tourism Lockdown to Tourism Recovery. *Current Issues in Tourism*, 1–10.

McDonald, N.C. (2015). Are Millennials Really the 'Go-nowhere' Generation?. *Journal of the American Planning Association*, 81(2), 90–103.

Miguéns, J., Baggio, R., & Costa, C. (2008). Social Media and Tourism Destinations: TripAdvisor Case Study. *Advances in tourism research*, 26(28), 1–6.

Molteni, F., Ladini, R., Biolcati, F., Chiesi, A.M., Dotti Sani, G.M., Guglielmi, S., . . ., &Vezzoni, C. (2021). Searching for Comfort in Religion: Insecurity and Religious Behaviour during the COVID-19 Pandemic in Italy. *European Societies*, 23(Supp. 1), S704–S720.

Montgomery, R.D., Schwarz, B.J., & Mitchell, M.A. (2016). Examining the Cross-Cultural Dimensionality of Prestige Sensitivity: An Empirical Analysis of Chinese and American Millennials. *Journal of East-West Business*, 22(2), 118–143.

Moran, R. (2017). Workplace Spirituality in Law Enforcement: A Content Analysis of the Literature. *Journal of Management, Spirituality & Religion*, 14(4), 343–364.

Parra-López, E., Gutiérrez-Taño, D., Diaz-Armas, R.J., &Bulchand-Gidumal, J. (2012). Travellers 2.0: Motivation, Opportunity and Ability to Use Social Media. *Social Media in Travel, Tourism and Hospitality: Theory, Practice and Cases*, 171–187.

Percy, M. (2019). Sketching a Shifting Landscape: Reflections on Emerging Patterns of Religion and Spirituality among Millennials. *Journal for the Study of Spirituality*, 9(2), 163–172.

Pfeiffer, D., Pearthree, G., & Ehlenz, M.M. (2019). Inventing What Millennials Want Downtown: Housing the Urban Generation in Low-density Metropolitan Regions. *Journal of Urbanism: International Research on Place Making and Urban Sustainability*, 12(4), 433–455.

Qiao, G., Zhao, X.L., Xin, L., & Kim, S. (2021). Concerns or Desires Post-Pandemic: An Extended MGB Model for Understanding South Korean Residents' Perceptions and Intentions to Travel to China. *International Journal of Environmental Research and Public Health*, 18(5), 2542.

Qin, M., Liu, X., & Zhou, X. (2020). COVID-19 Shock and Global Value Chains: Is There a Substitute for China?. *Emerging Markets Finance and Trade*, 56(15), 3588–3598.

Richards, G., & Morrill, W. (2020). Motivations of Global Millennial Travelers. *RevistaBrasileira de Pesquisaem Turismo*, 14(1), 126–139.

Ruggeri, K., Garcia-Garzon, E., Maguire, Á., Matz, S., & Huppert, F.A. (2020). Well-being is More Than Happiness and Life Satisfaction: A Multidimensional Analysis of 21 Countries. *Health and Quality of Life Outcomes*, 18(1), 1–16.

Sehlikoglu, S., & Karakas, F. (2016). We Can Have the Cake and Eat it Too: Leisure and Spirituality at 'Veiled' Hotels in Turkey. *Leisure studies*, 35(2), 157–169.

Sigala, M., Christou, E., & Gretzel, U. (Eds.). (2012). *Social Media in Travel, Tourism and Hospitality: Theory, Practice and Cases*. London: Ashgate Publishing, Ltd.

Sperry, L. (2016). Secular Spirituality and Spiritually Sensitive Clinical Practice. *Spirituality in Clinical Practice*, 3(4), 221.

Suar, D., Jha, A.K., Das, S.S., & Alat, P. (2019). The Structure and Predictors of Subjective Well-being among Millennials in India. *Cogent Psychology*, *6*(1), 1584083.

Turner, V., & Turner, E. (1978). Introduction: Pilgrimage as a Liminoid Phenomenon. *Image and Pilgrimage in Christian Culture: Anthropological Perspectives* (pp. 1–39). New York: Columbia University Press.

UNSDG. (2020). *COVID-19 and Transforming Tourism*. Geneva: United Nations

UNWTO (2011, October 11). *International Tourists to hit 1.8 billion by 2030*. https://www.unwto.org/archive/global/press-release/2011-10-11/international-tourists-hit-18-billion-2030

UNWTO (2022). *About Us*. https://www.unwto.org/about-us

Watts, G. (2016). *The Personal Politics of Spirituality: On the Lived Relationship between Contemporary Spirituality and Social Justice among Canadian Millennials* (Doctoral dissertation).

Withers, M., Henderson, S., & Shivakoti, R. (2021). International Migration, Remittances and COVID-19: Economic Implications and Policy Options for South Asia. *Journal of Asian Public Policy*, 1–16.

World Health Organization. (2001). *The World Health Report 2001: Mental Health: New Understanding, New Hope*. Geneva: WHO.

9

TURKEY'S TOURISM RECOVERY PROCESS DURING COVID-19

Policy, planning and management

In memory of Prof. Martin J. Haigh

Introduction

As elsewhere in the world, Turkey has been suffering from the COVID-19 pandemic and its economic impacts. The negative impact of the variants of coronaviruses on human health and health systems continues to be widespread. Meanwhile, within the tourism sector, this has resulted in stagnation and decline. The COVID-19 pandemic is an unprecedented crisis, not only because Turkey in the pre-COVID period ranks 12th and 6th with 22,4 and 34.5 billion dollars in total tourism revenues and a share in the country's economy with 2,6% and 4,6% in 2017 and 2019, respectively (Atlas Big, 2017; UNWTO, 2022). Lockdown in many countries, widespread travel restrictions, and airport and national border closures reduced the number of international tourist arrivals and arrivals were still 72% lower when compared to the pre-pandemic year of 2019. The pace of recovery remains slow and uneven across world regions due to the varying extent of mobility restrictions, vaccination rates, and traveller confidence.

Europe and the USA achieved the most robust results in 2021 compared to 2020 (+19% and +17% respectively), but both continents are still 63% below compared to those pre-pandemic levels (UNWTO, 2022). This decrease implies a big loss in tourism revenue, and according to UNWTO's crude estimation, the recovery could be achieved by 2025. In this manner, the COVID-19 pandemic and its effects are sensitive issues to many countries that are more dependent on tourism-induced incomes, such as Turkey, where the pandemic crisis has been entrenched by regional and global issues such as geopolitics and regional instabilities (Şeremet, 2016).

Scholars have devoted great effort to understanding the socio-economic effects of this pandemic in the context of spatiality and temporality. In so doing, they have tried to reveal the COVID-19 pandemic's interplay with the capacity of different societies to overcome, adapt and be resilient in the face of a rapidly evolving challenge (Zhang et al., 2021). In the same way, the Turkish experience and response to COVID-19 needs to be considered in the context of Turkish policy, planning and management perspectives. Although the literature provides some insight into the issues related to tourist motivation, sector workers, digitisation, resilience and policy, a 'holistic' way of evaluating the pandemic process from the angles of policy, planning and management in the context of the local cultural context remains to be examined. With this book chapter, these issues have been fleshed out with two case studies from two different regions of Turkey to highlight the relevancy of cultural context.

Although it is often not possible to prevent the emergence of crises, well-planned tourism crisis management that is implemented during an extraordinary set of circumstances and the results of the various mitigation actions taken to recover from the crisis (Shaen et al., 2021) are vital and reduce the impact of the crisis and help the post-crisis recovery (Yeh, 2021). The following part of this chapter presents the literature review to set the scene for the case studies of two Turkish tourism destinations, which are followed by a summary and conclusions.

Literature review

The last quarter of the 20th century and the early years of the 21st century have been a period in which the effects of different crises have been observed in the tourism sector and the country's economies. It is therefore the fact that the literature on crisis governance and planning has grown tremendously. This was accelerated by the COVID period. In this period, there has been a focus on the issues of having well thought-out tourism crisis and disaster management to mitigate the impact and help with post-crisis recovery (Yeh, 2021). A considerable number of studies on crisis-related scenarios and modelling at the beginning of the COVID-19 Pandemic have been published. Fotiadis et al. (2020) used a multi-perspective approach to evaluate the impact of crises, and they were able to foresee and calculate the expected drop in international tourist arrivals and found alarming results indicating that the drop in tourist arrivals could range between 30.8% and 76.3% and would persist at least until June 2021. The COVID-19 crisis left even this prediction behind and went down in history as the biggest pandemic that humanity has ever experienced.

Given that this topic is widely studied by multidisciplinary scholars, the web-based literature review on the tourism crises and the ways out of these crises have been undertaken. The review shows that studies on 'tourism recovery' emerged as a subject at the end of the 1970s (Figure 9.1). This minimal rise in this year shows that tourism has started to occupy a role in the economic and financial sectors. This review in Scopus focused on the dimensions of recovery and policy, planning and management by covering such terms as 'tourism recovery', or 'tourism recovery strategy', or 'tourism recovery planning', or 'tourism recovery management', or

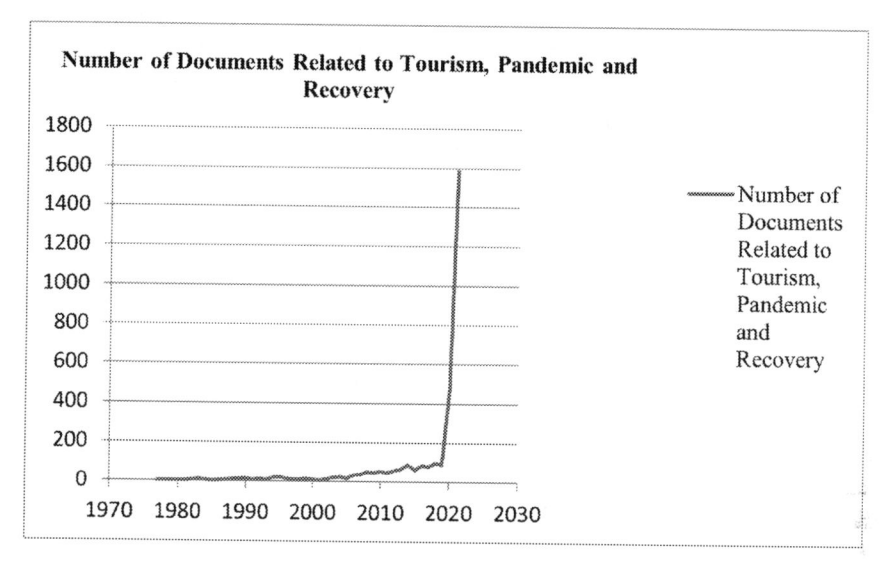

FIGURE 9.1 Literature survey: Number of publications on tourism crises and the recovery processes (January–February 2022)

'tourism planning legislation', or 'pandemic', or 'COVID-19', or 'coronavirus'. The period spanning the early 1970s to the end of 2021 in the first round of the obtained results was evaluated within the framework of this study. The fields of research were selected as title-abstract-keywords and the search was confined to academic documents (articles, conference papers, reviews, books, book chapters, and conference proceedings) from any discipline to contribute insights of international relevance.

The review shows that higher academic interest in this subject began in the 1990s, accelerated in the mid-2000s, and reached a peak with the COVID-19 pandemic. In addition, this study indicates that the number of papers from 2011 to 2021 accounts for over 83% of the total publications identified using the research parameters. The connection of 'tourism recovery' and 'tourism policy' with 'COVID-19-Pandemic-Coronovirus' has recently received growing attention, with remarkable peaks in the years 2020 with 5% and 2021 with 15% of the total papers published in the years given, respectively.

According to the subject's relevancy and timing, 77 studies published in 2020 and 2021 were reviewed in detail in addition to those undertaken in the field of direct tourism or interdisciplinary, especially those focusing on the COVID-19 Pandemic and recovery. Clustering over 400 keywords of these publications, Tourism Recovery and COVID-19 are used as wide-spread words in almost all studies. In addition, Coronavirus, Pandemic, Epidemic, Management, Management Effectiveness, Crisis Management, Crisis Recovery, Recovery Pattern, Sustainability, Environment, Resilience, Risk-Assessment, Nature-Based Tourism, Rural Tourism, Protected Area, Travel, Travel Restriction, Tourist Satisfaction, Perceived Risk

Tourist Hospitality, Tourist Behavioural Intentions, Tourism Destinations, Destination Brand, State Preferences emerge as the most studied areas regarding the recovery process. To a lesser extent, there have been studies that bring together the topics of Future of Tourism, Smart Tourism, Virtual Reality, Heritage Tourism, Scenario Planning, Pandemic, and Tourism. While the most studied disciplines in the field of Tourism Recovery are tourism, management, and economy; geography, urban and rural planning, public health, education, psychology, and computer science are flourishing interdisciplinary studies.

Although the studies involving a case are studies from all over the world (China, Australia, New Zealand, Africa, Hong Kong, Macau, Bucharest, Cyprus, Greece), the number of publications from China is one-third of the total (28.5%). Although publications from Japan, Mediterranean countries, Central European countries, and Australia were also noticeable, China occupies a prominent place in the literature. However, this does not necessarily suggest that China has a useful model of planning and management for recovery from crises.

Most of these studies are reviews and secondary data analyses accessible from the web, institutions and big data. This is principally explained by lockdowns and the COVID-19 risk of field studies. However, it has been observed that primary data were collected by online surveys and remote interviews. This showed, however, the need for direct field surveys on these subjects in the future. This study therefore contributes valuable fieldwork-based insights into the subject.

This review work has also shown that the findings of the studies on the effects of the crises on the tourism sector and on eliminating these effects can be assessed by taking into consideration the supply and demand sides as well. Therefore, at recovery times, it is more important to understand the choices tourists make, both from a scientific, managerial and policy point of view (Kemperman, 2021). Aliperti and Cruz (2019) highlight the need for tailor-made risk communication strategies, taking into consideration cross-country behavioural differences of international travellers. A further study by Chica et al. (2021) on a collective risk dilemma for tourism restrictions in the COVID-19 context, modelling lockdowns and mobility, suggested that enrichment by adding distances and/or in-out touristic flows among regions and social networks or spatial lattices will shape the latter effects. Given that sustainability is also an issue, an analysis based on Northern Cyprus by Seyedabolghasemi et al. (2022) measured tourist behavioural intentions after the first outbreak of the COVID-19 pandemic crisis. Further, it has also been analysed by Poulaki and Nikas (2021) using evidence from the Greek market. Both reflect the experience of the Mediterranean region.

As tourism activities have been highly and rapidly affected by crises in the fields of economic, political, social, environmental and pandemic, it is also important for research to respond quickly to the recovery process to suggest solutions or reduction of the problem, incentives and promotions. Accordingly, studies to find the best methods to predict the recovery of tourism from the devastating effects of COVID-19, such as econometric and combined forecasting models for the possible paths to tourism recovery were surveyed. For example, Zhang, et al. (2021)

modelled these issues in Hong Kong to help governments and businesses understand the specific losses caused by the COVID-19 pandemic and to take appropriate remedial measures to revive their tourism industries.

Given that tourism is a highly fragile and risky market, being able to manage crises in the tourism sector requires preparation in terms of policy, planning and management. Recovery necessitates being aware of the need for corporate action for and interdisciplinary research focusing on tourism preparedness; it also requires tailor-made risk communication strategies taking into consideration cross-country and regional behavioural differences of international travellers (Aliperti & Cruz, 2019). This might be achieved by establishing local, national and especially global networks. Thus, it is possible to adapt to the changing crisis conditions in the tourism sector and to make the necessary modifications to create and manage the demand.

As a concluding remark, the future of global economics after a two-year deep COVID-19 recession is still uncertain. Becken and Loehr (2021) assert that uncertainty is making planning extremely difficult for tourism for those involved in the tourism system (e.g., governments, businesses and other actors). Nevertheless, tourism is an integral part of strategic and inclusive planning and place-making, aimed at creating good places to live and good places to visit (Hartman et al., 2020: 215; Cihangir-Çamur et al., 2021). For this reason, recovery is vital not only for tourism revenues but also for wider society. Hence, the remaining part of the paper is organised to review the tourism recovery policy of Turkey through planning and management during COVID and will be followed by two differing planning and management case studies, namely Koycegiz-Dalyan and Kayseri-Erciyes.

Context: tourism crises in Turkey and tourism recovery policy, planning and management

This part of the study draws on the effects of the national and global crises that emerged in Turkey on the tourism sector and tourism policy. The first recognition of the importance of the tourism sector in Turkey began in the 1930s with the establishment of relevant institutions. Although the 'Tourism Institutions Incentive Law' no. 5647 was issued as the first incentive law in 1950, the remarkable growth of tourism was only observed in the 1980s; it was then placed into the heart of the economy in the early 2000s (Table 9.1). As Turkey is amongst the emerging economies, the tourism sector occupies an important place in the general budget revenues. Compared to the tourism destinations in the Mediterranean region, Turkey's tourism sector has been greatly affected by a variety of recent crises, as shown in Table 9.2.

Table 9.2 indicates the crises affecting Turkey's tourism industry, and the policy responses taken to these.

The reflection of these crises has been initially observed in the number of tourists visiting the country. In the meantime, there were significant decreases in the number of tourists (Figure 9.2). With the crises Turkey experienced in the 2000s, the discussions on what the recovery strategies developed by the sector against

TABLE 9.1 Tourism data of Turkey after 1980 and its place in the economy

Years	Number of incoming tourists	Tourism revenues (approx – $) (billion)	Share of tourism revenues in gross domestic product (GNP) (%)
1989	2.400.000	2,55	2,40
2000	10.428.153	7,63	2,90
2001	13.450.127	10,4	5,10
2005	25.045.142	20,32	4,10
2006	23.924.023	18,59	3,60
2007	27.239.630	20,94	3,10
2012	37.715.225	29,07	3,30
2015	41.114.069	31,46	3,70
2016	30.906.680	22,1	2,60
2017	37.969.824	26,28	3,10
2018	46.112.592	29,51	3,80
2019	51.747.198	34,52	4,60
2020	15.971.201	12	1,70
2021	30.038.961	24,48	N/A

Source: Ministry of Culture and Tourism (https://yigm.ktb.gov.tr/TR-201116/turizm-gelirleri-ve-giderleri.html)

TABLE 9.2 Chronological analysis of the crises affecting the tourism sector (1980–2021)

Years-Crises	Legal and institutional arrangements Steps towards crisis resolution
1980–90s • 1994 Gulf crisis – Iraq War • 1994 Economic crisis – April 5 Decisions • Terror attacks	1980 – Start of incentives in the neoliberal period in the economy 1982 – Tourism Incentive Law (Law no. 2634) 1985 – Transfer of planning authorities to municipalities with the Zoning Law
The 2000s • 1999 – Gölcük and Düzce earthquakes • 2001 – Economic crisis • 2003 – SARS virus outbreak • 2006 – Bird flu outbreak • 2003–2006 – Terror-bomb attacks on Istanbul and other tourism centres • 2007–2008 – America (mortgage) crisis and global crisis • 2009 – Swine influenza virus epidemic	2003 – Unification of Ministries of Culture and Tourism and Planning Authority in tourism centres
The 2010s • 2015 –Downing of the Russian plane • 2015–2016 – Istanbul-Ankara terror-bomb attacks • 2016 – 15 July military coup plot	Changes in Tourism Incentive Law: operating structures with a tourism look for the sales of property to foreigners and allocations to protected areas

Source: Adapted from Bozkurt (2019)

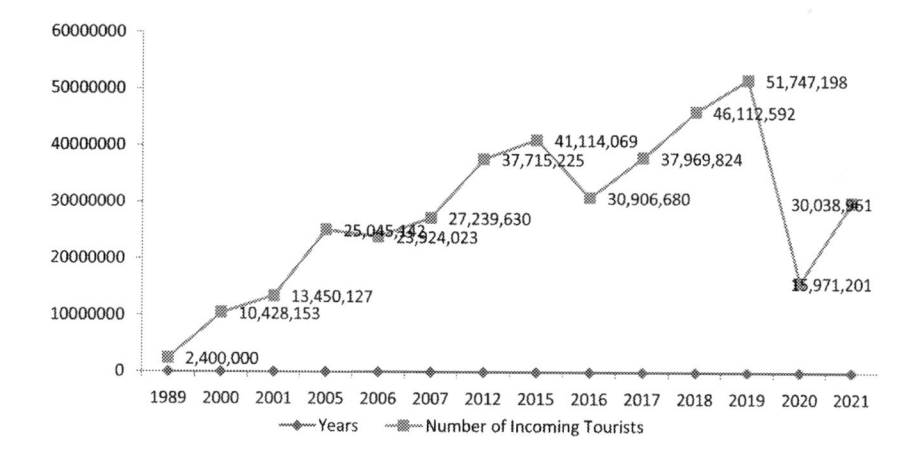

FIGURE 9.2 The effects of crises on the number of annual tourist arrivals (1989–2021)

TABLE 9.3 Distribution of foreigners arriving in Turkey by years (2002–2021)

Year	Foreigner	Rate of change foreigner (%)	Citizen (resident abroad)	Rate of change citizen (%)	Total	Rate of change total (%)
2002*	13.256.028	14,09	--------	--------	13.256.028	--------
2003	14.029.558	5,84	2.434.065	--------	16.463.623	24,20
2004	17.516.908	24,86	3.236.826	32,98	20.753.734	26,06
2005	21.124.886	20,60	3.920.256	21,11	25.045.142	20,68
2006	19.819.833	−6,18	4.104.190	4,69	23.924.023	−4,48
2007	23.340.911	17,77	3.898.719	−5,01	27.239.630	13,86
2008	26.336.677	12,83	4.801.097	23,15	31.137.774	14,31
2009	27.077.114	2,81	4.682.702	−2,47	31.759.816	2,00
2010	28.632.204	5,74	4.365.104	−6,78	32.997.308	3,90
2011	31.456.076	9,86	5.312.963	21,71	36.769.039	11,43
2012	31.782.832	1,04	5.932.393	11,66	37.715.225	2,57
2013	34.910.098	9,84	4.950.673	−16,55	39.860.771	5,69
2014	36.837.900	5,52	4.789.346	−3,26	41.627.246	4,43
2015	36.244.632	−1,61	4.869.437	1,67	41.114.069	−1,23
2016	25.352.213	−30,05	5.554.467	14,07	30.906.680	−24,83
2017	32.410.034	27,84	5.559.790	0,10	37.969.824	22,85
2018	39.488.401	21,84	6.624.191	19,14	46.112.592	21,45
2019	45.058.286	14,11	6.688.913	0,98	51.747.199	12,22
2020	12.734.213	−71,74	3.236.988	−51,61	15.971.201	−69,14
2021	24.712.266	94,06	5.326.695	64,56	30.038.961	88,08

Source: *The number of foreign resident citizen visitors was started to be calculated as of 2003. There is no number of citizens residing abroad in 2002.

these crises are and how this crisis process can be overcome were brought into the policy agenda of the country.

Table 9.3 shows that there were significant decreases in the number of tourists with the crises Turkey experienced in the 2000s, bringing along discussions on

TABLE 9.4 Incentives and measures implemented for the sustainability and revival of the tourism sector during the COVID-19 pandemic process

---

Steps towards crisis recovery (2019–2021 COVID-19 process)

- 2019* – 'Türkiye Tourism Promotion and Development Agency (TGA)' established with the Law on Turkish Tourism Promotion and Development Agency
- 2020 – Short-work incentive to support the sustainability of economic sectors
- 2020 – Safe Tourism Certification Strategy (https://Safetourismturkiye.Com/)
- 2020 – Vaccination certificate to facilitate mobility and support the tourism sector
- 2020 – Accelerated access to vaccination option for tourism employees only ('Enjoy I'm Vaccinated' campaign by Culture and Tourism Ministry)
- 2021–present – Tourism Incentive Law No. 7734 amending Law No. 2634 Tourism Incentive Law
- Creative solutions by visionary managers to coordinate and ease travel procedures (e.g., resolving flight-transportation restrictions with bus transfers)
- Supportive regulations for the construction sector (promoted sale of touristic properties and residence+hotel mixed uses to foreigners to revitalise the construction industry in tourism)

Source: Authors (produced as part of the study (February 2022).

*Although TGA was established in 2019, it was brought into operation with the COVID crisis.

what the recovery strategies developed by the sector against these crises are and how this crisis process can be overcome.

The 2016 coup attempt caused a political and security-related tourism crisis for Turkish tourism, and the number of tourists decreased from 35 million to 25 million, accounting for a 30% shrink (Table 9.3 and Figure 9.2). In the following years, although there had been a recovery period of 2017–2019 with a significant growth trend in tourism, the COVID-19 pandemic, which started in China in December 2019, caused the sector to face a global crisis. While the tourism sector had expected a higher number of visitors for 2020, the pandemic crises resulted in a decrease of 71.74% compared to 2019 (Table 9.3). In this period, in response to the COVID-19 closures, as other countries; Turkey also implemented a set of solutions featuring immediate, definite rules and restrictions to protect the health of its citizens as well as to keep the sector flourishing (Cihangir & Demirhan, 2021: 710; Erdoğanaras et al., 2020: 119). The COVID-19 pandemic, which started at the end of 2019, with its effects ongoing in the years 2020–2021, required new sustainability and recovery-revival policies to come to the fore. Table 9.4 shows the incentives and measures developed in this process.

Finally, the policies and strategies identified and adopted by Turkey in crisis processes, and especially after the 2010s, to remedy tourism, are categorised in two distinct clusters within the framework of the study. In this context, the supports that can be effective in the recovery of the tourism sector can also be examined as the 'direct support cluster' and 'indirect support cluster' as follows:

- **The cluster of direct support** (economic incentives, grants, low-interest lending, promotions, etc.):

  - *Short-work incentive* to support the sustainability of all economic sectors, as well as tourism;
  - *Fair supports* (as direct support in the form of financial, etc.);
  - *Fuel support* for aircraft (considered as one of the important supports and strategic approaches);
  - *Direct transportation financing supports.*
- **The cluster of indirect support** (legislation, etc.):
- *Promotion Supports* (Fairs, Agencies, etc.)

  - Safe Tourism Certification Strategy
  - Vaccination Certificate to Facilitate Mobility and Support the Tourism Sector
  - Accelerated Access to Vaccination Option for Tourism Employees Only
  - Fairs and Fair Supports can be positioned in the cluster of indirect supports because they have short-, mid-, and long-term effects on the tourism sector. Turkey has developed a new initiative by attending the Tourism Market 2015 with Tourism Fair in Russia. The biggest stand in the fair belonged to Turkey. In addition to the tourist facilities and agencies, there were representatives of health tourism, tourism associations from Antalya, Cappadocia, Kars and İzmir, and development agencies to make regional promotions.
  - *Support for Season Extensions*
  - After April, May and September, a new support program for October and November has been organised on the tourism agenda. In this way, it aims to prolong the tourism season and to resuscitate the dead months that are expressed as a low session.

- *Destination supports* (tourist budgets and making use of politics in tourist orientations)

  - Detailed analyses of the tourist generating countries and tourist behaviours for new and attractive destination combinations, package tours, etc. Accordingly, giving support to these source countries with varying promotions.
  - Supporting different tourism trends (according to the study titled 'ITB World Travel Trends Report 2014/2015 – ITB Berlin World Travel Trends Report 2014/2015' prepared by IPK International, knowing the preferences of tourists coming from different destinations plays an emerging role in determining the country's tourism policy and strategy).

- Coordination and ease of travel procedures
- *Tourism incentive regulations*
- Tourism incentive laws
- Supportive regulations for the construction sector (promoted sale of touristic properties and residence+hotel mixed uses to foreigners to revitalise the construction industry in tourism).

A general assessment of the two clusters suggests that the cluster size of support confirms a deficiency of direct supports. Hence, the tourism sector in Turkey is trying to survive and develop mainly through indirect incentives. Overcoming the crisis in the short- and mid-term necessitates re-evaluating the roles assigned to tourism in the future of the country. Also, new research is required and should be supported to scrutinise the effects of these clusters in the recovery of the tourism sector through the COVID-19 crisis.

Having laid out the context of Turkey's experience in the COVID process, our attention now turns to the case studies and the following part of this chapter, therefore, provides insight into the differences in tourism recovery management policies, strategies and plans of these professionally and non-professionally managed destinations in Turkey.

Case 1: Dalyan province of Köyceğiz in Muğla

Dalyan is a unique destination in the western part of Turkey, where there is protective law status for the Iztuzu beach, which connects the river channel through the sea, because it is the spawning ground of Caretta Turtles. The conservation of the local environment and habitat has increased the tourism potential of these areas, with some caveats that, particularly the provinces near the Antalya tourism area, were most negatively affected by the establishment of hotels throughout the beaches and estuary.

The early 1970s witnessed early growth in tourism from the UK and Germany towards the region's mass tourism destinations (Fethiye, Marmaris, Köyceğiz). This created a network of international communities' permanent and temporary settlements in the region, which later turned into the establishment of local international communities. Having burgeoning growth in tourism-driven urbanisation and second-home ownership towards Fethiye and Marmaris, Dalyan and its surrounding areas have become places where many international people's retirement plans have occurred. However, the distraction of the COVID process prevented many international people from visiting their second homes. Although these second houses and villas in the region have been considered a threat for the hospitality sector, this was later turned into an advantage to accommodate the tourists over the COVID period. Local tourism has been later informed by this development and caravan and camping tourism has been gaining traction alongside boutique hotels. This was also supported by a public policy initiative based on the fact that NBT-based PA areas have a great potential for tranquil spaces, allocated by the government's recent protection law, to develop this type of 'new' tourism.

Over the COVID period, villa tourism and boutique hotels in the region attracted both domestic and ex-pat tourists, who have become the main customers of the tourism sector in the region. Although some hotels have been closed during lockdowns, boutique hotels and villa tourism have been operational. So, a new sector has emerged, where many villa owners who are living abroad or in a different part of the country have marketed their places to customers over online marketing tools (e.g., Airbnb, Gumtree, Villa Plus). However, age might be a challenge for some people who are not technology friendly. In this case, some local agents have offered this service to people who bought a house while living abroad and were stranded during the lock-down period.

However, villa-based accommodation is not attractive to those who are fed up with cleaning, cooking and housekeeping for a larger family, who tend to replace the villas with hotels. A hotel owner reported that 'one of my regular visitors have given myself a phone to ask for an empty room, as his wife did not like the villa-based holiday as she was struggling to arrange cooking, cleaning and washing for two boys and her husband'. This might suggest that the future of villa tourism might not be a long-term tourism policy. With the changing trends, Generation Z's inclination towards tourism activities might change the focus more towards boutique hotels, bungalows and 'tiny' houses within the natural environment, which seem to offer more reliable accommodation in the future.

In this case study, the absence of DMOs in the destination might be an obstacle to the recovery of the destination in the post-COVID period. Not least because small destinations have financial constraints in the marketing and advertising process, the efforts of small hotels and tour agents are not necessarily sufficient to create recovery and management policies in times of austerity and recessions. This might also be dependent on the relationships between the local authorities and the national institutions. For example, Dalaman Airport is an important hub for close-proximity destinations. The lack of scheduled flights from the main tourism markets was a challenge for the destination. Therefore, many 'backpacker' tourists were put off by expensive flight prices and faced with few opportunities to visit the destination.

Overall, as Dalyan and its surrounding areas continue to receive tourists from European countries, it was most affected by the supra-national lock-down policy of the countries towards Turkey in the restriction period. Therefore, particularly those travelling with their cars and caravans became potential clients of this destination. This might also change the tourist profile from international tourists towards more Europeans with a Turkish background and, of course, domestic. As they were used to visiting and staying in 'all-inclusive' hotels in Antalya destinations, in the COVID period, with the villa and boutique hotels tourism, they have had a chance to enjoy the northern Aegean destinations' beauties and nature-based activities. The policy on tourism has played a role that the COVID process might bring to this change.

Case 2: Ski Resort destination's experience: Erciyes Mountain of Kayseri

The second case is a winter ski destination (Erciyes Mountain Ski Resort), managed by a DMO (Erciyes A.Ş.). This destination was opened in the early 1990s and declared a winter tourism development area of the country. Today, some 34 ski runs (six black, 15 blue, and 13 green) are available in the ski resort with over a 2000-bed capacity, with the city centre's additional capacity reaching an additional 6000 beds. The DMO of the ski resort began in 2011 with the effort of the metropolitan municipality of Kayseri (KMM). The marketing activity in the early development phase was earlier undertaken by the KMM with the support of international consultancy companies and later, the master plan of the potential destination was prepared by a company that also provides support to ski resorts in Austria and Switzerland. One of the main advantages of this master plan has been built on environmental sustainability principles. In the second step, the DMO was established in 2011 as a commercial company. This was aligned with the country's 2023 Tourism Strategy (TRTS2023) (KTB, 2007). The flourishing collaboration and cooperation of the city's governmental and private institutions have been the major reasons why the destination has flourished.

Turkish Airlines, as Turkey's flagship, helps in marketing the destination by bringing tour agents, bloggers and social media influencers as well as carrying the CEO of DMOs to international fairs and meetings with travel agents and tour operators. Turkish Airlines also provides additional services to customers, including carrying their ski equipment without extra charge, as well as sponsoring international sports organisations. Although lockdowns affected many ski destinations during COVID, Erciyes ski resort was operational during this time.

Although the destination offers the infrastructure for a wide range of ski activities, there are some shortages regarding 'after-ski' activities (social activities and accommodation). One of the major strengths of the destination within the COVID period for the destination is its proximity to Cappadocia. As earlier efforts were mainly related to forwarding the tourists of Cappadocia into the ski destination with a 'stopover' policy of travel agents, after the country's new direction towards bringing 'Muslim' tourists into the tourism destination, this policy was also locally facilitated by the Erciyes ski resort, which allowed the international clients to experience winter tourism. Given that the 'price-service' balance is affordable for many developing country citizens, many Gen-Z individuals opted for visiting Turkey's ski resort.

In the COVID period, although the lockdown process was only continued for three-weekends over the season, the Erciyes ski resort caught the attention of former Soviet countries, as the CEO of Kayseri Erciyes AŞ asserted that 'the tour operators [e.g., TUİ] formerly did not take my call, in this period, they come back to arrange rooms for their tours and charter flights, yet due to early reservation of the hotel rooms both in the mountain resorts and city hotels, we were not able to provide them accommodation places.' He also underscored that although geopolitical risks and political antagonism have largely affected sea–sun–sand tourism, winter tourism was less affected by these challenges, not least because he believes that skiing is a 'passion' for many people, not just filling their 'leisure time'. Therefore, although another region of the country has received larger tourist groups from the Middle East countries, this destination has not received large tourist groups either from Gulf countries or Middle Eastern countries. In the COVID period, there was also a 'flight-ban' to Kayseri Airport from Russia. To remedy this, they have picked up tourists from Ankara airport with a mini-bus shuttle service. In the meantime, the ski resort has been awarded as a 'safe ski resort' from an international independent company, because the resort has received 8,500 tourists (subject to PCR tests) to the destination without any positive cases in the meantime and the first COVID-19 period was closed without any interruption.

Conclusions

This book chapter attempted to understand the experience of the COVID process in the context of the Turkish experience, in which spatial-temporal perspectives were presented. The country's winter and summer destinations in two different locations were evaluated from the perspectives of policy, planning and management subjects. It has been principally seen that the DMO approach seems to be flourishing during the recovery period of the tourism destination. Although Turkey's TRTS2023 strategy mainly supports the DMOs in a 'holistic' way, the local-financially-independent DMO is more flexible in producing marketing strategies for the crisis's times and the politically unstable regions (Şeremet et al., 2022). This might be an example of the emerging role of DMO in creating resilient economies. While 'powerful' summer destinations suffer from the COVID-19 lock-down period, 'niche' tourism destinations have gained strength. Therefore, the winter destination seems to be less affected by this stagnation period.

The revitalisation of the tourism sector in the COVID period accrued to the small-scale region from the country's geopolitical discourse in recent years (Cihangir et al., 2022). The country's new geopolitical discourse was more operationalised through the country's flagship company and infrastructural investments in transportation. The widespread domestic airports spreading through the country's emerging destinations are bringing destinations closer to each other. In the Erciyes case, a new marketing strategy offering the amalgamation of the cultural with experience-based tourism created a combined marketing strategy. This comparison-based case study research evidenced that the Cappadocia destination was rejuvenated by the integration of experience-based tourism destination of ski tourism. As the variation is an important phenomenon for the rejuvenation process, the city's shopping centre and winter tourism resort have combined with Cappadocia's balloon tourism and cultural tourism assets. In this manner, the ski resort largely benefited from the partner destination's aligned tourism policy with the government's latest geopolitical initiative towards the east, including Russia, Ukraine and other eastern countries.

In the Dalyan case, the lack of networking and the challenge of 'new' geopolitical alignment have been more affected the destination, while villa tourism has created an alternative tourism approach to the town. Although the destination has sustained its tourism potential in the COVID period with this approach, this does not offer more job opportunities within the tourism sector, as it includes a closed circle. Nevertheless, the destination's boutique hotels and the country's 'new' tourism policy, as well as the support for the sector's workers, have to some extent helped to sustain the hopes of the tourism sector for the coming years. Alongside challenges in this period, some advantages emerged for the 'niche' market in shifting the tourist's perception towards the small hotels and boutique accommodation places. Given that there have been some incentives and regulations, small-scale accommodation businesses were not able to benefit from the government's financial support. The employees in the sector were only able to receive short-work payments for a limited period. Taken as a whole, while the COVID-19 period caused some challenges, the sector has learned to create new pathways for being resilient and creating alternative policies, even without the support of tourism authorities. This might 'spin-off' into the development of 'niche' accommodation places such as glamping, caravan, tiny-house, and camping tourism types in the summer tourism regions.

Overall, Turkey's experience in the COVID process allows us to recognise the structure and challenges of the tourism industry related to its interrelated and complex structure. It is a multi-sectoral eco-system and this characteristic of tourism demand and supply needs a more holistic perception and approach. These findings may help in the innovation of new generation tourism policies and in shaping the future by understanding what the pandemic taught us in different cultural contexts. This may direct politicians and decision-makers to a novel strategy, plan and management processes to repair the damage that the COVID-19 crisis has done to the tourism industry.

References

Aliperti, G., & Cruz, A. (2019). Investigating Tourists' Risk Information Processing. *Annals of Tourism Research, 79.* DOI: 10.1016/j.annals.2019.102803.

Atlas Big. (2017, February). www.atlasbig.com/tr/ulkelerin-turizm-gelirleri. Accessed 18 February 2022.

Becken, S., & Loehr, J. (2021). Asia – Pacific Tourism futures Emerging from COVID-19 Recovery Responses and Implications for Sustainability. *Journal of Tourism Futures, 1–14.* DOI: 10.1108/JTF-5-2021-0131.

Bozkurt, G. (2019). *Yerel ve Mekânsal Dinamiklerin Turizm Temelli Girişimcilik Üzerine Etkileri: Marmaris Yerleşmesindeki Girişimcilik Yapısı ve Girişimciliği Etkileyen Faktörlerin Çözümlemesi, Gazi Üniversitesi Fen Bilimleri Enstitüsü, Şehir ve Bölge Planlama Ana Bilim Dalı* (Unpublished PhD thesis).

Chica, M., Hernández, J.M., & Bulchand-Gidumal, J.A (2021). Collective Risk Dilemma for Tourism Restrictions under the COVID-19 Context. *Scientific Reports, 11,* 5043. DOI: 10.1038/s41598-021-84604-z.

Cihangir, E., & Demirhan, Ö. (2021). Van Tarihi Peynirciler Çarşısı'nın Turizm Sektörü ve Yerel Turizm Girişimciliği Açısından Restorasyon ve COVID-19 Sürecinde Değerlendirilmesi. *Kent Akademisi, 14*(3), 705–727.

Cihangir, E., Şeremet, M., & Cihangir-Çamur, K. (2022). Turkey at the Crossroads: A Study in Tourism Re-Alignment and Geopolitics. *Geography*, 3, 1–15.

Cihangir-Çamur, K., Şeremet, M., Cihangir E., & Özer, B., (2021). Kış Destinasyonlarında Başarı İçin Stratejik Planlama: Kayseri-Erciyes Kayak Merkezi Hikayesinden Çıkarımlar, *Destinasyon Konulu Güncel Araştırmalar-I*, 494–508.

Erdoğanaras, F., Cihangir-Çamur, K., Görer-Tamer, N., & Mercan, K. (2020). COVID-19, Mahalle, Müşterekler, Kentsel Yaşam ve Halk Sağlığı. *Türk Coğrafya Dergisi, 76*, 115–128.

Fotiadis A., Polyzos S., Tzung-Cheng T.C., & Huan, T.C. (2020). The Good, the Bad and the Ugly on COVID-19 Tourism Recovery. *Annals of Tourism Research*, 87. DOI: 10.1016/j.annals.2020.103117.

Hartman, S., Wielenga, B., & Heslinga, J.H. (2020). The Future of Tourism Destination Management: Building Productive Coalitions of Actor Networks for Complex Destination Development. *Journal of Tourism Futures, 6*(3), 213–218, DOI: 10.1108/JTF-11-2019-0123.

Kemperman, A. (2021). A Review of Research into Discrete Choice Experiments in Tourism: Launching. *Annals of Tourism Research*. DOI: 10.1016/j.annals.2020.103137.

KTB (Kültür ve Turizm Bakanlığı) (2007). *2023 Türkiye Turizm Stratejisi*. Ankara: Kültür ve Turizm Bakanlığı.

Poulaki, I., & Nikas I.A. (2021). Measuring Tourist Behavioral Intentions after the First Outbreak of COVID-19 Pandemic Crisis. Prima Facie Evidence from the Greek Market. *International Journal of Tourism Cities, 7*(3), 845–860. DOI: 10.1108/IJTC-09-2020-0218

Şeremet M. (2016). Geographical Education in Turkey: Challenges and Opportunities. *Geography, 101*(3), 146–155. DOI: 10.1080/00167487.2016.12093998.

Şeremet M., Cihangir E., & Cihangir-Çamur K. (2022). An Evaluation of Turkey's Nature-Based Tourism Agenda: Policy, Planning, and Management. In A. Mandić & K.S. Valia (Eds.), *The Routledge Handbook of the Nature-based Tourism Development*. London: Routledge.

Seyedabolghasemi, M.A., Kilic, H., Avci, T., Eluwole, K.K., & Lasisi, T.T. (2022). Residents' Perceptions of Sustainable Tourism Destination Recovery: The Case of Northern Cyprus. *Land, 2022*(11), 94. DOI: 10.3390/land11010094.

Shaen C., Marina E., Brian L., & John F.O. (2021). When Lightning Strikes Twice: The Tragedy-induced Demise and Attempted Corporate Resuscitation of Malaysia Airlines. *Annals of Tourism Research, 87*. DOI: 10.1016/j.annals.2020.103109.

UNWTO (2022). World Tourism Organization. *International Tourism Highlights*. www.e-unwto.org/doi/book/10.18111/9789284422456.

Yeh, S. (2021). Tourism Recovery Strategy against COVID-19 Pandemic. *Tourism Recreation Research, 46*(2), 188–194. DOI: 10.1080/02508281.2020.1805933

Zhang, H., Song. H., Wen, L., & Liu, C. (2021). Forecasting Tourism Recovery Amid COVID-19. *Annals of Tourism Research, 87*, 103149. DOI: 10.1016/j.annals.2021.103149.

10

RESTORE, REORIENT, AND REINVIGORATE

A localisation and sensemaking approach to crisis recovery

Isabella Qing Ye and Mireia Guix

Background

Despite the prevalence of micro and small businesses in tourism, the literature on crisis response and recovery remains limited to large international hospitality businesses (Ritchie & Jiang, 2019). The following case study on Binna Burra Lodge (BBL), an SME accommodation provider, sheds light on the importance of localised recovery by means of multi-faceted sensemaking activities. Nested in the Gondwana World Heritage-listed sub-tropical rainforests, BBL has championed applying international standards for sustainable tourism in its operations and won accolades such as the Green Globe Certification (Binna Burra Lodge, 2021). Interstate and international travellers and day-trippers engage in a wide range of open-air activities, such as guided tours, nature journaling, and bush tucker walks of Yugambeh country (BBL, n.d.). The natural and cultural values of the landscape create a strong place identity and a living history among the local community.

In September 2019, a climate change-induced, nationwide catastrophic bushfire destroyed BBL (Day & Noakes, 2021). Prior to the fire, Australia experienced record-breaking heat, minimal rainfalls, and extreme wind. The fire caused overwhelming destruction to the lodge, the surrounding subtropical rainforests, wildlife and its habitat, in turn hurting tourism to the Gold Coast Hinterland. The impacts triggered an outpouring of public sympathy for the loss of lodge and praise for brave acts of wildlife rescue, whilst raising awareness of urgent climate actions (Baldwin & Ross, 2020). The Australia-wide mega-fire also attracted global media traction and critique. Such reactions set a solid foundation for the collective recovery process.

A few months after the fire, Australia was hit by the COVID-19 pandemic, a global, extrinsic, human-induced crisis. Persistent restrictions in mobility altered the perception of geographical distances (Tomassini & Cavagnaro, 2020) and

DOI: 10.4324/9781003295839-13

brought about economic uncertainty across sectors (Gössling et al., 2020). Because Australia applied one of the world's strictest border closures, accommodation providers faced intermittent interstate lockdowns and border restrictions limiting their bookings (Tourism & Events Queensland, 2021). The period of depressed demand, however, provided BBL an opportunity to rebuild and recuperate from operations ceasing in 2019 due to the bushfires without losing international market share.

The ambiguity during a crisis can be leveraged as an opportunity for tourism destinations and organisations to transform existing practices (Berbekova et al., 2021). Accordingly, COVID-19 has presented an occasion to reflect on how to reset the course of tourism and critically reconsider sustainable and inclusive tourism growth (e.g., Gössling et al., 2020; Rastegar et al., 2021). Yet, the pandemic, being fast-paced, uncertain and unpredictable, complicated sensemaking (Christianson & Barton, 2021). Amidst the pandemic, organisations struggled to understand what happened ('what's the story') and decide how to respond and recover ('now what'?).

Sensemaking through a localised approach in times of crises

Sensemaking and situational awareness

The concepts of sensemaking and situational awareness help businesses understand crisis response and recovery actions because those concerned are forced to act outside their everyday routines and frames of reference. While there are multiple views on organisational sensemaking, a central notion is that members of organisations subjectively construct the reality in which they operate (Weick, 1993). Sensemaking is a socially constructed process in which organisational members attempt to understand issues by interacting with each other to interpret and make sense of the events, thus developing a 'shared sense of meaning' that enables action (Christianson & Barton, 2021; Maitlis, 2005). As Robert et al. (2007: 109) explain, sensemaking enables 'building mental models of the organisation and its surroundings.'

People engage in sensemaking processes as the crisis unfolds, apprehending what is happening (e.g., Kayes, 2004). Alternatively, people engage in retrospective sensemaking as they look back over the event to understand what happened postcrisis (e.g., Casto, 2014) to make their actions and experiences fit logically into their understanding of the world (Weick, 1995). When stakeholders reinterpret past events to construct a coherent vision and imagination of the future, they also engage in future-oriented sensemaking. This chapter explores BBL's crisis response and recovery actions that generated retrospective sensemaking cues for the organisational members, tourists and residents.

Crises involve rapid and unfamiliar changes in the organisational environment, which tend to 'shatter fundamental assumptions' (Maitlis & Christianson, 2014: 72) due to newly, often ambiguously emerged reality (Weick, 1993). Business-as-usual practices, routines and regular interactions are disrupted and usually fail during a crisis (Robert et al., 2007). Similarly, people's shared understandings break down due to fragmented information (Robert et al., 2007). Under such conditions, sensemaking activities are critical in creating and maintaining coherent understandings to sustain relationships and enable collective actions (Maitlis, 2005). Sensemaking is seen as central to an organisation's survival. Revans (1982) suggested that an organisation's rate of sensemaking must be the same or even more significant than the rate of change in its external environment. The importance of crisis sensemaking lies in empowering people to develop an appropriate mental model of a situation to process information and make informed choices (Olcott & Oliver, 2014). Crises require individuals and organisations to collectively construct these new mental models to accommodate the new environmental conditions so that coordinated actions are possible (Roth, 1997). While initial responses are limited under chaotic crisis conditions, sensemaking enhances an organisation's ability to respond collectively to the new environmental conditions. Thus, sensemaking is particularly relevant to the effective coordination and direction of recovery efforts (Olcott & Oliver, 2014).

However, sensemaking in times of crisis is challenging, as the process may break down. When crises hit, people typically cling to existing frames of reference for as long as possible by ignoring new information that cannot be reconciled until information about the crisis becomes impossible to ignore and are forced to abandon existing mental modes (Weick, 1995). In such an effort, people may experience challenges in integrating new information (Robert et al., 2007), falling into optimistic bias by overlooking information cues contradictory to their understandings of the event or false optimism bias by downplaying the severity of the crisis (Casto, 2014).

Sensemaking processes lead to what is known as situational awareness, which 'represents a detailed understanding of one's environment and the consequences of actions' (Olcott & Oliver, 2014: 12). Shared experiences build mutual understanding and a joint knowledge base for situational awareness that makes coordination and information exchange easier (Olcott & Oliver, 2014). Both sensemaking and end-state situational awareness are socially defined because they must be adapted to local circumstances (Weick et al., 2005).

Localisation

Localisation or locally led approaches encompass all activities and response models that originate with local actors or address locally specific issues in the aftermath of major crises (Wall & Hedlund, 2016). Locally led crisis recovery highlights the critical influences communities, indigenous custodians, charities, small businesses, private sectors, and diaspora bodies have on immediate crisis response and long-term recovery (Hofmann et al., 2019, Lin et al., 2018). Existential crises often trigger powerful community solidarity and collective mourning of loss among members of society, which prioritise common goals, encourage collaborations and voluntary recovery activities beyond government-mandated orders (Cappelen et al., 2021).

Such shared emotions activate an organisation's autonomous mode of self-help and a sense of agency, which motivate effective recoveries.

The notion of local actors is highly contextual and stretches beyond the geography of space, especially given the growing population of diasporas (Wall & Hedlund, 2016). COVID-19 prompts us to rethink the idea of belonging to the 'local' and its networks that tap into our innate rootedness and connections to place (Tomassini & Cavagnaro, 2020). The involvement of local actors is given varying priorities across different stages of destination/organisational development concerning resource allocations, trust-building, cooperation and drivers for change. During a major crisis, the accrued social capital through repeated interactions and normalised reciprocal relationships among local actors render swift resource mobilisation and distribution possible (Olcott & Oliver, 2014). A well-coordinated local response, in turn, facilitates a more holistic, nuanced and multi-faceted sensemaking process, leading to an equitable, inclusive and effective recovery.

Crises often present unexpected disruptions that challenge intricate relationships among local actors. Two pillars underpin a localised crisis recovery: effectiveness and power (Wall & Hedlund, 2016). Given the cultural proximity, knowledge of political power structures and communal trust, local recovery efforts hold greater legitimacy and relevance, thus resulting in effective responses and suitable protections for the affected populations (Roepstorff, 2020). Working alongside local actors with a clear goal construes a collective identity and fosters 'situating interactions', which derive from a shared sense of humanity and responsibility (van der Giessen et al., 2021: 12). The significance of a localised recovery can activate local actors' needs for self-worth, 'self-enhancement and self-efficacy' for meaningful changes (Brown et al., 2008, van der Giessen et al., 2021). The power dynamics among local actors and authorities also have mediating effects on crisis recovery. The urgency for certainty often intensifies conflicts over recovery priorities and undermines democratic local participation (Cretney, 2018). Understanding how alternative forms of power and marginalised voices are contested and negotiated helps build a more nuanced situational awareness during post-crisis recovery (Olcott & Oliver, 2014). Bureaucracy in response procedures and dominations of certain interest groups may engender shallow public consultations and a tokenistic local engagement, which defeats the very purpose of collective recovery (Cretney, 2018). Thus, empowering proactive and genuine local engagement calls for a combined approach of both participatory and beneficiary.

However, localised recovery is commonly confronted by several challenges due to the complex socio-political conditioned dynamics and power relations among local actors (Cohen & Neal, 2010). First, the meaning of 'local' is contested and culturally constructed. The binary framing of local, often geographically confined as opposed to global, overlooks the intricate involvement of global actors and the diaspora groups who may not be physically present (Wall & Hedlund, 2016). The diverse interpretations of who are considered as local, and what roles and responsibilities local actors should assume in the crisis recovery process further complicate an already chaotic post-crisis environment. Second, power imbalances among local actors raise the question of whether the local responses are representative (Wall & Hedlund, 2016). How do organisations gain clarity when navigating the complex and uncertain environment where crisis recovery takes place while not compromising inclusivity, fairness and sensitivity to the local context? Crisis recovery is never a linear progression. The crucial question is how to create synergy and situational awareness through local actors and their collective sensemaking efforts (Cohen & Neal, 2010).

The 3Rs framework: restore, reorient, reinvigorate

Through synergising BBL's myriad implemented practices and secondary data since the 2019 bushfire, this chapter proposes a 3Rs (restore, reorient and reinvigorate) framework to generate situational awareness and guide a transformational long-term recovery. The 3Rs framework, as shown in Figure 10.1, features a situational awareness and a futuristic vision, informed by BBL's localised sensemaking process (Figure 10.2). Specific to the BBL recovery, the local context and social dynamics are tightly integrated in generating a shared understanding, a renewed narrative, and a coordinated action to rise from the impacts of two coinciding crises. Rather than a sequential and reactive process, the 3Rs framework embraces continuous interactions among local actors while curating recovery actions in response to emerging changes.

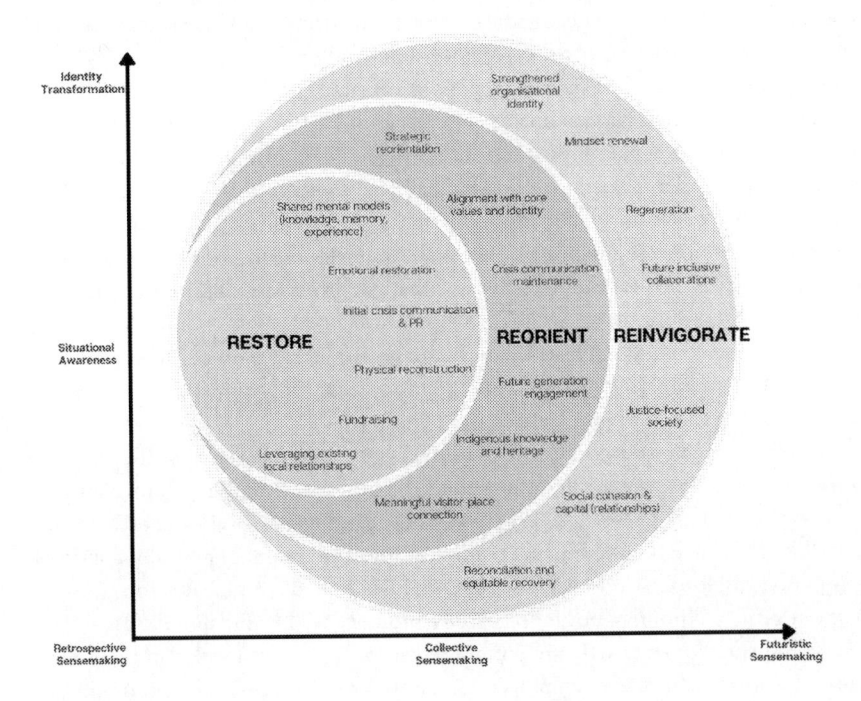

FIGURE 10.1 The 3Rs framework – restore, reorient and reinvigorate

▨ **RESTORE**	▨ **REORIENT**	▨ **REINVIGORATE**
• Employee transition support • Remembrance sites – Bushfire gallery and Phoenix Pavilion • Indigenous healing ceremony • Sole media spokesperson – Steve Noakes CEO • Unified media campaign #BringBackBinnaBurra • Global and national media attention • Zero-impact reconstruction • Rebuild critical infrastructure • Habitat rehabilitation (Friends of Binna Burra) • Grassroot crowdfunding (GoFundMe) • Micro-financing (Rights Issue)	• Strategic reorientation of recovery - engagement of Millennials and GenZ • Continuous media engagement and optimistic media narrative • Adoption of regenerative principles • Building collective resilience (people, nature, & wildlife) • Fostering reconciliation with indigenous community and knowledge • Crafting new cultural awareness training and visitor interpretive programmes.	• Aligning BBL actions with UN SDGs • Advocating regenerative tourism practices and climate actions • Commitment to Reconciliation Action Plan (RAP) • Balancing distributive justice and restorative justice in promoting inclusive and long-term recovery efforts. • Establishing transdisciplinary local advisory groups – Binna Burra Foundation & PALs (Partnership, Alliances & Links) to enhance resilience and strategic capacity

FIGURE 10.2   Binna Burra Lodge recovery using the 3Rs framework

Restore

Restoration encompasses activities and processes that reinstate normality to an affected organisation (Cretney, 2018, Wut et al., 2021), including but not limited to funding acquisition, impact assessments, stakeholder communication and collaboration, and infrastructure reconstruction. BBL carried out an immediate collective restoration in the aftermath of the fire to rebuild critical infrastructure (road access, water and telecommunications), support employee transition, organise booking refunds, and secure financial resources (Cotterell & Gardiner, 2019, Day & Noakes, 2021).

Many restorative actions were situated within the existing collaborative structures and pre-crisis mental models, echoing conservation and sustainability. BBL has developed and exercised a renewed mentality to 'build back better' that transcends the traditional build-back-to-normal mindset (Day et al., 2021). The bushfire posited climate change adaptation as central to the recovery narrative, shaping the reconstruction under zero-waste, zero-emissions principles, with water-sensitive and light-sensitive design with minimal disturbance to nocturnal animals and birds. Similarly, habitat rehabilitations through participatory structures, such as the Friends of Binna Burra, were successful in securing grants while moving the narrative from conservation to regenerative land management practices (BBL, 2021a).

The bushfire generated significant media interest in BBL from around the world. Swift formation of the local government recovery task force and visits from the Queensland Premier and the Prime Minister of Australia also attracted publicity to secure public and private funding. Immediately after the fire, BBL established the '#*BringBackBinnaBurra*' campaign and grassroots crowdfunding initiatives (Schultz & Barnett, 2020). Much of the crowdfunding contributions came from Millennials, who resonated with the 'spirit of Binna Burra'. By proactively undertaking fundraising and mission-driven activities, such as outdoor smoke ban during fire season, millennials became a pivotal group that BBL engages moving forward. A call to attract like-minded millennial shareholders was launched in 2020 through a Rights Issue for capital expansion (Schultz & Barnett, 2020). It invited investors to buy $1.00 shares (500 minimum) until 14 April 2022 (BBL, 2021a). Building on the original frame of reference of being Australia's first tourism crowdfunded initiative, the call for micro shareholders aimed to continue with BBL as Australia's oldest ecotourism collective (BBL, n.d.).

Beyond financial and physical rehabilitation, BBL emphasised collective emotional restoration through positive media narrative and stakeholder communication, as well as setting up community remembrance sites. Crisis communication with local stakeholders was critical in managing the public narrative of the bushfire. As one of the most common strategies undertaken post-crises (Berbekova et al., 2021), crisis communication, both internal and external, can affect the crisis lifecycle and scope, mitigating or exacerbating negative consequences (Ritchie & Jiang, 2019). The tragic burndown of the heritage BBL in 2019 gained wide coverage, from local (*ABC News*) to global (*New York Times*), from print (*The Australian*) to digital media (Instagram and YouTube). To ensure a coordinated communication response to the public and the media, the chairman, Steve Noakes, became the sole spokesperson for BBL. A unified #*BringBackBinnaBurra* discourse also weaved a collective story that portrays BBL as a resilient, confident, community-focused, and responsible local heritage business. Such collective sensemaking evoked fond public memories and emotional connections to the place from the local community, national and international guests, as Schultz and Barnett (2020: 3) put it: the fire 'revealed the love people have, locally, nationally and globally, for Binna Burra'.

Positive transformation and recovery began with various local actors reflecting on what happened and constructing stories about shared memories or experiences of the crisis (Day et al., 2021). Remembrance sites such as *Bushfire gallery* and *the Phoenix Pavilion* served as manifestations of collective retrospective sensemaking and healing activities for impacted local actors. Post-crisis trauma may impose long-term psychological distress, which deems a social dimension of recovery necessary (Mair et al., 2016). The remembrance sites enabled people to share memories, testimonials, anecdotes and remembrances of their connections to Binna Burra, forging a collective storytelling and recollection. These activities generated a shared narrative of the 'spirit of Binna Burra', one that links individuals and their stories to the site, connects present time to the future, and involves emerging generations in the conversations. Both facilities contributed to situational awareness as 'an intergenerational attachment where the person-to-place bonds have evolved through individual meaning and understanding' (BBL, 2020: 7). The renewed, shared understanding of the crises, the world, and the organisation empowered

BBL to enter a process of strategic reorientation grounded on situational awareness and deep emotional connection to the place.

Reorient

Recovery from the initial shock requires an organisation to reorient actions and relationships by crafting new activities, ways of thinking and collaborations (Margo, 2020). In the event of compounding disruptions from two existential crises, an organisation's ability to challenge the status quo, reorient strategic direction, and activate multi-faceted local coordination reduces the chance of a fragmented recovery response (OECD, 2021), and assists resilience building and long-term transformations. BBL has adopted pioneering practices that balance its immediate goals (*reopening, physical recovery, emotional healing, functional repurposing, and stakeholder communications*) and long-term visions (*regenerative operation, advancing reconciliation initiatives, and climate commitments in line with SDG goals*) (Day et al., 2021). Unlike other pandemic-torn destinations and businesses, BBL was almost shielded from severe disruptions due to its closure in 2020 and Australia's strict border policy. Such conditions provided a golden opportunity to recuperate and reflect on bushfire impacts, preparing for future strategic reorientation.

Rather than 'bouncing back' to the pre-crisis state, BBL's response and recovery efforts were directed towards what Demiroz and Haase (2019) called 'bouncing forward.' BBL engaged in collective sensemaking and forward thinking in 2020, starting a journey of strategic reorientation after the bushfires to provide an answer to 'what's next?' and 'how to stay relevant, authentic and creative?' Millennials and Generation Z were invited as co-narrators to imagine the BBL and Lamington National Park transformations. Striving to be a meaningful connection between nature and heritage, BBL proactively adopted regenerative principles to guide recovery and build collective resilience, whilst leveraging existing social capital to rewrite an optimistic narrative (Day et al., 2021). The bushfires and COVID-19 pandemic allowed BBL to 'reset, re-imagine and recreate focusing on the future 86 years of Binna Burra, while acknowledging and staying true to the past 86' (Schultz & Barnett, 2020: 39). Such a process entailed developing 'narratives of understanding to validate and inform past, present and future actions in ways that reflect their own identity-related beliefs and assumptions' (van der Giessen et al., 2021: 5).

The strategic reorientation also illustrates a reconciliation with the indigenous community and knowledge. A retrospective sensemaking exercise fostered a meaningful understanding of 'how we talk about our surrounding environment and its pasts, presents, and futures' (BBL, 2021b: 9). The endorsement of the *Reconciliation Action Plan (RAP)* represented a significant leap towards BBL's continued commitment to respect and acknowledge the traditional custodians (Yugambeh people) of the land and apply Indigenous knowledge to its narrative (BBL, 2021b). Working in tandem with the BBL's visioning and Masterplan, the RAP placed prominence on heritage, with a particular focus on identification, protection, conservation, presentation and transmission to future generations of cultural and natural heritage. In line with the Queensland First Nations Tourism Plan 2020–2025, the RAP aims to strengthen the tie between the Indigenous people and non-Indigenous people, between visitors and the Binna Burra land, culture and history while shaping a living identity for the communities. A partnership with the Yugambeh community and aboriginal-led design agency facilitated conversations to apply Yugambeh stories, knowledge, rights and history to cultural awareness training, site interpretive programmes, and visitor experience design (BBL, 2021b). Learning about the Indigenous stories enriched authentic and meaningful visitor-place connections, which contributes to the BBL's path to reconciliation (BBL, 2021b). The strategic reorientation laid the foundation for a transformative revival of BBL.

Reinvigorate

Reinvigorate, as to give new energy to the organisation, came from strengthening the organisational identity and its relationship with others. Sensemaking activities reinvigorated a responsible business mindset, promoting a justice-focused society and equitable recovery (Day & Noakes, 2021; BBL, 2021b). The twin crises presented a volatile context, where unprecedented challenges unveil and evolve continuously and unexpectedly. Conventional business models often fail, thus breeding paradigm-shifting innovations and radical changes. The new strength of a responsible business mindset was evident in aligning BBL's practices with the UN SDG goals, advocating climate actions and regenerative tourism. BBL Is committed to regenerative mindset, resilient business ecosystems and transformative visitor experiences (Binna Burra Lodge, 2020). Regenerative resilience and inclusive practices (reflected in Day et al., 2021) promoted the ongoing regeneration of natural and cultural landscapes.

Moreover, the indigenous reconciliation process formed a crucial part of BBL's vision towards an equitable recovery and a justice-focused society. Reconciliation is seen as part of the new DNA (BBL, 2021b), that transformed a purely nature-based tourism business into a respectful and culturally inclusive business. In recognition of the local needs and rights, BBL acknowledged the 'histories, stories and living knowledge of Aboriginal people and culture' as a key component to the Binna Burra narrative' (Schultz & Barnett, 2020: 49). BBL strived to engage procedural justice by involving Aboriginal people in decision-making, while practising caution regarding information transparency, the enactment of power, and power imbalances among local actors during sensemaking activities. In addition, the reconciliation journey to an equitable recovery (Rastegar et al., 2021) is a continuous process. It is crucial to maintain fairness of recovery costs and benefits distribution (distributive justice) while exploring and implementing actions for an equitable and just future (restorative justice). BBL's aspirations towards strengthening relationships with Aboriginal people include developing meaningful employment opportunities, sourcing from indigenous-owned suppliers and designing trail interpretations that feature indigenous stories.

The proactive local assistance and coordinated actions were reconciled and manifested as a collective and futuristic sensemaking effort that made BBL's transformation and reinvigoration possible. Sensemaking activities created opportunities to further leverage social capital. Extending connectedness through a shared sense of belonging to the community of BBL while strengthening old and forging new meaningful relationships also contributed to reinvigorate social cohesion, echoing that sensemaking contributes to coordinated action (Roth, 1997). BBL's community-centred values attracted local support and contributions. During the BBL rebuilding stage, the solidarity and voluntary support reinforced BBL's existing relationship and social contracts with local actors while forming new networks to tackle novel challenges. For example, the Partnership, Alliances & Links for enhancing resilience and strategic capacity, welcomed Griffith University, Ecotourism Australia, the National Parks Association of Australia, and The Tourism CoLab to explore innovative science-based practices on the regenerative economy and social enterprise (Binna Burra Lodge, 2020). Similarly, community members and local experts joined Binna Burra Foundation, tapping into the community knowledge in geosciences, environmental education, ecology, climate change and sustainability to explore future collaborations. Furthermore, emergent relationships with Aboriginal representatives are a step towards integrating traditional custodian knowledge into a holistic understanding and identity of BBL.

The story of BBL exemplifies how the organisational reality of the future is constructed through a collective sensemaking process and situational awareness (Robert et al., 2007). Such a process guided the restoration, reorientation and reinvigoration of the organisational identity, networks and relationships. When confronting multiple existential crises, organisations often lose sight of the systemic effects by dwelling in the immediate damages, loss, while hoping for pre-crisis normality. In seeking to build a holistic situational awareness, we advocate for a collective and futuristic sensemaking approach that positions the local dynamic at the centre of recovery. On an organisational level, the iterative and entwined nature of the 3Rs framework offers flexibility as it allows the affected organisation to drive recovery direction and stakeholders' narratives in terms of expressing locally relevant stories and meanings attached to the place.

Conclusions

This chapter has explored a localised sensemaking approach in the crisis response and recovery of Binna Burra Lodge during an environmental crisis, the 2019 Australian bushfires, and a human-induced crisis, the COVID-19 pandemic. This case is unique in advancing our knowledge of the added complexity and synergetic impacts of coinciding crises at an organisational level. There is currently limited research into coinciding crises (Berbekova et al., 2021), with only two studies (e.g., Cohen & Neal, 2010; Page et al., 2012) exploring how concurring events of different origins intertwine on a national level. In contributing toward addressing this gap in knowledge, discussions in this chapter demonstrated how the two crises forged transformational effects on the BBL narratives, from conservation to regeneration and climate adaptation, from natural heritage to a more meaningful cultural heritage connection to the land and shifting public focus from sadness and loss to optimism and hope.

A collective sensemaking framework enabled the co-construction of a narrative change and fostered effective crisis recovery (Berbekova et al., 2021). However, to date, it has not been widely used to advance tourism research. This research demonstrates that sensemaking can provide new insights into the 'resolution and reflection' stage that have yet to be explored fully in prior literature. BBL's case shows that sensemaking exercises are critical in crisis response, as they enable collective actions from a shared understanding and shared frames of reference. In turn, retrospective sensemaking fuels collective introspections on organisational beliefs and identity, thus leading to a renewed understanding of the organisation, its surrounding environment and its past, present and future. While the crisis scale and nature may complicate recovery, sensemaking actions laid a regenerative, equitable and just recovery path for BBL by renewing organisational identity, fostering emotional person-to-place bonds, and strengthening social cohesion and capital towards inclusive collaborations.

Further, this chapter responds to the dominance of technical and procedural aspects in crisis literature and proposes the *3Rs Recovery Framework* guided by a holistic and place-based sensemaking approach. The 3Rs framework highlights the meaning (co)construction and (re)construction by local actors as multiple crises develop over time and space. Localised sensemaking returns agency to resource-poor SMEs who determine locally relevant recovery priorities and trajectories as they navigate the ongoing challenges from both crises. Crises bring disruptions, but they also present opportunities to deepen human-nature bonding, cultivate hopeful transformations and foster community renewals. While global or government-led support is key to crisis recovery, this chapter enhances the visibility of local initiatives and sensemaking activities that offer multi-faceted perspectives into the complex crisis context that businesses face.

While this chapter contributes to case study research that offers limited frameworks and knowledge (Mair et al., 2016), we provide a first-of-its-kind attempt to apply a localised sensemaking framework to advance knowledge in tourism crisis literature. Contributions are limited by reliance on secondary data. Future research may study sensemaking efforts longitudinally as a crisis unfolds using interviews or retrospectively relying on individual and collective stakeholder narratives.

References

Baldwin, C., & Ross, H. (2020). Beyond a Tragic Fire Season: A Window of Opportunity to Address Climate Change? *Australasian Journal of Environmental Management*, 27(1), 1–5

BBL (2020). *Annual Report 2019–2020*. Australia: Queensland.

BBL (2021a). *Annual Report 2020–2021*. Australia: Queensland.

BBL (2021b). *Reflect Reconciliation Action Plan: Reset – Reimagine – Recreate*. Australia: Queensland.

BBL (n.d.). *Binna Burra Lodge*. www.binnaburralodge.com.au/

Berbekova, A., Uysal, M., & Assaf, G. (2021). A Thematic Analysis of Crisis Management in Tourism: A Theoretical Perspective. *Tourism Management*, 104342.

Binna Burra Lodge. (2020). *Recovery PALs for Binna Burra* [Media Release]. www.binnaburralodge.com.au/wp-content/uploads/2020/02/Media-Release-Feb-2020.pdf

Binna Burra Lodge. (2021). *Binna Burra Joins the Global Sustainable Tourism Council (GSTC)*. *[Media Release]*. https://www.binnaburralodge.com.au/news/binna-burra-joins-the-global-sustainable-tourism-council-gstc/

Brown, D., Stacey, P., & Nandhakumar, J. (2008). Making Sense of Sensemaking Narratives. *Human Relations*, *61*(8), 1035–1062.

Cappelen, A., Falch, R., Sorensen, E., & Rungodden, B. (2021). Solidarity and Fairness in Times of Crisis. *Journal of Economic Behaviour and Organisation*, *186*, 1–11

Casto, C.A. (2014). *Crisis Management: A Qualitative Study of Extreme Event Leadership* (PhD thesis, Kennesaw State University, Kennesaw, GA).

Christianson, M.K., & Barton, M.A. (2021). Sensemaking in the Time of COVID-19. *Journal of Management Studies*, *58*(2), 572–576.

Cohen, E., & Neal, M. (2010). Coinciding Crises and Tourism in Contemporary Thailand. *Current Issues in Tourism*, *13*(5), 455–475.

Cotterell, D., & Gardiner, S. (2019). Bushfire at Binna Burra Lodge: A case study. *Griffith Institute for Tourism*. www.griffith.edu.au/__data/assets/pdf_file/0027/926433/Binna-Burra-case-study_FINAL-GIFT-Website.pdf

Cretney, R. (2018). Beyond Public Meetings: Diverse Forms of Community Led Recovery Following Disaster. *International Journal of Disaster Risk Reduction*, *28*, 122–130

Day, J., & Noakes, S. (2021). Ecotourism and Climate Change. In D. Fennel (Ed.), *Routledge Handbook of Ecotourism* (pp. 216–230). London: Routledge.

Day, J., Sydnor, S., Marshall, M., & Noakes, S. (2021). Ecotourism, Regenerative Tourism, and the Circular Economy – Emerging Trends and Ecotourism. In D. Fennel (Ed.), *Routledge Handbook of Ecotourism* (pp. 23–36). London: Routledge.

Demiroz, F., & Haase, T. W. (2019). The Concept of Resilience: A Bibliometric Analysis of the Emergency and Disaster Management Literature. *Local Government Studies*, *45*(3), 308–327.

Gössling, S., Scott, D., & Hall, C.M. (2020). Pandemics, Tourism and Global Change: A Rapid Assessment of COVID-19. *Journal of Sustainable Tourism*, *29*(1), 1–20.

Hofmann, J., Altreiter, C., Flecker, J., Schindler, S., & Simsa, R. (2019). Symbolic Struggles Over Solidarity in Times of Crisis: Trade Unions, Civil Society Actors and the Political Far Right in Austria. *European Societies*, *21*(5), 649–671

Kayes, D.C. (2004). The 1996 Mount Everest Climbing Disaster: The Breakdown of Learning in Teams. *Human Relations*, *57*(10), 1263–1284.

Lin, Y., Kelemen, M., & Tresidder, R. (2018). Post-disaster Tourism: Building Resilience through Community-led Approaches in the Aftermath of the 2011 Disasters in Japan. *Journal of Sustainable Tourism*, *26*(10), 1766–1783

Mair, J., Ritchie, B., & Walters, G. (2016). Towards a Research Agenda for Post-disaster and Post-crisis Recovery Strategies for Tourist Destinations: A Narrative Review. *Current Issues in Tourism*, *19*(1), 1–26

Maitlis, S. (2005). The Social Processes of Organizational Sensemaking. *Academy of Management Journal*, *48*(1), 21–49.

Maitlis, S., & Christianson, M. (2014). Sensemaking in Organizations: Taking Stock and Moving Forward. *Academy of Management Annals*, *8*, 57–125.

Margo, E. (2020). *Towards Recovery: Renewal and Reorientation as Regional Strategies for a Post-COVID-19 Era*, Orkestra. www.orkestra.deusto.es/en/latest-news/news-events/

beyondcompetitiveness/1924-towards-recovery-renewal-reorientation-regional-strate-gies-post-covid-19-era

OECD (2021). *The Territorial Impact of COVID-19: Managing the Crisis and Recovery across Levels of Government*. OECD. Oecd.org/coronavirus

Olcott, G., & Oliver, N. (2014). Social Capital, Sense-Making and Recovery from Disaster: Japanese Companies and the March 2011 Earthquake. *California Management Review, 56*(2), 5–22.

Page, S., Song, H., & Wu, D.C. (2012). Assessing the Impacts of the Global Economic Crisis and Swine Flu on Inbound Tourism Demand in the United Kingdom. *Journal of Travel Research, 51*(2), 142–153.

Rastegar, R., Higgins-Desbiolles, F., & Ruhanen, L. (2021). COVID-19 and a Justice Framework to Guide Tourism Recovery. *Annals of Tourism Research*, 103161

Revans, R.W. (1982). What is Action Learning? *Journal of Management Development, 1*(3), 64–75.

Ritchie, B.W., & Jiang, Y. (2019). A Review of Research on Tourism Risk, Crisis and Disaster Management: Launching the Annals of Tourism Research Curated Collection on Tourism Risk, Crisis and Disaster Management. *Annals of Tourism Research, 79*, 102812.

Robert, K.H., Madsen, P., & Desai, V. (2007). Organizational Sensemaking during Crisis. In C.M. Pearson, C. Roux-Dufort, & J.A. Clair (Eds.), *International Handbook of Organizational Crisis Management* (1st ed., pp. 107–122). London: Sage.

Roepstorff, K. (2020). A Call for Critical Reflection on the Localisation Agenda in Humanitarian Action. *Third World Quarterly, 41*(2), 284–301

Roth, R.J. (1997). Insurable Risks, Regulation, and the Changing Insurance Environment. In H.F. Diaz, & R.S. Pulwarthy (Eds.), *Hurricanes: Climate and Socioeconomic Impacts* (pp. 261–272). New York: Springer.

Schultz, T., & Barnett, B. (2020). *Binna Burra Strategic Visions, Masterplan, and RAP Background Summary Report*. Queensland: Binna Burra.

Tomassini, L., & Cavagnaro, E. (2020). The Novel Spaces and Power-geometries in Tourism and Hospitality after 2020 Will Belong to the 'Local'. *Tourism Geographies, 22*(3), 713–719

Tourism and Events Queensland. (2021). *Domestic Tourism Snapshot*. Queensland: Tourism and Events Queensland

van der Giessen, M., Langenbusch, C., Jacobs, G., & Cornelissen, J. (2021). Collective Sensemaking in the Local Response to a Grand Challenge: Recovery, Alleviation and Change-oriented Responses to a Refugee Crisis. *Human Relations, 75*(5), 903–930.

Wall, I., & Hedlund, K. (2016). Localisation and Locally-led Crisis Response: A Literature Review, Swiss Agency for Development and Cooperation. www.local2global.info

Weick, K.E. (1993). The Collapse of Sensemaking in Organizations: The Mann Gulch Disaster. *Administrative Science Quarterly, 38*, 628–52.

Weick, K.E. (1995). *Sensemaking in Organizations*. London: Sage.

Weick, K.E., Sutcliff, K.M., & Obstfeld, D. (2005). Organizing and the Process of Sensemaking. *Organization Science, 16*(4), 409–421.

Wut, T.M., Xu, J., & Wong, S. (2021). Crisis Management Research (1985–2020) in the Hospitality and Tourism Industry: A Review and Research Agenda. *Tourism Management, 85*, 104307.

11

BUILDING TRUST AMONG TOURISTS IN THE POST-COVID-19 PERIOD

The role of external quality certifications

Thais González-Torres, José-Luis Rodríguez-Sánchez and Eva Pelechano-Barahona

Introduction

During the year 2020, the world suffered the worst health crisis in recent history with the COVID-19 pandemic. Its consequences are spread all over the world and in all sectors of activity. Tourism is a very sensitive and vulnerable sector to any risk situation caused by external factors, and this pandemic caused a significant drop in the demand, affecting companies' performance. The rapid spread of the COVID-19 outbreak has led to economic disruption as a result of border closures and mandatory mass quarantine, which has had a major impact on the tourism industry. All this has exposed the tourism industry to unprecedented pressure, causing a significant reduction in revenue and creating liquidity issues (De Rosa et al., 2020). In addition, customer trust in hotels and other tourism services has been seriously damaged (Reznik et al., 2020; Addo et al., 2020).

Hospitality operators are striving to find appropriate solutions to maintain and improve or adapt quality standards in order to mitigate customer uncertainty. The quality of the service is a key aspect when competing in the hospitality industry since it influences the efficiency and profitability of the sector and, therefore, its competitiveness. The analysis of quality in the hotel sector has always aroused much interest in the literature both from the point of view of consumers and hospitality firms (Benavides & Ortega, 2014).

In the context of the current health crisis, it is necessary to focus on the measures needed to eliminate any risks, such as the adoption of external quality certifications. The implementation of internationally recognised quality systems such as ISO certifications is widely recognised as an instrument to demonstrate a firm's commitment to quality by applying internal communication systems, protocols and standards (Ortega et al., 2013). However, in recent years, under the framework of their own quality departments, large hotel chains have developed their own quality

DOI: 10.4324/9781003295839-14

labels, following their own protocols and standards. This contrasts with the lack of resources for small independent hotels to promote their own quality standards. To the best of our knowledge, this literature has not addressed this issue related to pandemics and similar global societal risks.

To fill this research gap, this study examines the role and usefulness of external certifications in the context of the COVID-19 epidemic outbreak. The main research questions are:

RQ1. What role do quality certifications play in health crisis situations?

RQ2. Are external quality certifications useful for all types of hotels?

RQ3. What are the main approaches followed by hotels to generating trust among their potential clients?

In view of the importance of certifications in overcoming crises and the existence of independent hotels and large hotel chains in the Spanish hotel industry, this study makes two major contributions. First, it argues that external quality certifications are not useful for all types of hotels, and second, it identifies that the main approaches followed by hotels to generate trust among their potential clients in this health COVID-19 crisis are to comply with health recommendations while continuing to generate customer experiences.

Theoretical framework: external quality certifications in the tourism and hospitality industry

In recent years, higher-quality tourism has been promoted through the creation of a quality culture among all hotels and employees, improving the service offered through innovation and continuous improvement (Benavides & Ortega, 2014). Implementing quality practices allows managers to rethink the way of doing things by enhancing both products and internal processes. Quality practices can eliminate and improve less productive activities, for example, by reducing errors or complaints and creating new tasks. In addition, high-quality standards will improve the experience of the customer, who will be willing to pay a higher price for the products. This allows firms to reduce costs, increase sales, and improve customer loyalty and the image and reputation of the company (Alonso-Almeida et al., 2012; Bagur-Femenías et al., 2016).

Rodríguez Antón and Alonso-Almeida (2011) point out the key role of quality management in hotels due to the high degree of customer contact, where the attention paid by employees has a great influence on customer satisfaction. This means that it is necessary to establish policies in order to standardise processes and implement programs to motivate and engage employees, such as training programs in specific knowledge and skills. Having standardised processes forces workers to follow these behavioural patterns, leading to higher-quality services as well as customer and employee satisfaction.

The choice of tourist accommodation is a decision surrounded by great uncertainty. Quality is a key attribute, given its intangible nature, which implies that each consumer may perceive it in a very different way, being very difficult to observe and evaluate. This means that the appreciation of quality depends on the confidence of the consumer in the veracity of the information he or she receives (Carimentrand & Ballet, 2004). In this sense, the adoption of certifications can encourage a more objective view of quality, thus providing an external guarantee to companies. Quality seals or labels attempt to symbolise elements such as information, legitimacy and confidence, which are crucial for both consumer recognition and market valorisation (Valceschini & Nicolas, 1995). The relevance of these certifications lies in the client's lack of resources – time and/or knowledge – to analyse the characteristics of each product or service (Carimentrand & Ballet, 2004).

Besides the advantages for customers, companies adopting quality certifications, whether large chains or independent hotels, obtain better financial or operational results. This derives both from improvements in their internal processes as well as from customers' perceptions of the company (Sutherland et al., 2021). Among the relevant outcomes are reduced costs and waste, improved image, improved relations with suppliers, or satisfaction of customers, employees or other stakeholders (Segarra-Oña et al., 2012). The implementation of certifications, seals or labels involves costs that companies must assume. The value obtained depends on factors such as types of certification, locations, industries, organisations and products (Sutherland et al., 2021). The most relevant internationally recognised quality systems are ISO 9001, UNE 182001 or 'Q de calidad turística' certificate (Institute for Spanish Tourist Quality – ICTE). In terms of environmental quality, the green certifications ISO 14001 or Eco-Label are also adopted.

For many years, large hotel chains have focused on generating an image of their own brand that is recognised by customers by offering a homogeneous quality service in all their hotels. However, in small companies, quality control has been carried out through informal control systems, especially by managers, because of easier and simpler structures to supervise (Bagur-Femenías et al., 2016).

The traditional experience in continuous improvement and quality enhancement is proving useful in dealing with a COVID-19 pandemic, establishing hygiene protocols and conveying safety to customers. Rodríguez-Anton et al. (2011) point out the importance of having certified quality systems in place to optimise internal procedures and serve as strategic tools when facing an economic crisis. For this reason, many hotels have considered developing their own COVID-free quality labels.

Materials and methods

Sampling procedure and data collection

In order to achieve the main purpose of this study, hotel chains in Spain were selected. The sample for this study consisted of three international hotel chains located among the 60 hotel chains with more than a mere presence in Spain

TABLE 11.1 Stages of the case study approach

Profile
Review of literature (Web of Science and Scopus)
Sample selection
Hotel Chain A (72 hotels)
Hotel Chain B (35 hotels)
Hotel Chain C (36 hotels)
Units of analysis
Hotel Chain A CEO
Hotel Chain B CEO
Hotel Chain C CEO
Total CEOs: 3 respondents
Hotel Chain A area managers (operations and human resources)
Hotel Chain B area managers (operations and human resources)
Hotel Chain C area managers (operations and human resources)
Total senior managers: 6 respondents
Information gathering
6 semi-structured interviews: 2020 senior managers (operations and human resources)
3 open interviews: 2020 (CEO)
Internal and external documents: 2020
(Principle of triangulation)
Information transcription
ATLAS.ti (qualitative data analysis)
Data records and classification:
(1) internal documents, (2) external documents, (3) interviews, and (4) field notes
Results and conclusions
Conformity with the analysis results
Conclusions, along with literature and professional implications

Source: Adapted from Rodríguez-Sánchez et al. (2019)

(Table 11.1). All three companies have establishments located in urban and beach destinations.

This study adopts a qualitative-based approach to an exploratory case study (Flick, 2009). The respondents were chosen for their expertise, that is, as key informants. Following the purposive sampling method (Sangpikul & Kim 2009), only top-level hotel executives and managers were sampled, given their high position in the information hierarchy (Kruesi et al., 2017). The number of interviews and informants was not specified at the beginning of the research, and it was decided that a strategy of 'theoretical saturation' would be followed to determine this.

In order to promote an open dialogue, evidence was collected through open and semi-structured interviews that began with broad open-ended questions followed by focused and directed questions as the interviews progressed within and between interviews (Manuj & Mentzer, 2008). Interviews continued until it was perceived that informants did not reveal any new information and reported similar and consistent information – theoretical saturation (Yin, 1998).

Results

The role and usefulness of external quality certifications in the COVID-19 context were discussed with the respondents. The main approaches followed by hotels to generate trust among potential clients were also explored.

The role of quality certifications in health crisis situations

Initially and according to diverse studies, the role of quality certifications was demonstrated to force companies to review internal processes and plan improvement actions in health crisis situations (Rodríguez-Anton et al., 2011; Alonso-Almeida et al., 2013; Sutherland et al., 2021). The following quote shows how a Hotel Chain B senior manager stresses the need for guidelines to respond to the current situation:

> It is clear to us that the cleaning and disinfection processes are going to be more in-depth. Costs, cleaning times and room rotation will increase. The processes and spaces in the restoration or reception will also be longer. It is necessary to promote digitalised processes that avoid contact and agglomeration of people (check in, check out, consultations). Even so, we continue to think about what and how we need to do it.

Certifications help improve brand image and enhance customer confidence (Segarra-Oña et al., 2012; Alonso-Almeida et al., 2013). Hotel Chain A manager pointed out:

> We are working to obtain external certification by a third party. It wouldn't be so much for the technical expertise they can provide us with, but to give the customer that perception of safety. It is about showing the client that we take hygiene and prevention measures very seriously in our facilities.

However, following Sutherland et al. (2021) factors such as location and type of industry can affect the value obtained from the certification. Hotel Chain C CEO stresses that the relevance and global dimension of this health crisis requires ensuring safety at the individual hotel, destination and country level:

> The fundamental aspect of the certifications is the generation of security through sectorial labels or even associated with the Spain brand.
> An additional effort is required, thinking of the 80 million tourists who come to Spain.
> We must rebuild our brand and reinforce the idea that this has made us stronger and we know more than anyone else. We need our destinations to be perceived as COVID-free and to create a specific seal for each country at international level.

In this line of thought, the three hotel chains have sought external recognition, especially at the international level, by applying World Health Organization recommendations as well as other Spanish rules such as the advice of the Institute for Spanish Tourist Quality (ICTE). In addition, the three companies have agreements with nationally and internationally certified suppliers such as Diversey (specialised in hygiene solutions for the hotel sector) and are advised and audited by external consultants such as Quiron Prevención (specialised in occupational risk prevention) or Bio 9000 (specialised in food and environmental safety).

However, the observation made by the Hotel Chain C CEO is in line with the need for more explicit, external and objective recognition in order to mitigate distrust:

> We seek to reinforce our anti-COVID protocol by improving current measures as well as adhering to new ones. This is why we have recently obtained the 'Clean and Safe' certificate.

External quality certifications and hotel chains

According to Bagur-Femenías et al. (2016) for large hotel chains, it is crucial to provide a homogeneous quality service in all their hotels in order to meet customer expectations and brand differentiation. The following quote shows how a Hotel Chain A senior manager stresses the need to develop their own quality procedures:

> A great number of large hotel chains are creating their own label to ensure that they meet presumably international standards. They have allocated a great deal of economic resources to create them and to disseminate them through their own channels.

Large hospitality companies collaborate amongst themselves to address environmental threats, with the main goal of destination marketing and development activities being to improve the competitive position by increasing trial and repurchase (Chathoth & Olsen, 2003; von Friedrichs Grängsjö & Gummesson, 2006). The senior manager of hotel chain B suggested collaboration by focusing on safety and quality as key sources of reputation and efficiency (Tapper & Font, 2004; Benavides-Chicón & Ortega, 2014).

> Collaboration at sector level to create health standards and/or COVID-free certifications would be a very useful way not to lose competitiveness. The individual development of these standards is very demanding in terms of resources. Cooperating and sharing resources is a more efficient way. In addition, this common effort will allow for greater visibility to project a positive and homogeneous image of the sector.

From a sectoral perspective, collaboration with competitors is crucial to increasing bargaining power at the industry level to address issues such as the creation of sector-specific regulation (Chathoth & Olsen, 2003). In order to do so, the relative relevance of individual sectors within an industry is crucial (Zhang et al., 2009). However, the senior manager of hotel chain B reveals the lack of coordination mechanisms at both institutional and industry levels, which is the main reason for developing individual COVID free procedures:

> *In my opinion, things could have been done better. We could have organised ourselves at the sectorial level with the support of governments and an international marketing campaign we only have minimum standards. Everyone is waging war on their own.*

The implementation of certifications, seals or labels involves high costs (Sutherland et al., 2021). Consistent with Bagur-Femenías et al. (2016), Hotel Chain C senior manager is aware of the need of small hospitality firms to achieve this type of external recognition:

> *It is a useful measure for independent hotels. Hotel chains have their own quality departments (we have designed our own protocols). The brand image of small, independent hotels is weaker than that of the chains. These companies do not have specialists, so it is interesting that a third party certifies that they follow certain processes and standards that guarantee to minimise the risk will help consumer confidence.*

Main approaches to generating trust among potential clients in the COVID-19 era

Customer satisfaction comes not only from the basic functional qualities of the service, but also from emotional dimensions such as security (Berry et al., 2002). To overcome this crisis, the three companies consider it crucial to implement protocols to ensure the health safety of guests and employees. The following Hotel Chain C senior manager discusses the critical role of security in the customer experience, considering the current health context:

> *We are aware that the client's priorities will change: they will be especially demanding with hygiene and safety. However, it does not make any sense to turn the experience into a hospital. No one wants to travel to a hospital; travellers want to be safe and comfortable in hotels. A holiday service with health guarantees should be provided, but we must be careful to prevent the customer from losing the experience.*

Similarly, a Hotel Chain B senior manager claims:

> *We all think that the client is going to be very concerned about security, about the possibility of getting infected or spreading the virus. We will need to continually show the customer a security image. Hotel companies must assess the possibility that some customers may want to avoid any kind of contact.*

The following respondents insist on the requirement to redefine the internal processes to ensure a safe environment for guests and employees. In this vein, Hotel Chain A senior manager indicated:

> *We are considering the impact on the guest experience of switching from traditional service kits to personal protective equipment kits (mask, gloves and hydroalcoholic gel). We believe that if we do this through a fun and friendly message to the customer, it will not cause him or her a panic attack.*

The existence of a quality culture among hotel employees is crucial to improve the service (Benavides & Ortega, 2014). Internal processes cannot be redefined without the commitment of employees (Alonso-Almeida et al., 2012; Bagur-Femenías et al., 2016). Accordingly, there is a need for standardised processes to enhance the customer experience and to improve employee satisfaction (Rodríguez-Antón & Alonso-Almeida, 2011; Bagur-Femenías et al., 2016). Hotel Chain A CEO illustrates this issue:

> *It is very important to make employees aware of the relevance of their behavior to the company's image with customers. There are five fundamental pillars. First, hygiene: frequent hand washing with soap and water and hydroalcoholic gel dispensers in work areas. Second, prevention: COVID-19 diagnostic test, temperature control and protective elements. Third, training: staff have received specific training in hygiene and safety. Fourth, information: quality department team assists hotels with hygiene and safety measures. Fifth, back office: also we applied hygiene and safety measures, and social distancing.*

Discussion

The rapid spatial spread of the recent COVID-19 outbreak, together with its unpredictable scaling and ripple effect, has resulted in one of the greatest economic disruptions in recent decades, especially for the tourism industry (Kuo et al., 2008), where customer trust in hotels may have been seriously damaged.

The high quality of Spanish hotels has been amply demonstrated to be a very important value in creating unique service experiences and building customer loyalty. The sector has been working for many years to achieve high levels of service quality and to be able to have a competitive position at an international level. Hotel companies have always had to work to comply with very demanding legislation in terms of hygiene, food safety, health and safety, fire prevention, etc., thus achieving a know-how of great value to be able to overcome any crisis, such as the current one, guaranteeing a good service experience. In this sense, it is worth mentioning the efforts made to obtain ISO, AENOR, Q for tourism quality and Biosphere company certifications, among others, that guarantee their good work, their commitment to sustainability and to their employees, and so on. These seals have become a requirement to compete, given the high levels of competition and demands of today's customers. For this reason, in recent years, this sector has decided to redefine its processes by seeking entities that certify its excellence.

This COVID-19 crisis demands that companies increase security in their facilities following national and international recommendations, and that protocols are implemented for both employees and guest security. In this sense, companies already had a long way to go, which allows them to offer a good customer experience.

The interviews conducted in this research allow us to show that certifications are highly valued by hotel managers as they generate security for guests when choosing hotel accommodation. Certified companies have made a greater effort to improve their internal processes than those that are not certified and to train their employees. This effort is perceived by their guests. In this sense, large hotel chains, normally internationalised, have implemented a culture of quality at all levels of the company, in line with Benavides and Ortega (2014), and have established very strict protocols internally for all their hotels. These guarantee homogeneous standards of service in each of them that the guest recognises and values. This trajectory allowed them to generate their own quality seals, which translate into better service and which have allowed them to face other previous crises, in line with what authors such as Rodríguez-Anton et al. (2011) point out.

For these large chains with their own quality seals, obtaining global seals such as 'Clean and Safe' is considered a marketing tool only, allowing them to reinforce their good image in terms of prevention and safety, with a view to attracting international clients. Nowadays, hotels must face the opinions of their customers on social networks, so they must also improve the image they project to the outside world. These social networks have a great influence on the choice of hotel, so certifications help to improve the image of the company and the sector by increasing trust (Segarra-Oña et al., 2012; Alonso-Almeida et al., 2013, Sutherland et al., 2021).

However, the companies analysed consider that despite the great effort being made by the hotel sector, this crisis is so global that it goes beyond the individual limits of each company, requiring the effort and collaboration of all entities in the tourism industry and the public administration. Therefore, it is essential to generate a certification at the country level that is internationally recognised in order to be able to compete with guarantees of safety and excellence. On the other hand, small and independent hotels have a weaker image because they have fewer resources to rely on quality specialists and establish protocols. Their operating standards are much less well known and may not even be set out in a specific procedure, following Bagur-Femenías et al. (2016). Thus, small hotels can derive the most value from external certifications in terms of image and in terms of being able to improve their internal procedures and offer a better service experience.

The experience accumulated by the companies in the sector, together with their capacity for innovation and adaptation to the new challenges of the environment, such as technology, has made it possible to face COVID-19 with great guarantees of safety and hygiene. All the companies analysed have pointed out the importance of establishing protocols focused mainly on the use of masks, increasing the hygiene of their facilities, providing protective equipment for their employees and maintaining safety distances by reducing capacity, implementing online check-in and check-out, as well as including medical assistance among their services. It is also very important to make these protocols known to both employees and guests, so all the companies have established different communication channels. Along with these steps, in a health crisis period, it is essential that companies improve their human resources management policies in terms of health and safety training, internal quality protocols, as well as skills to improve customer relations.

Conclusions, limitations and future research agenda

In situations of health crises, external certifications improve the customer's perception of Spanish hotel establishments, reducing uncertainties and improving the customer's image and trust. Hotel chains with well-established internal quality protocols are able to improve their image as safe companies through certifications. However, small and independent hotels achieve, in addition to this improvement in the customer's image, an improvement in their internal processes, which translates into better quality and customer experience. Certifications force companies to redesign their internal management models by modifying and standardising their processes. It also forces them to establish a culture of quality at all levels of the company to ensure safety standards.

During the pandemic, the whole sector is carrying out the recommendations given by the health authorities at national and international levels, trying to improve the customer's perception. Hotels must continue to work on improving the customer experience with all the health guarantees and achieve a safe environment free of COVID, but without forgetting that the customer does not want to have the feeling of being in a hospital. The role of staff is key to achieving this.

However, the magnitude of the pandemic and its international nature require measures beyond the individual actions of each of the hotels, being necessary to establish collaborations between all the agents that form the value chain of the industry. Administrations must also collaborate to ensure that Spain is a safe destination that complies with all health recommendations.

The results obtained in this research should be interpreted with caution. First, the qualitative methodology does not allow us to understand the phenomenon studied in other contexts or to draw conclusions that can be extrapolated to other sectors. Second, only three Spanish hotel chains were analysed. Therefore, as a future line of research, a questionnaire should be developed to expand the number of companies analysed.

References

Addo, P.C., Jiaming, F., Kulbo, N.B., & Liangqiang, L. (2020). COVID-19: Fear Appeal Favoring Purchase Behavior towards Personal Protective Equipment. *The Service Industries Journal, 40*(7–8), 471–490. DOI: 10.1080/02642069.2020.1751823

Alonso-Almeida, M., Marimon, F., & Bernardo, M. (2013). Diffusion of Quality Standards in the Hospitality Sector. *International Journal of Operations & Production Management, 33*(5), 504–527. DOI: 10.1108/01443571311322706

Alonso-Almeida, M.M., Rodríguez-Antón, J.M., & Rubio-Andrada, L. (2012). Reasons for Implementing Certified Quality Systems and Impact on Performance: An Analysis of the Hotel Industry. *The Service Industry Journal, 32*, 919–936, DOI: 10.1080/02642069.2010.545886.

Bagur-Femenías, L., Celma, D., & Patau, J. (2016). The Adoption of Environmental Practices in Small Hotels. Voluntary or Mandatory? An Empirical Approach. *Sustainability, 8*, 695, DOI: 10.3390/su8070695.

Benavides-Chicón, C.G., & Ortega, B. (2014). The Impact of Quality Management on Productivity in the Hospitality Sector. *International Journal of Hospitality Management, 42*, 165–173. DOI: 10.1016/j.ijhm.2014.07.004

Berry, L.L., Carbone, L.P., & Haeckel, S.H. (2002). Managing the Total Customer Experience. *MIT Sloan Management Review, 43*(3), 85–89.

Carimentrand, A., & Ballet, J. (2004). Le commerce équitable entre éthique de la consommation et signes de qualité. *Proceedings Agroindustria Rural y Territorio, December 2004*, 1–4.

Chathoth, P.K., & Olsen, M.D. (2003). Strategic Alliances: A Hospitality Industry Perspective. *International Journal of Hospitality Management, 22*(4), 419–434. DOI: 10.1016/j.ijhm.2003.07.001

De Rosa, M., Lanzilotta, B., Perazzo, I., & Vigorito, A. (2020). *Las políticas económicas y sociales frente a la expansión de la pandemia de COVID-19: aportes para el debate. Aportes y análisis en tiempos de coronavirus*. Montevedio: University of the Republic of Uruguay.

Flick, U. (2009). *The Sage Qualitative Research Kit: Collection*. London: SAGE Publications Limited.

Kruesi, M., Kim, P.B., & Hemmington, N. (2017). Evaluating Foreign Market Entry Mode Theories from a Hotel Industry Perspective. *International Journal of Hospitality Management, 62*, 88–100. DOI: 10.1016/j.ijhm.2016.12.005

Kuo, H.I., Chen, C.C., Tseng, W.C., Ju, L.F., & Huang, B.W. (2008). Assessing Impacts of SARS and Avian Flu on International Tourism Demand to Asia. *Tourism Management, 29*(5), 917–928. DOI: 10.1016/j.tourman.2007.10.006

Manuj, I., & Mentzer, J.T. (2008). Global Supply Chain Risk Management Strategies. *International Journal of Physical Distribution & Logistics Management, 38*(3), 192–223. DOI: 10.1108/09600030810866986

Ortega, E.M.P., Guilló, J.J.T., Moliner, J.P., Azorín, J.F.M., & Gamero, M.D.L. (2013). Certificación en calidad, resultados empresariales y estructura organizativa en el sector hotelero español. *Intangible Capital, 9*(1), 199–224.

Reznik, A., Gritsenko, V., Konstantinov, V., Khamenka, N., & Isralowitz, R. (2020). COVID-19 Fear in Eastern Europe: Validation of the Fear of COVID-19 Scale. *International Journal of Mental Health and Addiction*, 1–6. DOI: 10.1007/s11469-020-00283-3

Rodríguez-Antón, J.M., & Alonso-Almeida, M.M. (2011). Quality Certification Systems and their Impact on Employee Satisfaction in Services with High Levels of Customer Contact. *Total Quality Management, 22*(2), 145–147. DOI: 10.1080/14783363.2010.529640

Rodríguez-Anton, J.M., Alonso-Almeida, M.M., & Rubio-Andrada, L. (2011). Shedding More Light on the Impacts of Quality Certified Systems in Small Service Enterprises: A Multidimensional Analysis. *African Journal of Business Management, 5*(19), 7911–7922. DOI: 10.5897/AJBM11.531

Rodríguez-Sánchez, J.L., Mora-Valentín, E.M., & Ortiz-de-Urbina-Criado, M. (2019). Human Resource Management in Merger and Acquisition Planning. *Journal of Organizational Change Management, 33*(1), 16–28.

Sangpikul, A., & Kim, S. (2009). An Overview and Identification of Barriers Affecting the Meeting and Convention Industry in Thailand. *Journal of Convention & Event Tourism, 10*(3), 185–210. DOI: 10.1080/15470140903131822

Segarra-Oña, M.A., Peiró-Signes, A., Rohit, V., & Miret-Pastor, L. (2012). Does Environmental Certification Help the Economic Performance of Hotels? Evidence from the Spanish Hotel Industry. *Cornell Hospitality Quarterly, 53*, 242–256. DOI: 10.1177/1938965512446417

Sutherland, I., Sim, Y., & Lee, S.K. (2021). Impacts of Quality Certification on Online Reviews and Pricing Strategies in the Hospitality Industry. *International Journal of Hospitality Management, 93*. DOI: 10.1016/j.ijhm.2020.102776

Tapper, R., & Font, X. (2004). *Tourism Supply Chains. Report of a Desk Research Project for The Travel Foundation.* Leeds: Metropolitan University.

Valceschini, E., & Nicolas, F. (1995). La dynamique économique de la qualité agroalimentaire. In F. Nicolas & E. Valceschini (Eds.), *Agroalimentaire: une économie da la qualité* (pp. 15–37). Paris: Inra Económica.

von Friedrichs Grängsjö, Y., & Gummesson, E. (2006). Hotel Networks and Social Capital in Destination Marketing. *International Journal of Service Industry Management, 17*(1), 58–75. DOI: 10.1108/09564230610651589

Yin, R.K. (1998). The Abridged Version of Case Study Research. In L. Bickman & D.J. Rog (Eds.), *Handbook of Applied Social Research Methods* (pp. 229–259). Thousand Oaks, CA: Sage Publications.

Zhang, X., Song, H., & Huang, G.Q. (2009). Tourism Supply Chain Management: A New Research Agenda. *Tourism Management, 30*(3), 345–358. DOI: 10.1016/j.tourman.20

12

JUDGING THE RESILIENCE OF ONLINE LEARNING FOR HOSPITALITY COURSES DURING COVID-19

Rekha Maitra and Shantanu Jain

Hospitality education

Hospitality education has been recognised as a motivating force for the still-developing economies which have recognised the hospitality sector as a driving force for growth and development (Mill & Morrison, 1999). India, a developing country, identifies the potential of hospitality and the tourism sector as sources of employment. (Honey & Gilpin, 2009). In 1984, the Ministry of Tourism, Government of India (MoT) was responsible for India's hospitality and hotel management courses, with the National Council for Hotel Management & Catering Technology (NCHMCT) emerging as an autonomous body. NCHMCT, a nodal and affiliating organisation, started monitoring education standards for all institutes run by the Government of India with a standard syllabus and universal norms. During this phase, many food crafts institutes were also upgraded to hotel management institutes. Presently, there are 21 central government colleges and 33 State Government colleges, and many private colleges affiliated with NCHMCT (Kumar, 2014).

Due to pandemics, hospitality and tourism educational institutions adopted a COVID-19 mode of delivery. The Academy of Online Tourism Education inaugurated the North-East Tourism Academy (NETA) as a step to resuscitate the sector. This initiative is intended to improve the management skills used in tourism, promote entrepreneurial acumen in tourism, and sector-specific research to support small-scale operators. (Bhutia, 2020)

The COVID-19 pandemic posed many challenges to faculties as well as students. The majority of adult education techniques involve group work and practical activities. This was not feasible or practical due to the lockdown. Imparting hospitality skills that require practical exposure to understand different types of operations, i.e., chopping, cutting, cooking, boiling, poaching, broiling, welcoming, serving, dressing, designing, decorating, etc., became cumbersome in theoretical form, and so later faculty members opted for demonstration sessions.

DOI: 10.4324/9781003295839-15

During a three-year degree programme in hospitality and hotel administration, a hotel management professional is taught to utilise the five senses (i.e., sight, sound, smell, taste and touch), to produce the best products. They also learn to use their sensory organs to check the cleanliness, supervise the area, and sense hidden dangers. These skills could not have been offered without practical exposure in core departments, including low/high flame, food and beverages, welcoming guests, and other functional activities. Given the COVID-19 pandemic, the state government and nodal agencies encouraged all first-year and first-semester students at the undergraduate and postgraduate levels to enrol in universities and degree colleges without exams. Specific skill sets will be prioritised for development to have a lasting career in hospitality. The teachers and facilitators must focus on increasing fragility in one phase and changing social values in the second phase. Resilience must be developed, and other skills required post-COVID time include facility management, soft skills, and emotional intelligence. (EHL, 2020).

During online education, parents were also working from home and could observe the lectures extended by institutions. Therefore, institutions place more emphasis on academic inputs to justify these. Lei and So (2021) validated that online learning emerged as the preferred option for following social distancing and COVID safety protocols due to the pandemic outbreak. A study by Milton and Moyeenudin (2022) suggests that the efficacy of online education has remained a research topic. Skill-based professional courses such as Hotel Management consist of 50% theory and 50% practical sessions for nurturing the overall development of the students. Therefore, the student-centric methods were designed to deliver a practical lecture, and study time was reduced from 1 hour to 40 minutes for an online session. (Naik, 2020) The semester-end examinations were conducted through AON's platform Co-cubes with a multiple-choice-based question pattern. The faculty did live proctoring by accessing the student's system camera and microphone.

In a study conducted by Chhetri et al. (2020), it was found that 26.2% of students were not very satisfied with the effectiveness of online classes compared to classroom teaching, and only 18.9% were satisfied. A total of 30.9% were happy with the course coverage, whereas 18.4% were not. Because of such a new teaching pedagogy, 41.3% were satisfied with the online lectures, PDFs and videos, whereas 6.5% were not. Teachers did their best to put the point forth, but sometimes just hearing was not enough. Thus, 28.9% understood the taught topics, whereas 19.9% did not. Lastly, support from the facilitator is essential throughout the curriculum, which might have been hampered in the case of online classes, as evident from the 23% of the samples voting towards it, though about 50% voted that they were satisfied. The study also investigated specific challenges that students face while taking online classes. The biggest challenge was technical issues while joining and attending the course, with around 42% of samples agreeing to it, followed by lack of in-person interaction with the students, and lastly, distractions, including the prevalence of notifications & updates on laptops.

A Chinese study was conducted by Lei and So (2021) on 491 students and 117 faculty members from 15 colleges using T-tests and multi-group structural equation modelling. Even though enough literature is available on online education and teaching, hardly any study has analysed the experiences the faculty and students go through while participating in an online platform, especially for practical-oriented skill-based courses like Hospitality and Tourism. It was found that both groups – students and faculty—did not find the online setup in classes beneficial. External factors also came into play here, and the faculty stated that university-related factors, such as support and training, also affected the overall experience. The further analysis also questioned the effectiveness of a virtual environment for conducting lectures in Tourism & Hospitality courses, which are practically oriented. It did, however, conclude that technology did not hinder the process, as in today's age, everyone is used to it, and the faculty use information systems to prepare the lectures and so do the students. (Lei & So, 2021)

Though it is possible to conduct online lectures using edX, Zoom, Google Meet and some region-specific apps like Weibo and Cisco Webex, for subjects like Hospitality and Tourism, as evident across the country where colleges have adopted the online method to deliver lectures, the feasibility is still in question considering the amalgamation of practical concepts into online classes. There could be many reasons for this. The external factors are the most important, such as the faculty not finding a rhythm in conducting practical lectures online. Some are not familiar with technology, while others do not entirely believe in the practical applications of an online teaching model. (Sigala, 2004).

Any natural disaster, in this case a pandemic, can create huge hassles and problems in people's daily lives, which can cause concentration lapse, anxiety and stress. (Di Pietro, 2017). A paper by Dani et al. (2020) validated that almost 97% of the students agreed about how COVID has affected their internship programmes and the hospitality industry on a global scale. 73% of the students believed that the online teaching method was beneficial during the lockdown times, though 75% also agreed that they got full support from their facilitators. Another study concluded that 80% of the samples agreed that offline, face-to-face classes are more effective than online classes, and their preference lies with the former. (Sciarini et al., 2012).

Maitra (2021: 8–9) emphasised that 'the role of technology is constantly changing; due to the changing environment, people employed in the teaching sector need to upgrade their skill sets, particularly in the case of using technology platforms'. It is expected that teachers and students will have to opt for hybrid (combination of online and offline) teaching. Pencarelli (2019: 455) identified that the 'Tourism and hospitality system is well integrated with technological advancements and uses features, i.e., real-time data regarding location, traffic and metrological forecasts. Analytical tools are service-oriented, with modulation principles and virtual presence'.

Impact of pandemic COVID-19

The impact of COVID-19 was felt in all industries, including the hospitality teaching industry, where it was never before the case that education was affected globally. In March 2020, many parts of the world were told to shift to an online platform for

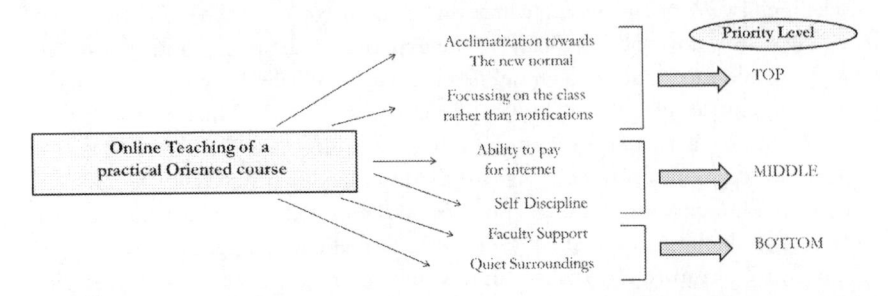

FIGURE 12.1   Descriptive model depicting suggested priority levels during online classes

taking classes at short notice of 3 days, which made it very difficult, specifically for the practically oriented courses which are hands-on, skill-based and work majorly on physical interaction. India's educational institute shut down offline. Operations for the students were instructed to remain closed till March 31st (TOI-Online, 2020). Though the instructions were given until March 31, it was extended until May 1, and it kept rising, resulting in massive losses. According to UNESCO (2020), one hundred and forty-three million primary school students, one hundred and thirty-three million middle school students, and four million graduate and postgraduate students were affected by COVID-19; almost 320 million students were impacted.

This situation led to alternative methods of streaming the learning process, mainly the online teaching model. Academic committees were involved in designing teaching models to make online classes enjoyable with video lectures, such as YouTube. Students commenced learning through online platforms like Zoom, Microsoft and Google Classroom, and a record surge in the number of people using online learning platforms increased gradually. Before the pandemic hit the world, these modes were practically non-existing/less utilised. (Raheem, 2020)

Based on the review presented thus far, Figure 12.1 represents the priorities for teaching practically oriented online classes. Faculty support and quiet surroundings fall into the low level, self-discipline of students, ability to pay for internet charges by the institution, fall into the middle level of priority and proper focus on the class contents by students to understand the concept considering it as the new normal is the most significant priority.

Objectives of the study

The literature review suggests that online teaching in hospitality was not explored before the pandemic. The research emphasises that student engagement is low during online education, primarily due to learning a practical-oriented subject during the ongoing impact of COVID-19. Considering the research gap, the following objectives were framed.

- To understand the impact of the COVID-19 pandemic on the education system of India

- To judge the effectiveness of online learning for a skill-based course in hospitality
- To analyse online studying from a student perspective

Methods

This chapter intends to determine student satisfaction levels while attending a practical skill-based course such as hospitality online. Subjects like food and beverage production and service need hands-on training using kitchen tools and equipment. Similarly, rooms division subjects like housekeeping also require cleaning agents and equipment, which cannot be learned online.

The research methodology was divided into two parts. The first was to develop a questionnaire on the impact of online teaching on hospitality courses. The questionnaire was in English and was distributed to the students of various hotel management institutes scattered across the country to ensure comprehensive country-wide inclusion. The questionnaire was made via Google Forms and was divided into different segments, including demographics, preferences of students and parameters about the faculty, which were analysed using Likert scales. The second was to investigate the faculty parameters using factor analysis, T-test, and ANOVA to determine their significance.

Sample and data collection

A total sample of 711 responses was received from hotel management students, although the scope of potential students was 2000+. The response rate can be related to questionnaires being often ignored, even when the authors personally persuade the samples (Semley et al., 2017). Students from all three years of hotel management colleges participated, and the demographics were as follows:

Table 12.1 represents the number of respondents/students from each year of the course. The data shows the maximum participation from students in the first year with 61.3% or 436 samples, third-year hotel management students followed by 26% respondents or 187 samples in the third year and lastly 12.4% or 88 samples, forming the second-year students of the hospitality course.

Table 12.2 reflects maximum participation from male students with 78.1% responses in 555 samples and 21.9% or 156 sample participation from the female students.

TABLE 12.1 Demographic classification

Year	No. of respondents	Percentage
1st year	436	61.3
2nd year	88	12.4
3rd year	187	26.3
Total	711	100.0

TABLE 12.2 Gender classification

Gender	No. of respondents	Percentage
Male	555	78.1
Female	156	21.9
Total	711	100.0

TABLE 12.3 Familiarity with online sessions

Experience	No. of respondents	Percentage
Yes	619	87.1
No	92	12.9
Total	711	100.0

TABLE 12.4 Preferences for online vs. classroom sessions

Preference	No. of respondents	Percentage
Yes	175	24.6
No	474	66.7
No difference	62	8.7
Total	711	100.0

Results and discussion

Experience with online sessions

Table 12.3 shows that 87% of students have already experienced online sessions, whereas 13% have not experienced them before.

Preference for online classes over classroom teaching

As shown in Table 12.4, students were asked if they would prefer online classes over classroom teaching; their responses reflect that 67% of students were against online courses, as it does not give them enough exposure to understand the practical aspects, followed by 25% who were in favour of the online sessions. The remaining 9% of students were unaffected by online/offline sessions, which did not make any difference, even if the practical sessions were conducted online.

Reasons that make online classes preferable over classroom teaching

In Table 12.5, Hotel Management students were asked why online sessions are preferable to classroom teaching. 37% of students said home comfort while studying makes it easy to attend the sessions. 16% of students prefer online sessions due

TABLE 12.5 Parameters of preference for online classes

Reasons	Respondents	Percentage
Personal preference	111	15.6
The comfort of home while studying	262	36.8
More flexibility	91	12.8
Induces self-reliance	37	5.2
Promotes self-study	142	20
Parents can attend and analyse	68	9.6
Total	711	100.0

TABLE 12.6 Preferences for classroom teaching

Reasons	Respondents	Percentage
Traditionally adapted	66	9
No network issues	115	16
Personal attention	112	16
Better concept grasping	233	33
More faculty support	64	9
More engaging	121	17
Total	711	100.0

to their personal preference, and 13% find an online mode more flexible. The lowest reason was 'induces self-reliance,' with only 5.9% of students voting for it as a preference over the offline classes.

Reasons that make classroom teaching preferable over online classes

Table 12.6 shows the results when students were also asked about why they opt for classroom teaching over online classes. 33% of students believed that they could understand the concepts more easily in the class, 17% of students find this to be more engaging, 16.2% of students feel that in the classroom, they do not have to face any network issues, and 16% think that the classroom sessions are more engaging in comparison to online classes.

Problems faced while learning in an online class

Students were asked, as shown in Table 12.7, if they faced any problems during online classes. From the responses, it was discovered that 40% of students faced the problem of unstable networks, and 20% of students feel they cannot concentrate due to their home environment. They found it more ineffective than classroom teaching, as the teacher did not directly view them. 19% of students found it difficult to understand concepts, and 8% saw it as massive confusion.

TABLE 12.7 Problems faced in online sessions

Problems	Respondents	Percentage
Unstable network	287	40.4
Power cuts	26	3.7
Non-habitual	57	8
Ineffective than classroom teaching	144	20.3
Difficult to understand concepts	137	19.3
Massive confusion	60	8.4
Total	711	100.0

Faculty parameters

Three parameters were utilised to judge faculty performance: teaching ability, faculty commitment, and classroom engagement. The variables that comprise the perception of faculty component were factor analysed using Principal Component analysis after ascertaining the appropriateness of factor analysis using Bartlett's Test of Sphericity (significant at the 0.05 level) and Kaiser-Meyer-Olkin (KMO) statistic (>0.6). Factors with an eigenvalue more effective than one and loading of 0.5 and above were then rotated using varimax rotation with Kaiser normalisation.

A smaller number of factors should be extracted to summarise the information contained in the original variables. This research uses approaches based on eigenvalues (eigenvalue > 1) and a Scree plot to determine the number of factors. To ensure that the variables for each of the elements were internally related, their Cronbach's coefficient alpha was measured and found to have acceptable internal consistency reliabilities, that is, greater than 0.7 (Nunnally, 1978)

Perception factors

The Perception component comprised seven variables analysed using Principal Component Analysis, and seven factors emerged, explaining 86.62% of the Variance. The summary results of all the elements and sub-elements for the Satisfaction component are presented in Table 12.8. The factor analysis yielded three dimensions labelled 'teaching ability,' 'faculty commitment,' and 'classroom engagement.'

The first factor identified is 'Teaching Ability', which has a factor mean of 3.26 and consists of three items: Ability to control the class, Put the point across and doubt addressing. This factor accounts for a 75.5% variance. The second factor identified is 'Faculty Commitment,' which accounts for 6.47% variance, has a factor mean of 3.35 and consists of two items: Personal Support from Faculty and Interest shown by the faculty. The third factor identified is 'Classroom Engagement,' which has a factor mean of 3.13 and consists of two items: Class Engagement and Concept Clarity. This factor accounts for a 4.62% variance. T-tests were conducted to assess whether male and female students differed in their perception

TABLE 12.8 Summary of factor analysis results

Factors	Significant Variables	Factor Loadings	Item Mean	Factor Mean	Eigen Values	% of Variance	Coefficient alpha
F1: Teaching ability	Ability to control the class	.842	3.21	3.26	5.28	75.5%	.901
	Putting the point across	.753	3.25				
	Doubt addressing	.687	3.32				
F2: Faculty commitment	Personal support from faculty	.842	3.20	3.35	1.45	6.47%	.857
	The faculty showed interest	.761	3.49				
F3: Classroom engagement	Class engagement	.833	3.05	3.13	1.32	4.62%	.862
	Concept clarity	.551	3.22				
Total variance explained		*86.62%*					
Kaiser-Meyer-Olkin measure of sampling adequacy		*.938*					
Bartlett's Test of sphericity		*.000*					

TABLE 12.9 Summary of T-test- faculty perception

	Variable	N	Mean	Std. Deviation	Std. Error Mean	T	df	Sig. (2-tailed)
Teaching ability	Female	156	3.2350	1.11053	.08891	−.349	267.541	.727
	Male	555	3.2709	1.21087	.05140			
Faculty commitment	Female	156	3.3878	1.19350	.09556	.470	709	.639
	Male	555	3.3351	1.25039	.05308			
Classroom engagement	Female	156	3.1186	1.15579	.09254	−.134	709	.893
	Male	555	3.1333	1.22926	.05218			

of teaching ability, faculty commitment and classroom engagement. The summary of the t-test results is given in Table 12.9.

There was no significant difference observed in the case of perception of teaching ability ($t(267.5) = -.349, p > .05$), faculty commitment ($t(709) = .470, p > .05$) or classroom engagement ($t(709) = -.134, p > .05$).

One-way ANOVA was conducted to assess whether students studying in different years differed significantly in their perception of teaching ability, faculty commitment and classroom engagement. The summary of the ANOVA results is presented in Table 12.10.

The students from the three different years of study did not differ significantly in terms of their perception of the faculty members' teaching ability ($F(2,708) = .149$, $p > .05$), faculty commitment ($F(2,708) = .698, p > .05$) or classroom engagement ($F(2,708) = .149, p > .05$). A high mean score (1.473) of classroom engagement

TABLE 12.10 Summary of analysis of variance (ANOVA)

		Sum of Squares	df	Mean Score	F	Sig.
Teaching ability	Between groups	.422	2	.211	.149	.862
	Within groups	1003.173	708	1.417		
	Total	1003.595	710			
Faculty commitment	Between groups	2.141	2	1.070	.698	.498
	Within groups	1085.149	708	1.533		
	Total	1087.290	710			
Classroom engagement	Between groups	1.095	2	.548	.372	.690
	Within groups	1043.120	708	1.473		
	Total	1044.216	710			

signifies that students are influenced by the faculty's capability of making the sessions interesting and engaging.

This research study revolves around the efficacy of online teaching sessions in a practical-oriented course – hospitality and hotel administration. The results of the statistical tests present the findings in the Indian context. The paper introduced a brief history and the current online teaching trends followed in the country during the COVID-19 pandemic. Analysis of Variance (ANOVA) implies that faculty commitment in online education is a significant factor; faculty should give personal attention to students to understand the concepts. Due to pandemic situations, students are unable to connect with faculty.

Conclusions

This exploratory paper set out to identify the COVID effect on a skill-based course, such as hospitality, in the context of India. This country is still affected by factors like unstable internet, evident in 287 samples, about 40% of the sample, who voted for this reason as a significant problem faced in online education. Although the study agreed with extant literature on recent trends in hospitality education, it was evident that apart from switching platforms, no pedagogical changes were witnessed, in contrast to tourism education, where an exclusive online academy was inaugurated to adopt the new normal. A scale was used to measure parameters in the classroom relating to online teaching, where 233 samples voted for 'better concept grasping' and 'online education over a classroom', and 263 samples voted for 'the comfort of home while studying' and the 'problems faced during online teaching'.

The faculty parameters were analysed with factor analysis, which yielded that faculty commitment is of the highest importance along with the significant factors of faculty's support and the interest shown by the faculty.

To conclude, this chapter emphasises that hybrid teaching has become a need of the hour. To simplify the learning and teaching process, students and faculty must be adaptive to technology platforms, making teaching seamless for students. The technology adoption will require a change in the organisation's processes duly supported by a robust internet connection. Tourism and hospitality teaching must adopt technology to simplify communication among students and faculty. The demand for blended teaching will increase. Faculty and students will have to upskill themselves to use learning platforms to undertake further study. Educational institutions will have to reform their policies to make all of this possible.

Recommendations

The pandemic has impacted various institutions and organisations; therefore, teachers and students must remain adaptive to online learning platforms. A mixed blend of online and offline teaching can solve the issues faced by hospitality students. Hotel management is a practice-oriented course that requires more practical exposure than theoretical sessions. There are two central departments and four core subjects taught in hotel management courses across India: Food Production and Food & Beverage Service consisting of the Food & Beverage (F&B) Department and Front Office & Housekeeping consisting of the Rooms Division Department. Students who find learning challenging can observe videos to better grasp and participate in virtual practical activities.

They can be asked to procure raw cooking ingredients for practical food production sessions. To better adapt this blended approach, the syllabus has to be fine-tuned to the convenience of procuring the ingredients and simplifying the technique, which can be executed in a home kitchen. In addition, it is suggested that faculty give real-time cooking demonstrations to the students through online platforms to grasp the concepts better. Similarly, colleges could organise cook-alongs so that students prepare the dishes at home at the same time as faculty members cook on campus. Students need to be involved practically to help them understand the concepts.

For other subjects like front office, where reservations and bookings are taught on software which is usually paid, technology can again be the saviour, and the platform 'Any desk' can be used to access software-loaded college computers, accessed from the student at their house. Housekeeping practices would be relatively easy, as bedmaking and flower arrangement are possible in online sessions. Lastly, the food and beverage service, table laying, clearance and beverage service simulations can again be efficiently conducted as cutlery, crockery and flatware are available at home.

References

Bhutia, P.D. (2020). An Online Academy for Tourism Studies Launched – ET Travel World. *ET TravelWorld.com*. https://travel.economictimes.indiatimes.com/news/education/institutesnline-academy-for-tourism-studies-launched/76887460. Accessed 29 July 2021.

Chhetri, S., & Dambhare, A., & Kakkar, P. (2020). *A Study on Evaluating The Satisfaction Level of Indian Hospitality Students with Online Education System During COVID Pandemic.* https://www.researchgate.net/profile/Ankit-Dambhare/publication/347910271_A_STUDY_ON_EVALUATING_THE_SATISFACTION_LEVEL_OF_INDIAN_HOSPITALITY_STUDENTS_WITH_ONLINE_EDUCATION_SYSTEM_DURING_COVID_PANDEMIC/links/5fe6f214299bf140884418d3/A-STUDY-ON-EVALUATING-THE-SATISFACTION-LEVEL-OF-INDIAN-HOSPITALITY-STUDENTS-WITH-ONLINE-EDUCATION-SYSTEM-DURING-COVID-PANDEMIC.pdf

Dani, R., Kukreti, R., Negi, A., & Kholiya, D. (2020). Impact of COVID-19 on Education and Internships of Hospitality Students. *International Journal of Current Research and Review*, 86–90. DOI: 10.31782/ijcrr.2020.sp54

Di Pietro, G. (2017). The Academic Impact of Natural Disasters: Evidence from L'Aquila Earthquake. *Education Economics, 26*(1), 62–77. DOI: 10.1080/09645292.2017.1394984

EHL. (2020). A Look into the Future: Hospitality Management Studies after COVID-19. *Hospitality News & Business Insights by EHL.* https://hospitalityinsights.ehl.edu/future-hospitality-education-after-COVID-19

Honey, M., & Gilpin, R. (2009). *Tourism in the Developing Countries-promoting Peace & Reducing Poverty.* Washington, DC: US Institute of Peace.

Kumar, M. (2014). Hospitality Education in India- Present Status, Challenges & Opportunities. *African Journal of Hospitality, Tourism & Leisure, 3*(2), 1–12.

Lei, S.I., & So, A.S. (2021). Online Teaching and Learning Experiences during the COVID-19 Pandemic – Comparing Teacher and Student Perceptions. *Journal of Hospitality & Tourism Education, 33*(3), 148–162. DOI: 10.1080/10963758.2021.1907196

Maitra, R. (2021). Adoption and Implementation of Digital Transformation for the Sustainability of Tourism and Hospitality Business in India. *Journal of Services Research, 21*(1), 88–111.

Mill, R., & Morrison, A. (1999). *The Tourism System: An Introductory Text.* 3rd ed. Iowa: Kendall/Hunt Publishers.

Milton, T., & Moyeenudin, H.M. (2022). A Meta-Analysis on Online Classes for Hotel Management Students at Chennai During COVID-19. In S. Fong, N. Dey, & A. Joshi (Eds.), *ICT Analysis and Applications. Lecture Notes in Networks and Systems*, Vol. 314. Singapore: Springer. DOI: 10.1007/978-981-16-5655-2_57

Naik, P. (2020). Hospitality Education: During and Post COVID-19. In V. Zutshi, N. Chowdhary, A. Singh, & P. Lakhawat (Eds.), *Rebuilding Tourism & Hospitality Sectors: COVID-19 Crisis, Policy Solutions & the Way Forward* (pp. 114–122). New Delhi: Bharti Publications.

Nunnally, J.C. (1978). *Psychometric Theory.* 2nd ed. New York McGraw-Hill.

Pencarelli, T. (2019). The Digital Revolution in the Travel and Tourism Industry. *Information Technology & Tourism, 22*(3), 455–476.

Raheem, B.R. (2020). The Role of E-Learning in COVID-19 Crisis. *International Journal of Creative Research Thoughts, 8*(3), 3135–3138.

Sciarini, M., Beck, J., & Seaman, J. (2012). Online Learning in Hospitality and Tourism Higher Education Worldwide: A Descriptive Report as of January 2012. *Journal of Hospitality & Tourism Education, 24*(2–3), 41–44. DOI: 10.1080/10963758.2012.10696668

Semley, N., Horner, S., & Brunt, P. (2017). Research Methods in Tourism, Hospitality and Events Management. *Research Methods in Tourism, Hospitality and Events Management.* London: Sage.

Sigala, M. (2004). Investigating the Factors Determining E-learning Effectiveness in Tourism & Hospitality Education. *Journal of Hospitality and Tourism Education, 16*(2), 11–21. DOI: 10.1080/10963758.2004.10696789

TOI-Online. (2020, March 16). Govt Announces Closure of All Educational Establishments Across India till March 31. *The Times of India.* https://timesofindia.indiatimes.com/home/education/news/govt-announces-closure-of-all-educational-establishments-across-india-till-march-31/articleshow/74659627.cms#:~:text=NEW%20DELHI%3A%20The%20government%20of,the%20spread%20of%20coronavirus%20infection. Accessed 28 January 2021.

UNESCO. (2020). *Education: From Disruption to Recovery.* Govt, Announces Closure of all Educational Establishments across India. Accessed 28 January 2021.

Vohra, M. (2020). *How the Corona Crash Hit Indian Financial Markets in March 2020–6 Charts – Views on News from Equitymaster.* www.equitymaster.com/detail.asp?date=04%2F02%2F2020&story=4&title=How-Corona-Crash-Hit-Indian-Financial-Markets-in-March-2020-6-Charts. Accessed 28 January 2021.

13

THE USE OF FOOD DELIVERY APPLICATIONS IN THE RESTAURANT INDUSTRY DURING THE COVID-19 CRISIS

Consumers' perspectives

Gonçalo Barbosa, Jaime Coelho, Marta Fernandes and Makhabbat Ramazanova

Introduction

The tourism and hospitality sectors are characterised by being dynamic, as they are constantly evolving, undergoing various changes over time. What is certain, during past decades, the sector has proved its role and value in the economy of many tourist destinations. However, tourism and hospitality, like any other economic sector, are fragile because, as new phenomena arise and influence their normal state, they have the need to reinvent themselves to enhance their activity. A notable example of this process is the constant and accelerated evolution of technology, which is increasingly forcing the area of tourism and hospitality to adapt in order not only to satisfy consumer needs, but also to meet their expectations.

Just as in the past it was necessary for an individual to travel to the production site of goods and services, now everything is possible at the distance of a simple 'click'. In this sense, technological progress can be seen as an advantage or disadvantage to tourism development, depending on the environment in question. Therefore, an appropriate context that can be approached to assess this issue is the case of COVID-19 and how technology was an aid for the tourism and hospitality sector to survive.

With the emergence of COVID-19, a huge gap between the populations became evident in terms of interpersonal relations. Faced with this void, digital technology occupied a space that needed to be filled, and in a way, people began to understand that they could maintain their daily lives in an artificial way, but one that was effectively safe, fast and accessible to all. For example, during the pandemic, people were unable to travel, but it was up to digital to promote dreams to these people, as they carried out research on destinations and looked forward to visiting them. Another case related to restaurants, one of the segments of tourism

DOI: 10.4324/9781003295839-16

and hospitality, which were closed for months without being able to serve their customers and had to find new ways to subsist. It is specifically on this point that we want to focus our attention—that is, to understand the effect of the consequences of the pandemic and how home delivery applications became a lifeline for the tourism and hospitality sector.

In this way, this chapter uses qualitative and quantitative methodologies to analyse the influence of information and communication technologies on tourism and hospitality, as well as which technical and professional characteristics are necessary to make the digitalisation process work. In addition, an analysis of the use of FDAs (food delivery applications) and how they affect restaurants will be conducted. Finally, the case study concerns consumer perceptions of home delivery applications in Portugal.

Literature review

Information and communication technologies involve new ways of processing and analysing information using other means such as artificial intelligence, big data and virtual reality, among others (Mundy, 2018). Moreover, these types of tools are strongly integrated with human life since more and more people are dependent on the virtual. On the other hand, digital tools can be seen as a new form of consumption and communication besides having a shaping role in human behaviour. The progressive evolution of digital technology has led to new consumption patterns that have forced the tourism and hospitality sector to adapt to a new context. This phenomenon was already evident before the appearance of COVID-19, but its recognition and use grew abruptly during the pandemic.

The role and positive effect of ICT on tourism is widely recognised. Some authors have found a positive correlation between ICT application and tourism demand at tourist destinations (Shehzad et al., 2019; Rehman et al., 2020). In the case of small and medium tourism enterprises, Feshari (2017) stated that the possibility of accessing the internet and other ICT tools in a company helps to improve the competitive status and quality process and reduce costs. Reflecting on the consumer's perspective regarding tourism and hospitality, ICT have rapidly changed the needs and preferences of tourists to something more complex and difficult to obtain. Therefore, it is considered that the model of offers and services made available within the industry had to undergo a reform in order to be able to meet consumer expectations. This remodelling has been notorious since the moment that technological support began to appear that complemented the tourist activity as well as the tourist experience itself. With the use of a mobile phone or any other mobile device, it is possible to access a wide range of tools in a safe, fast, accessible and dynamic way, such as geographic information systems (maps, GPS), reservation systems (flights, accommodation units, transport, tickets), translators, communication applications (email, weather applications), and home delivery applications (UberEats, Glovo) (Morozov & Morozova, 2019). The previously mentioned tools have a considerable impact on tourist experience by facilitating it and enhancing its stay in a destination. Thus, as argued by Abrhám and Wang (2017), tourism service providers should further invest in information and communication technologies, following new trends and offering new digital tourism services.

From another perspective, digitalisation in the business structure in the field of tourism and hospitality has led to an increase in the level of requirements and demands regarding personal skills and those of a technical and professional nature (Morozov & Morozova, 2019). According to this perspective, it is necessary to reflect on the fact that the functionality and effectiveness of the digitalisation process in the field of tourism and hospitality can only be successful when human resources are able to meet expectations; therefore, education programmes must provide opportunities that allow them to learn specific skills that are useful for the digitalisation process. To be able to work effectively within the digitalisation process, it is necessary to have some knowledge of digital practices (knowing how to work with electronic devices), the ability to adapt (to different contexts and be able to respond), focus and self-development, the ability to solve non–standard tasks and the decision-making on uncertainty (Morozov & Morozova, 2019).

Knowing and understanding the needs and expectations of the target group are crucial in order to provide high-quality services and products, especially in restaurant businesses. Consumer needs are diverse, which challenges hospitality and restaurant managers to consider different characteristics and design their products and services accordingly. In this context, several factors may influence restaurant selection, such as service quality, food quality and hygiene, diversification in food offerings, dining atmosphere and positive experiences (Yüksel & Yüksel, 2003). According to the literature, the quality of a restaurant can be analysed according to two distinct panoramas: tangible (equipment, environment) and intangible (service quality) elements (Kim et al., 2006). The implementation and further development of information and communication technologies can influence the basis that supports the entire restaurant system.

The application of digital technology in restaurants does not aim to replace previous methods but to improve the operating standards in order to increase the effectiveness of the service, generating a value chain that perhaps could be a differentiating element in terms of competitiveness. The use of ICT enables restaurants to reformulate their service packages, allowing them to innovate or specialise to capture new or groups of customers. Therefore, the digitalisation process can be inserted at the internal level of the restaurant (the sales, operations and resource management component), allowing for the maximising of labour productivity to generate a higher quality in terms of service (Sigala, 2004). On the other hand, there is a set of other technological components essential to the business, such as the reservation and purchasing system, revenue management, payroll and customer database that reflect digital and that help in the smooth running of the restaurant. Thus, it can be concluded that digitalisation brings together all kinds of tools needed to improve the business structure and operation of a restaurant.

Now, it is necessary to reflect that the appearance of the coronavirus has shaken all that was considered normal, and the restaurant sector was not left out of this development. Since the restaurant industry relies on human interaction, it was considerably affected by COVID-19 (Albuquerque et al., 2022). On the other hand, the pandemic caused the rise in Food Delivery Applications (FDAs) use as a form of consumption that was not previously used with such prominence and frequency. FDAs have seen an exponential increase in the number of users who, according to certain criteria, have found it to be the best way of consuming their products in a quick, safe and efficient manner. Before assessing the importance of these tools for the catering industry today, it is fundamentally important to really understand what FDAs are and why people want to take advantage of this service.

Food delivery services can be of two types: online format (in the case of digital applications dedicated to this type of service) and private (when establishments have their own mechanisms to provide this service). The online food delivery service is an innovative and dynamic service where the consumer, through a digital application, orders his purchases and these arrive at his home quickly and safely. This purchase model has been increasing, as it is something recent due to the controversial times we are going through and the near ubiquity of smartphones. According to Mundy (2018), the sustainability of a food delivery app is dependent on two factors, such as the ability to meet the needs and expectations of its consumers and the emergence of more such apps increasing competitiveness among them. The author also argues that it is necessary to understand the reason for the use of applications to know how it is possible to capture the attention of potential consumers, as well as the need to realise that continuous use and gratification will contribute to the increase of knowledge and enrichment of the subject. In addition, factors such as the ease of ordering, the friendliness of the courier, the quality of delivery, flexible prices, past experiences and time savings make this a quality service and attract more and more consumers.

Context of the empirical study

Tourism is one of the main strategic sectors for the Portuguese economy for its social, economic and environmental development (Oliveira, 2014). Recognising its crucial place in the economy of the country, policymakers and tourism stakeholders have made strong efforts to develop this industry. The tourism sector represented 15.4% of national GDP in 2019, which demonstrates an increasing demand for the country as a tourist destination, both among Portuguese and foreigners.

Research interest has broadened among academics in selecting the Portuguese context as a case study from various tourism perspectives. Andraz and Rodrigues (2016) explored the relation between the economic context and tourism flows of domestic tourists and international tourists to Portugal. de Freitas et al. (2021) stressed the historical value of the country and examined the urban landscape perceptions of the residents in the city of Porto. Magano and Cunha (2020) state that digital marketing and recent internet technologies are key factors influencing the attitudes and behaviour of visitors in the Portuguese context. However, a lack of research was observed in the use of ICT and digital technologies in the restaurant sector of Portugal. Among a few studies, the work of Brochado et al. (2021) to be referred, attempting to investigate the impact of COVID-19 in ICT introduction in the restaurant sector in Portugal. Thus, it is essential to understand the role of ICT in the restaurant sector in Portugal, especially during the pandemic crisis, because it may have been one of the segments that most benefited from this era of modernisation. For this, it is necessary to understand how information and communication technologies can be used as differentiating and supporting tools in restaurants.

Methodology

Data collection

The target audience of the empirical study is consumers living in Portugal. This study aims to understand how FDAs can positively or negatively impact the daily lives of Portuguese consumers. Due to the impossibility of identifying all the individuals of the population, a convenience sampling approach was used to select them and include them in the sample. The questionnaire consisting of two parts was distributed. The first part consisted of socio-demographic questions, such as gender, age group, nationality, academic qualifications, and current consumer situation. The second part of the questionnaire, on the other hand, is composed of questions related to the behaviour and the way consumers interact with FDAs, such as how often they use the applications, motivations for using them, potential advantages and disadvantages and, finally, questions related to the ordering process. This questionnaire was disseminated virtually through various social networks between 7 and 17 December 2020. As a result, a total of 414 responses were collected, 363 valid, which corresponds to an 88% response rate. To analyse the data obtained through the questionnaires, the researchers used Excel software.

Results and discussion

Sample profile

Table 13.1 outlines the socio-demographic data obtained, that is, general characteristics of the respondents such as country of origin, gender, age, education and occupation.

According to the data obtained, there was a prominence of the Portuguese nationals in the sample that accounts for 344 people, which translates into 95% of the total respondents. The remaining 5% were of foreign origin. Furthermore, it is possible to identify that the majority of respondents were female (71.6%). With regard to the age criterion, it can be stated that the majority of respondents were in the 18–29 age bracket (62.8%). Table 13.1 shows that secondary education predominates in relation to the others, corresponding to a value of 57.6% (209 people). This is followed by university degrees (25.6%), 3rd cycle (6.3%), masters

TABLE 13.1 Social demographic data

Variables		N	%
Country of origin	Domestic	344	95
	Foreigner	19	5
Gender	Male	102	28.1
	Female	260	71.6
	Other	1	0.3
Age	<18	44	12.1
	18–29	228	62.8
	30–49	64	17.6
	50–68	25	6.9
	68 or more	2	0.6
Education	Elementary school	1	0.3
	Middle school (5th-6th grade)	7	1.9
	Middle school (7th-9th grade)	23	6.3
	High school	209	57.6
	College	93	25.6
	Masters	30	8.3
Occupation	Student	214	59
	Unemployed	25	6.9
	Employee	108	29.8
	Retired	5	1.4
	Other	11	3

and other degrees (8.3%), 2nd cycle (1.9%) and lastly, 1st cycle (0.3%). With regard to the last factor, it can be seen that the student class stands out in comparison to the other hypotheses, occupying a value of 59%, which corresponds to 214 respondents.

Consumer perceptions of the use of FDAs

The following section is based on the analysis of the questions concerning each specific part, such as the respondents' view as consumers of products and services delivered by the intermediaries in the food delivery sector. First, it is essential to understand the frequency of using the internet by the respondents. Most answers focused on the time frequency 'always' (72%), demonstrating that the great majority of respondents constantly need to use the digital medium. This hypothesis gains strength when the 'often' category comes in second place (25%). On the other hand, only a small portion of respondents reported little use of the internet, 2% are those who use 'sometimes' and only 1% of those who never use it.

Next, respondents were asked to indicate whether they are familiar with, and use, FDAs in their daily lives. It can be seen that there is very little significant difference between those who are users (54.8%) and those who are not (45.2%). This equality on both sides may mean that ICT, such as home delivery applications, has gained prominence in recent times, with their number of users growing more and more. However, it also expresses that this evolution is not yet fully accepted since the number of those who use these tools is still not dominant. This situation may be a result of the little dissemination of the existence of FDAs or of other factors of a personal nature, such as the lack or reduced purchasing power of a younger age group which is more familiar with this type of technology, the inherent fear (losing money, leakage of personal data, the order never arriving at its destination, etc.) which people have in using digital platforms when buying products and services.

In terms of which FDAs are most used, Uber Eats is favoured (55.8%), followed by its biggest competitor Glovo (25.4%). In third place, the preference falls on the 'other apps' (12.2%), followed by Takeaway.com (3.8%) and Too Good to Go (2.8%). The leadership of the first app can be explained by its 'parent app', Uber (transport booking app), being the leader in its field (private transport). Specifically, the Uber user can order their meals whether or not they have their own Uber Eats app and also have other benefits, such as accumulating discounts through the trips they make. Therefore, it is understandable that the option of 'Uber Eats' is in first place due to all the associated advantages.

Regarding the frequency of use of the FDA, there is a great disparity in the results. Specifically, the 'sometimes' option emerges as the most frequent response (54.3%), which corresponds to a total of 139 respondents. This is followed by 'rarely' (34.8%) and 'frequently' (9.8%). It should also be noted that only 3 respondents out of a total of 363 answered 'almost always' use of the applications. Having said this, it can be seen that although they are users of these technological tools, their use varies greatly. This may be a reflection of the economic power of the respondents, since home delivery carries an additional fee for the service beyond the food itself, or people will resort to the applications according to their availability during their daily lives. Because of this, we tried to understand the reasons that led users to resort to this type of application. The most selected option was effectively the 'sanitary issues' (30.2%), which was obvious in the pandemic context. On the other hand, the issue of 'unavailability' of time (23.8%) corresponds to 75 people. After this, and in a decreasing way, reasons such as 'other reasons' (19.7%), 'diversified offer' (16.8%) and lastly the issue of 'geographical location' (9.5%). Having said this, it may be considered that there is a mix of reasons that lead people to use these applications since, in some way, they facilitate their daily lives in addition to satisfying their desires. From another point of view, we must also highlight that the environment (in this case, the pandemic situation) directly affects the consumers' way of acting.

Table 13.2 summarises the advantages and disadvantages pointed out by the respondents in addition to expressing their frequency and percentage value.

Regarding the advantages, it is noticeable that the vast majority considers that it is easy to order products through home delivery applications (53.19%). In addition to the time efficiency associated with the service (20.92%), in a reduced margin of time, the order arrives at its destination. The criterion of being able to track the order comes in third place (17.73%), as, somehow, users feel more secure when

TABLE 13.2 Advantages and disadvantages of home delivery applications

Advantages	Frequency	%	Disadvantages	Frequency	%
Ease of order	193	53.19	Waiting time	94	25.97
Time efficiency	75	20.92	Meal status	84	23.26
Order tracking	64	17.73	Contact loss	73	20.16
Reasonable prices	18	4.96	Order exchange	60	16.67
Courier kindness	11	3.19	Order customisation	50	13.95

purchasing their products through the availability of this function. Next is the question of the prices being reasonable and of quality (4.96%), as it is easy to order different types of gastronomy at very affordable prices. Finally, the friendliness of the delivery people (3.19%), which appears as the least relevant criterion when compared with the previous ones, may be a differentiating moment for the consumer when receiving the delivery.

Regarding the disadvantages of using home delivery applications, the most relevant is waiting time (25.97%). This factor is very variable, as it depends on numerous issues such as the distance between the place of preparation and the destination, the volume of traffic at that moment, and the type of vehicle used to transport the order. Second, the state of the meal (23.26%), which is a fundamental criterion because, if the meal is not well packed and arrives in good condition to the consumer, it may generate problems not only with the courier but also with the restaurant itself, which may lead to the consumer giving up using digital for this type of service. Next is the issue of the loss of contact and interaction with the employees (20.16%), which is considered an important moment of the experience when we physically go to the restaurant, and something that does not exist when we resort to the virtual one. The exchange of orders (16.67%) and the customisation of the dish (13.95%) are the least relevant disadvantages since it is not very common to have exchanges of orders because there is a whole set of data associated with a single order and the customisation of the dish, which may bring additional costs, is only used by those who already know that they are subject to an increased fee.

In relation to the first part of the question, it can be understood that there is not a very significant disparity between the options, since 198 people state that they have no fear of using digital as a means for their orders (54.5%), but 165 of the total respondents' state that they have some fear of using this type of application (45.5%). Therefore, it was essential to understand the reasons why people were afraid of digitalisation for this type of service (Figure 13.1). The most prominent is 'access to bank details' (31%), which is a legitimate concern, since in order to make any virtual purchase, all bank credentials must be entered in order to carry out the purchase. Next were 'possible problems with the order' (25%), problems related to the quality, the way of packing meals or the waiting time, among others. Then, 'access to the address' (16%) and the 'credibility of the applications' (12%), since if you are not confident about the effectiveness and efficiency of the application, you are also not willing to provide your address. There was less emphasis on all the 'undesirable

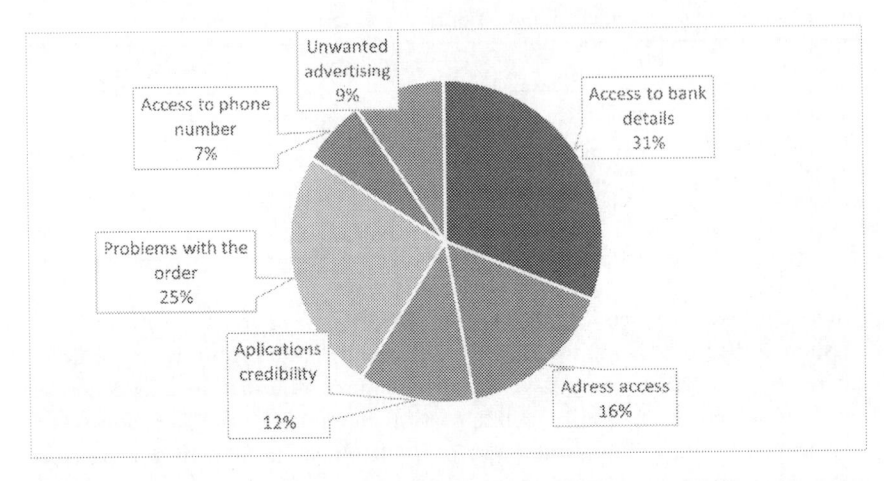

FIGURE 13.1 Reasons to feel insecure when ordering online

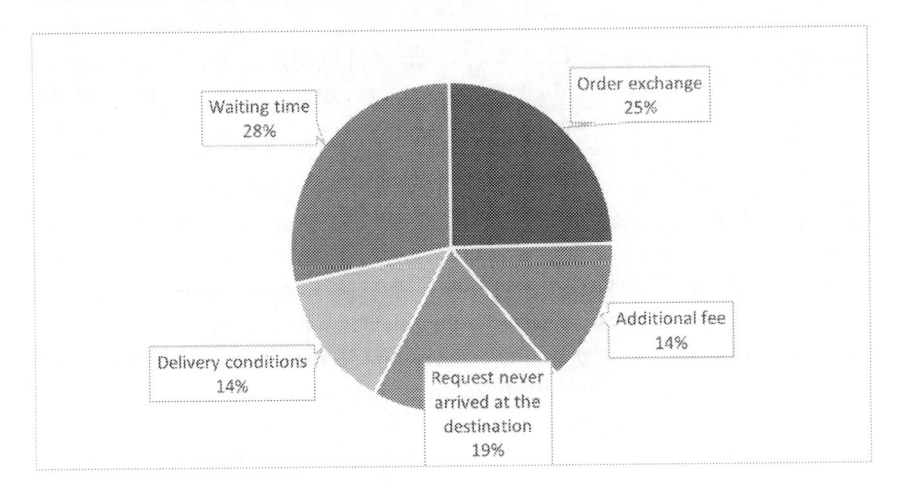

FIGURE 13.2 Delivery concerns

publicity, through the email obtained when registering in the application' leading to unwanted advertising (9%) and the 'access to the telephone number' (7%).

Also in this phase, it was necessary to ascertain the number of respondents who had already experienced any type of problem when using this type of information and communication technology. This being the case, the vast majority responded that they had never had problems when using home delivery applications (61.9%), something that is quite expressive between those who are afraid and those who are not, since one hundred and sixty-five people (38.1%) say that they have already had problems ordering their meals through the digital channel.

Next, there was the intention to understand the reason for the respondents' insecurity in ordering online (Figure 13.2). In this way, the hypotheses drawn up arise according to some response possibilities and there may be other types of valid scenarios. Therefore, the most prominent options are 'waiting time' (28%) and 'change of order' (25%), which is quite natural given the general human condition, as by nature we are incapable of waiting a long time for something that we want/need, as well as being little empathetic towards the mistakes made by others when we are paying for the service. Next is the fact that the order never arrived at its destination (19%), which calls into question the relevance and effectiveness of the application used. Lastly, the 'high surcharge' (14%) and 'delivery conditions' (14%) appear as less frequent causes, but they equally leave a bad impression of the service itself and may lead to a loss of loyalty.

Conclusion

This chapter aimed to analyse the role of digital and information and communication technologies as tools for the development of the tourism and hospitality sector. In this sense, it was necessary to assess how digital technology influences the normal state of the sector, and it can be seen as a progressive or hindering factor depending on the segment in question.

In this way, it was possible to understand that technological evolution contributed positively to the development and innovation of the hospitality sector, namely, in the restaurant sector during the pandemic in Portugal. This digital progress allowed for the continued existence of a connection between companies and their customers, so that there is a mutual benefit. However, it can also be seen that the use of home delivery applications is a fashionable topic, but it is not fully accepted, as there are a number of barriers that somehow condition most people to be users of this type of digital application. On the other hand, most of the users who use this type of application are from a young age group and therefore do not have a higher purchasing power, while those that do are not so familiar with digital technology. In addition, these applications are contrary to some existing traditions in Portugal. However, we believe that there was only an abrupt growth in the use of home delivery apps due to all the surrounding circumstances that affected the normal behaviour of consumers in Portugal during the pandemic. Finally, this work allowed us to understand the function and fundamental role of digitalisation in tourism, mainly in the way we should approach the potential customer using different techniques and changing our strategies according to the factors that influence the normal state of tourism.

References

Abrhám, J., & Wang, J. (2017). Novel Trends of Using ICTs In The Modern Tourism Industry. *Czech Journal of Social Science, Business and Economics, 6*(1).

Albuquerque, H., Ramazanova, M., Borges, I., Silva, F.M., & Marques, J. (2022). Analysis of the Consumer Behaviour Regarding the Use of Online Food Delivery Apps during COVID-19 Sanitary Restrictions in Portugal. In *Advances in Tourism, Technology and Systems* (pp. 385–396). Singapore: Springer.

Andraz, J.M., & Rodrigues, P.M. (2016). Monitoring Tourism Flows and Destination Management: Empirical Evidence for Portugal. *Tourism Management, 56*, 1–7.

Brochado, D., Silva, C., Silva, S., & Azevedo, D. (2021). Digital Technologies to Minimize the Impact of the COVID-19 Pandemic in Restaurant Sector. In *4th International Conference on Tourism Research* (pp. 92–100). London: Academic Publishing.

de Freitas, I.V., Sousa, C., & Ramazanova, M. (2021). Historical Landscape Monitoring through Residents' Perceptions for Tourism: The World Heritage Porto City. *Tourism Planning & Development, 18*(3), 294–313.

Feshari, M. (2017). The Role of ICT Indices In tourism Demand of Iran (the FMOLS co-Integrating Approach). *Iranian Journal of Economic Studies, 5*(2), 209–221.

Kim, W.G., Lee, Y.-K., & Yoo, Y.-J. (2006). Predictors of Relationship Quality and Relationship Outcomes in Luxury Restaurants. *Journal of Hospitality & Tourism Research, 30*(2), 143–169.

Magano, J., & Cunha, M.N. (2020). Digital Marketing Impact on Tourism in Portugal: A Quantitative Study. *African Journal of Hospitality, Tourism and Leisure, 9*(1), 1–19.

Morozov, M., & Morozova, N. (2019). Innovative Staff Training Strategies for the Tourism and Hospitality Industry. *5th International Conference on Economics, Marketing, Law and Education: Advanced in Economics, Business and Management Research, 110*, 1–4.

Mundy, S. (2018). Competition Heats up in India's Online Food Delivery Market. *Financial Times*. https://www.ft.com/content/365617e6-f239-11e8-ae55-df4bf40f9d0d

Oliveira, E. (2014). The Tourism Potential of Northern Portugal and its Relevance for a Regional Branding Strategy. *Advances in Hospitality and Tourism Research (AHTR), 2*(2), 54–78. http://static.dergipark.org.tr/article-download/dd06/30d9/c250/imp-JA93Y-C93RB-0.pdf

Rehman, O.U., Liu, X., Rauf, A., Slama, M.B., & Amin, W. (2020). Internet Tradition and Tourism Development: A Causality Analysis on BRI Listed Economies. *Tourism Economics, 26*(6), 926–957.

Shehzad, K., Liu, X., Rauf, A., Arif, M., Mazhar, S., Sohail, N., & Amin, W. (2019). Revolutionising Tourism Development in China: An Effective Role of ICT and Western Silk Road Project. *Asia Pacific Journal of Tourism Research, 24*(9), 965–977.

Sigala, M. (2004). Integrating and Exploiting Information and Communication Technologies (ICT) in Restaurant Operations. *Journal of Foodservice Business Research, 6*(3), 55–76.

Yüksel, A., & Yüksel, F. (2003). Measurement of Tourist Satisfaction with Restaurant Services: A Segment-based Approach. *Journal of Vacation Marketing, 9*(1), 52–68.

14

THE COVID-19 PANDEMIC AND (RE)CONSIDERATIONS OF OCCUPATIONAL STRESS IN NEW YORK CITY'S HOSPITALITY INDUSTRY

Lauren A. Siegel

Introduction

Proper staffing is a key pillar of any hospitality business, as industry staff provide the product experience for customers in this industry. When the global COVID-19 pandemic hit in 2020, many hospitality businesses were forced to shut their doors, at least temporarily, and then when restrictions were eventually lifted, many hospitality businesses faced difficulties in reacquiring staff – both previously existing and new staff. These challenges have continued for nearly two years without a viable solution in sight. This has been especially true for the restaurant industry of New York City, United States – one of the largest restaurant workforces in the world.

Staffing shortages have always been an issue faced within the hospitality industry, but the COVID-19 pandemic has brought new and onerous challenges. The continued staff shortage has been blamed on a variety of antecedents, including government subsidies for the unemployed during the pandemic, an increase in childcare expenses, and the safety and security of workers in crowded hospitality settings. To truly understand the essence of the issue, the potential employee's perspective must be considered. Parker and DeCotiis (1983) defined occupational stress as the result of dysfunctional working conditions. Every occupation has idiosyncratic stressors that will ultimately determine an employee's levels of occupational stress.

Prior to the pandemic, root causes of occupational stress in the hospitality industry were found to include characteristics such as job security, social support, pay, work schedule and work hazards (Cho et al., 2008; Elovainio et al., 2002; Krantz & Östergren, 2000; Murray-Gibbons & Gibbons, 2007; Vatankhah et al., 2020; Yousaf et al., 2019). There have been several studies that have considered occupational stress post-pandemic, with exposure to infection considered the highest stressor (Said & El-Shafei, 2021), and even some studies in the area

DOI: 10.4324/9781003295839-17

of occupational stress in hospitality post-pandemic (Lippert et al., 2021; Sonmez et al., 2020; Tsui, 2021); however, because the restaurant industry of New York City (NYC) has had an inimitable and unique course through the pandemic, with restrictions constantly changing and additional stressors like lack of healthcare for hospitality workers (Sonmez et al., 2020), the existing literature on occupational stress and its effects on restaurant employees must be reconsidered.

Thus, this chapter aims to explore and identify the specific occupational stress factors facing hospitality workers post-COVID by focusing on one of the largest hospitality markets in the world, the New York metropolitan region of the United States. The existing literature will be reconsidered in the shadow of the specific circumstances faced by NYC's restaurant industry with an aim to build on existing theory. This chapter will also explore the management implications of these factors to create a sustainable workforce for hospitality businesses post-pandemic, especially those facing extreme crises and a demand for complete reorganisation in response to the crises.

Background

Overview of occupational stress and hospitality industry workers

Occupational stress was defined in 1983 as a symptom associated with personal dysfunction as a result of conditions unfolding in a work setting (Parker & DeCotiis, 1983). The consequences of occupational stress in job performance include a variety of adverse outcomes: absenteeism, high staff turnover or even service failure.

The World Health Organization (WHO) declared in 2020 that occupational stress had become a worldwide health epidemic (WHO, 2020) with stressors causing severe depression, high levels of anxiety and even suicidal thoughts or feelings of self-harm. The WHO states that occupational stress is more deeply triggered when employees feel they have little support from supervisors and colleagues. Excessive stress experienced can not only dramatically impact an employee's work performance but also spill over into their interpersonal relationships and severely damage their overall well-being (Rehman & Mubashar, 2017).

While occupational stress is described to mean a phenomenon caused by work pressures, environmental conditions and responsibilities experienced by employees, Hart and Cooper (2002) suggest addressing occupational stress from both the perspective of employee well-being along with organisational performance. Hence, the anticipation that an employee might have of their employer's expectations will therefore negatively impact their individual performance.

The hospitality industry ranks as one of the most stressful work industries due to its customer-facing nature (Ross, 1995). Those working in the hospitality industry are expected to act in a kind and gracious manner that is aligned with the nature of the sector. Any emotional burden must be suppressed, which weakens the motivation to achieve good performance (Wang, 2020).

Compared to the general workforce (O'Neill & Davis, 2011), a sizeable increase in occupational stress has already been observed in the hospitality/tourism sector over the past 15–20 years (Karatepe & Tizabi, 2011; Ross, 2005). For this reason, occupational stress has emerged as an important topic of research and practice in the hospitality industry (Hwang et al., 2014; O'Neill & Davis, 2011; Yousaf et al., 2019).

There is also a significantly high turnover rate in the hospitality industry; such a high turnover rate not only has direct economic costs in terms of recruiting and training for new employees, but also hidden costs in terms of service quality and customer satisfaction (Yang et al., 2019). These considerable expenses associated with employee turnover, which would otherwise be shouldered by business owners, can be mitigated by providing significant support for staff in several areas (Carbery et al., 2003; Hwang et al., 2014).

In studies conducted prior to the COVID-19 pandemic that focus on occupational stress in the hospitality industry, social support is prescribed as the most common recommendation as an alleviant for employees; social support has been found to be strongly connected to lower turnover intention. Yousaf et al. (2019) found that hospitality workers with high social support are less vulnerable to negative effects of occupational stress, and that higher engagement with their organisation will lower the rate of turnover intention. Because restaurants are social centres, social support is an even more salient factor in employee well-being (Hwang et al., 2014).

Challenges

COVID-19 pandemic and hospitality employment

This book has already highlighted many of the numerous challenges faced by the hospitality and tourism industries in the wake of the COVID-19 pandemic. Thousands (potentially millions) of food service businesses around the world have lost tremendous revenue and the industry is facing unprecedented challenges amid economic losses. Even after restrictions have lifted in many places, diners are choosing to stay home after seeing their accrued savings from cooking at home during lockdowns.

Several studies have considered the impacts of the COVID-19 pandemic on occupational stress among hospitality employees (Lippert et al., 2021; Sonmez et al., 2020; Tsui, 2021). Sonmez et al. (2020) researched the impact that the pandemic had on immigrant workers in the United States, shining a light on the harsh conditions these workers face without universal healthcare and without paid sick leave. Their study also emphasised that these are frontline and 'essential' workers whose roles pose a significant threat to their emotional well-being, but often without the same social support received by other frontline/essential workers.

Tsui (2021) studied the effects job stress had on wellness on hotel workers in Taiwan's hospitality industry during the COVID-19 pandemic and found a significant relationship between employees' perceived expectations from organisational management and job stress. This indicates that if employees have internalised that their managers will continue to require the same high job performance, especially during a time when external stressors are also very high like they were during the pandemic, there is more likelihood that the employees will feel higher levels of job stress. There is a significant correlation between job stress and turnover intention. Therefore, if these same employees continue to feel extremely high levels of job stress without an intervention, they are even more likely to leave their jobs.

Lippert et al. (2021) explored the occupational stressors experienced by Chicago's restaurant and food service workers during the COVID-19 pandemic. They highlighted five themes: fear of being exposed to the virus while working, job insecurity, inconsistent pay and hours and a lack of health benefits and paid time off. These stressors led to uncertainty among the respondents regarding whether they would continue to work in the restaurant industry. Among the five stressors that Lippert et al. defined, some are consistent with past research conducted in the area of occupational stress (like job insecurity) but also new stressors that have emerged with the pandemic (like fear of exposure to the virus). Lippert et al. also highlighted that hardships associated with the pandemic could be mitigated by the support and connections fostered by the communities within the organisational structure of their employer.

Also worth consideration is that Lippert et al.'s study was conducted in Chicago, one of the largest cities in the United States, and therefore their found stressors can also be considered uniquely American. For example, the US is the only industrialised nation without universal healthcare available and this lack of healthcare benefits has become a significant stressor during the pandemic.

New York City restaurant industry's COVID-19 timeline

The hospitality industry is a major source of economic activity in New York City and was one of the hardest hit during the COVID-19 pandemic. The city of New York has particularly faced a myriad of additional and unique challenges over and above what other regions were experiencing during the same timeframe (see Table 14.1). Prior to the pandemic, the restaurant industry was one of the largest sources of employment; in 2019, there were 317,800 workers in the NYC restaurant industry, earning $10.7 billion in total wages citywide (NYC Hospitality Alliance, 2022). As of January 2022, the hospitality sector employs 30% less than the numbers experienced in 2019 and more than 1,000 NYC restaurants have permanently closed since the onset of the pandemic in March 2020.

On March 16, 2020, New York Governor Andrew Cuomo put the first ban on indoor dining in response to surging COVID cases. Quickly, restaurants had to rush to put infrastructure in place to accommodate outdoor dining. To do so, the parking spaces of the city's streets, sidewalks and even backyards were transformed into elaborate outdoor dining spaces – something that was never previously done in the history of the city. This sudden shift to outdoor dining was meant as a temporary solution to offset the losses incurred from the ban on indoor dining, with

TABLE 14.1 Timeline of events affecting the New York City restaurant industry in the wake of the COVID-19 pandemic

March 2020	*First ban on indoor dining in New York*
April 2020	*Restaurants begin to board up due to vandalism and burglary*
June 2020	*Outdoor dining plan is introduced allowing restaurants to expand onto sidewalks, parking spaces and backyards*
August 2020	*Six months into the pandemic, more than 1,000 NYC restaurants had closed*
September 2020	*Indoor dining set to return at 25% capacity*
October 2020	*10% surcharge on diners' bills approved by city council to make up for lost revenue*
November 2020	*New curfew introduced by Mayor DeBlasio and bars and restaurants must shut at 10 pm*
December 2020	*Indoor dining banned (again)*
January 2021	*Many restaurants report complications with outdoor dining amid cold winter months*
March 2021	Excelsior Pass *introduced in NY state which allows proof of negative COVID test*
June 2021	*To-go liquor discontinued by Governor Cuomo*
August 2021	*New York City is first major US city to require proof of vaccination to eat indoors*
November 2021	*Supply chain issues drive up costs for food sellers*
December 2021	*Restaurant workers fight for liveable wages in protests*
December 2021	*Omicron COVID strain causes mass cancellations of restaurant bookings amid busy holiday time*
February 2022	*Ongoing security concerns from 'anti-vax' customers*

some places seeing success more than others. This became extremely apparent as more and more New York restaurants began to shut their doors for good, unable to sustain operations through outdoor-only service. This included infamous restaurants like Blue Smoke, 21 Club, Fedora, Good Stuff Diner, Otto, Sidecar and Toro, many of which were steeped in history and had a longstanding record among the NYC restaurant 'scene'.

There was also an extreme uptick in demand for delivery and takeout orders, with much of the burden going to low-paid immigrant workers serving as delivery drivers. There are high risks of delivery service coupled with a lack of healthcare; many delivery drivers have reported injury on the job and subsequent medical care that they were forced to pay for out of their own pocket (Olszewski, 2021). The lack of proper healthcare for delivery drivers demonstrates the adverse working conditions for the 'essential workers' upon whom most residents relied heavily during the pandemic (Sonmez et al., 2020).

As the vaccine became widely available beginning in March 2021, New York state introduced the 'Excelsior Pass,' which was a smartphone application that, once registered, would allow individuals to display their proof of negative COVID test or vaccine. While this showed promise of a return to indoor dining, this positivity was short-lived, as this resulted in restaurant employees having another responsibility in their duties: to police the vaccination or negative testing status of diners. One worker told Eater New York that asking for proof of vaccination at the door feels dystopian, like a governmental official asking to see someone's papers (Alunan, 2021). This new role also brings a new threat of dangerous confrontations over vaccination status.

At the famous Carmine's restaurant on New York's Upper West Side, there was an incident in which three tourists were arrested for allegedly assaulting a restaurant hostess who asked for proof of vaccine to dine in the restaurant (Pruitt-Young, 2021). Video footage shows the attackers repeatedly punching a 22-year-old hostess after she asked them to show proof of vaccination before entering the restaurant in accordance with local regulations. The hostess had to be taken to the hospital for treatment of her injuries. While in response to such attacks, there were calls for the NYC mayor to impose greater penalties for those who assault restaurant workers, little was done to compensate or protect employees against this type of violence. Alunan (2021) posed the question, 'With restaurant employees striving to keep indoor dining safe for customers, who is ensuring the safety of the employees?'

There have been some reports of restaurant owners spending money on security to protect staff against unruly diners (something that was never needed prior to the COVID-19 pandemic); however, it is still quite rare, especially amid the other difficulties being faced because of the pandemic circumstances like rising costs and supply chain issues (Hur, 2022). As if all of this was not enough, now supply chain difficulties occurring around the globe have been affecting many industries due to rising costs, delayed shipments and slimmer margins. These issues are affecting the food business more than most (Feldman, 2021), after feeling much fatigue from an already very difficult period of time. As this article goes to press, proof of vaccination is still required to dine indoors in New York City.

Undoubtedly, this myriad of events and unending revolving door of challenges have had immense impacts on the occupational stress of NYC hospitality workers, levels of which were not previously seen. These unprecedented times have led to foggy territory for the research stream into occupational stress factors and how they would apply to restaurant workers in NYC during this time. New stressors seem to be emerging almost monthly, without an end in sight. In response, NYC restaurant workers have begun to fight for liveable wages, with hundreds threatening not to continue working until the minimum wage is raised (Moses, 2021). The option to find work that offers remote working options has tempted restaurant employees looking for a lifestyle change and a hopeful departure from the restaurant industry altogether in the wake of the pandemic.

Implications

As the last section described, there are a number of additional stressors that NYC restaurant workers had to face, including dangerous working conditions, low wages, job uncertainty and burnout. In considering occupational stress in light of this timeline of events, it is apparent that NYC restaurant workers have been and are continuing to be pushed to their limits.

Lazarus and Folkman (1984) postulate that employees will suffer more occupational stress if they are not given the proper resources to cope with difficult events; however, when employees are equipped with adequate personal resources, the levels of occupational stress can be mitigated (Bakker et al., 2014). Thus, it is essential to consider the most salient approaches to mitigating occupational stress for NYC restaurant workers by seeking the most appropriate and necessary resources to provide them.

In studies that explored occupational stress both pre- and post-pandemic, social support was the primary factor in alleviating stressors. Restaurants are by nature a social outlet, with employees experiencing positive social interaction with customers and also within the community of other service-industry colleagues. Therefore, the stress associated with the loss of this community due to COVID-19-related shutdowns was especially significant in the service industry (Lippert et al., 2021). Sense of community among workers and social support is at the heart of employee retention and recruitment in New York's hospitality industry and it is highly encouraged to foster positive social relations to counteract the negative stressors unfolding during the pandemic. This can be implemented at the restaurant-management level by introducing small methods of communication among employees during times of uncertainty. Such acts can include a group text thread among all management and employees of a particular business to keep communication flowing and a sense of social support for times when physical presence at the workplace is not possible.

Likewise, the research suggests that engaging with communities negatively impacted by the pandemic could help improve employee retention as a sense of psychological capital will be obtained through community-based philanthropic activities (Li et al., 2021). To instill a sense of community engagement for employees, visits to local homeless shelters or food-related charities can be organised, although it is highly recommended to offer employees some kind of additional incentive, either financial or non-financial, to participate if these activities happen outside of normal working hours so that it does not come to be viewed as another essential task (Yousaf et al., 2019). Beyond community outreach, there are a variety of activities that would foster social capital among hospitality employees, including developing teamwork training and sports competitions or leagues.

When imagining a morale-boosting response for employees, it is vital to remember that the experience of COVID-19 for the restaurant industry of NYC was nonlinear and because of the spectrum of difficulties, a complex prescription for employee support is still not completely obvious.

Conclusion

This chapter was based on past research both pre- and post-COVID-19 pandemic on occupational stress in the hospitality industry and aimed to identify the specific occupational stressors that were heightened due to the pandemic scenario with a targeted focus on the restaurant industry of New York, New York, USA. It was found that past research conducted on occupational stress does not fully consider the complicated situation that NYC's hospitality industry has faced for the duration of the COVID-19 pandemic, which is still ongoing.

Along with studies conducted prior to the pandemic, social support is a strong recommendation to help combat occupational stress; however, it is not a one-size-fits-all solution. Thus, more work needs to be done in this area to investigate innovative mitigation techniques for newly emerged stressors caused by pandemic circumstances. For example, a uniquely American source of occupational stress is the lack of universal health insurance for restaurant workers, which was exacerbated during a *public health* pandemic such as the COVID-19 crisis. Any solutions that would be created to mitigate this particular stressor would need to happen at a higher governmental level and unfortunately cannot be alleviated by social support. This study stresses the regional variance of occupational stress, which is dependent on local social and cultural factors as well as the agendas of regional decision makers.

The past research done in this area is not entirely applicable to the specific situation now facing NYC restaurant employees. The COVID-19 pandemic has further exacerbated this variance because of the changing restrictions and regulations imposed on different regions, cities and countries. As such, a study that was conducted in the same vein on Chicago's restaurant workers (Lippert et al., 2021) is not necessarily applicable to the restaurant workers in NYC. Because of this complexity, more exploration is needed and this study lays the groundwork for several paths for future research, such as destination-specific stressors of occupational stress during COVID-19. Work in this area will be valuable for rebuilding the industry when the COVID-19 pandemic subsides, whenever that may be.

Additionally, a limitation of this study was the lack of interviews conducted with employees personally facing these challenges, although this research lays the groundwork for more empirical research to be done in this area. This can include conducting interviews with restaurant workers closely affected by the events described in this chapter, as it is important to include their lived experiences and obtain a full narrative.

References

Alunan, A. (2021). What It's Like to Be a Restaurant's 'Vaccine Bouncer'. *Eater New York.* https://ny.eater.com/2021/12/14/22834678/vaccine-mandate-restaurant-workers-host-safety-nyc.

Bakker, A.B., Demerouti, E., Sanz Vergel, A. (2014). Burnout and Work Engagement: The JD-R Approach. *Annual Review of Organizational Psychology and Organizational Behavior, 1,* 389–411.

Cho, J.J., Kim, J.Y., Chang, S., Fiedler, N., Koh, S., Crabtree, B., Kang, D., Kim Y., & Choi, Y. (2008). Occupational Stress and Depression in Korean Employees. *International Archives of Occupational and Environmental Health, 8*(1), 47–57.

Elovainio, M., Kivimäki, M., & Vahtera, J. (2002). Organizational Justice: Evidence of a New Psychosocial Predictor of Health. *American Journal of Public Health, 92*(1), 105–108.

Feldman, A.E. (2021). As Supply Chain Problems Drive Prices Up, New York City Food Sellers Try to Manage. *New York One Spectrum News*. www.ny1.com/nyc/all-boroughs/business/2021/11/19/as-supply-chain-problems-drive-prices-up-new-york-city-food-sellers-try-to-manage.

Hart, P.M., & Cooper, C.L. (2002). Occupational Stress: Toward a More Integrated Framework. In N. Anderson, D.S. Ones, H.K. Sinangil, & C. Viswesvaran (Eds.), *Handbook of Industrial, Work and Organization Psychology*, Vol. 2. London: Sage Publications Inc.

Hur, K. (2022). Restauranteur Says He Spends Around $750,000 on Security to Deal with Unruly Diners. *CNBC*. www.cnbc.com/2022/02/16/restauranteur-says-he-spends-around-750000-on-security-to-deal-with-unruly-diners.html.

Hwang, J., Lee, J., Park, S., Chang, H., & Kim, S. (2014). The Impact of Occupational Stress on Employee's Turnover Intention in the Luxury Hotel Segment. *International Journal of Hospitality and Tourism Administration*, 15(1), 60–77.

Karatepe, O.S., & Tizabi, L.Z. (2011). Work-related Depression in the Hotel Industry: A Study in the United Arab Emirates. *International Journal of Contemporary Hospitality Management*, 23(5), 608–623.

Krantz, G., & Östergren, P.O. (2000). Common Symptoms in Middle Aged Women: Their Relation to Employment Status, Psychosocial Work Conditions and Social Support in a Swedish Setting. *Journal of Epidemiology & Community Health*, 54(3), 192–199.

Lazarus, R., & Folkman, S. (1984). *Stress, Appraisal and Coping*. London: Springer Publishing.

Li, Z., Yu, Z., Huang, S., Zhou, J., Yu, M., & Gu, R. (2021). The Effects of Psychological Capital, Social Capital, and Human Capital on Hotel Employees' Occupational Stress and Turnover Intention. *International Journal of Hospitality Management*, 98, 103046.

Lippert, J.F., Furnari, M.B., & Kriebel, C.W. (2021). The Impact of the COVID-19 Pandemic on Occupational Stress in Restaurant Work: A Qualitative Study. *International Journal of Environmental Research and Public Health*, 18, 10378.

Moses, D. (2021). Fight, Don't Starve: NYC Restaurant Workers Threaten Mass Exodus Amid Omicron Unless Paid Livable Wage. *AMNY The Villager*. www.amny.com/news/nyc-restaurant-workers-threaten-mass-exodus-amid-omicron/.

Murray-Gibbons, R., & Gibbons, C. (2007). Occupational Stress in the Chef Profession. *International Journal of Contemporary Hospitality Management*, 19(1), 32–42.

NYC Hospitality Alliance. (2022). *Industry Statistics*. https://www.thenycalliance.org/industry-statistics/

O'Neill, J., & Davis, K. (2011). Work Stress and Well-being in the Hotel Industry. *International Journal of Hospitality Management*, 30, 385–390.

Olszewski, S. (2021). NYC Food Delivery Workers Face a 'Harrowing World'. *Cornell Chronicle*. https://news.cornell.edu/stories/2021/09/nyc-food-delivery-workers-face-harrowing-world.

Parker, D., & DeCotiis, T. (1983). Organizational Determinants of Job Stress. *Organizational Behavior & Human Performance*, 32(2), 160–177.

Pruitt-Young, S. (2021). 3 Tourists Allegedly Attacked a Restaurant Hostess Who Asked for Vaccine Proof at a Restaurant. *NPR*. www.npr.org/sections/coronavirus-live-updates/2021/09/17/1038392877/new-york-tourists-attack-hostess-restaurant-vaccine?t=1645271614481.

Rehman, N., & Mubashar, T. (2017). Job Stress, Psychological Capital and Turnover Intentions in Employees of the Hospitality Industry. *Journal of Behavioral Science*, 27, 27–57.

Ross, G.F. (1995). Work Stress and Personality Measures among Hospitality Industry Employees. *International Journal of Contemporary Hospitality Management*, 6, 9–13.

Ross, G.F. (2005). Tourism Industry Employee Work Stress – A Present and Future Crisis. *Journal of Travel and Tourism Marketing*, 19(2–3), 133–147.

Said, R.M., & El-Shafei, D.A. (2021). Occupational Stress, Job Satisfaction, and Intent to Leave: Nurses Working on Front Lines during COVID-19 Pandemic in Zagazig City, Egypt. *Environmental Science and Pollution Research, 28*(7), 8791–8801.

Sonmez, S., Apostolopoulos, Y., Lemke, M.K., & Hsieh, Y.C. (2020). Understanding the Effects of COVID-19 on the Health and Safety of Immigrant Hospitality Workers in the United States. *Tourism Management Perspectives, 35*, 100717.

Tsui, P.L. (2021). Would Organizational Climate and Job Stress Affect Wellness? An Empirical Study on the Hospitality Industry in Taiwan during COVID-19. *International Journal of Environmental Research and Public Health, 18*, 10491.

Vatankhah, S., Bouzari, M., & Safavi, H. (2020). Unraveling the Fuzzy Predictors of Stress at Work. *International Journal of Organizational Analysis, 29*(2), 277–300.

Wang, C.J. (2020). Managing Emotional Labor for Service Quality: A Cross-level Analysis among Hotel Employees. *International Journal of Hospitality Management, 88*, 102396.

World Health Organization. (2020). *Occupational Health: Stress at the Workplace*. www.who. int/news-room/q-a-detail/ccupational-health-stress-at-the-workplace.

Yang, C., Guo, N., Wang, Y., & Li, C. (2019). The Effects of Mentoring on Hotel Staff Turnover: Organizational and Occupational Embeddedness as Mediators. *International Journal of Contemporary Hospitality Management, 31*(10), 4086–4104.

Yousaf, S., Rasheed, M.I., Hameed, Z., & Luqman, A. (2019). Occupational Stress and its Outcomes: The Role of Work-social Support in the Hospitality Industry. *Personnel Review, 49*(3), 755–773.

15

COMMUNITY-BASED TOURISM AS A POST-COVID-19 DEVELOPMENT STRATEGY IN AGRICULTURAL COMMUNITIES

Rolando Torres Aguilera, Erick Sergio Andrés Rodríguez, Oswaldo Muñoz Rubio and María Angélica Rojas Bernal

Introduction

The current economic crisis in Colombian agriculture has sharpened due to COVID-19. This is also the case for the farmers who belong to the Organización Campesino Construyendo Futuro, located in the town of Jardin, Antioquia, which found in tourism a sustainable path to handle the crisis. This revealed the poor preparation and vulnerability of their socioeconomic system to physical shocks. Physical shocks originate when ecological and social borders are crossed, generating economic collapse (Cárdenas et al., 2020). This is especially due to price instability and changes in atmospheric conditions, which increase the economic vulnerability of farmers. Generating a sustainable solution requires an innovative strategy.

In this regard Morales Zamorano et al. (2015), state that agrotourism can function as an instrument for regional economic development, since when implemented it generates positive benefits, turning it into an income generator. For this, adequate training is required. Tourism in rural areas includes the participation and active observation by the tourist within agricultural activities and/or provision of accommodation services, entertainment, learning, gastronomy and commercialisation of agro-food, whether fresh or processed products.

This leads us to ask if it is possible to propose sustainable development alternatives based on tourism; however, due to the breadth of this problem, we have decided to delimit the research object by focusing exclusively on the Municipality of Jardín Antioquia. The methodology used and the results obtained will be useful for other communities with more or less tourist visitation.

DOI: 10.4324/9781003295839-18

Methods

The present investigation is of an applied type, understood in the terms defined by Mario Tamayo y Tamayo (2004). The project arises from the Investigation Action Participation (IAP). Seen as much more than an investigation, since it is conceived as a particularly educational process that helps self-training and self-knowledge of reality, so that the people of the community could carry out, define the research project and produce the knowledge of their reality (Bernal, 2010).

For the analysis of the information of this project, a multiple triangulation method was used, which is defined as the combination of two or more types of triangulation, such as methodological, theoretical, data and observer triangulation. It is based on using more than one level of analysis. (Aguilar & Barroso, 2015). Due to the complexity of the research, a case study was carried out. This type of research is appropriate in situations in which it is desired to intensively study the basic characteristics of the current situation and interactions with the environment of a few units, such as individuals, groups, institutions or communities (Tamayo y Tamayo, 2004). To collect the data, information was collected from the Strategic Plan for Tourism Development of the Municipality and the main OTAs, but for the validation of tourist products, an expert judgment model was used, based on a sample of 195 surveys from the 8817 travel agencies in Colombia, a sample with a confidence level of 95% and a 7% margin of error.

Literature review

Any development proposal that is generated from tourism must be framed within the concepts of sustainable development. The most widely used definition of sustainable development was published in a document known as the Brundtland Report. In this report, sustainable development was defined as that which 'meets the needs of the present without compromising the needs of future generations' (UN Brundtland Commission, 1987: 41). In this context, it is important because it is expected that tourism will not only help the inhabitants of a municipality to overcome the economic difficulties generated by COVID-19, but that this solution will contribute to the sustainable development of the municipality in the long term.

In this context, it is also necessary to be clear about the concept of community tourism. For García (2016: 597), community tourism is defined as 'any solidarity tourism activity that allows the active participation of the community from an intercultural perspective and the proper management of cultural heritage, based on a principle of equity in the distribution of local benefits'. One of its essential characteristics is the role of the community. Community tourism is a model of collective action in a community's territory to stop them from being passive objects of a Fordist model of tourism and instead become active actors in a post-Fordist model of territorial development (Álamo et al., 2015).

When community tourism is developed in rural settings, one can speak of rural tourism. In this way, the community can generate wealth in rural areas of Latin

American countries through the participation of the local community in tourism management. Thus, the benefits obtained have an impact on the community itself (Jaime et al., 2018). Rural tourism can promote the integral development of communities, trying to reduce poverty through the generation of employment and the obtaining of complementary income. This tourism modality offers the opportunity to create small businesses that are intensive in labour and employ a relatively higher percentage of women than in other sectors. It is also important to note that the local community is the essential part of this type of tourism product (Jaime et al., 2018)

Case study setting

The Municipality of Jardín is located 138 kilometres from the city of Medellín. It is bordered to the west by the Andes, to the north with the town of Jericó, to the east with the Municipality of Támesis and to the south with the Caldas department; it has an area of 224 km². It is located 1,750 metres above sea level and has an average temperature of 19°C, has 14,518 inhabitants and a population density of 64.81 Inhabitants/km². The population is primary urban, 7.651, which corresponds to 52.7%, and the rural population, 6,867, which is equivalent to 47,3% (Rendon, 2020)

The Municipality of Jardín is considered a tourist centre in the Southwest Region for its various cultural, natural and built attractions. It was greatly strengthened by the declaration as a National Monument of its temple and its Main Square during the government of Belisario Betancur. In addition to its architectural beauty and ecological significance, Jardín is a clean and organised town, framed in fresh mountain landscapes that harmonise with the quality of the human group that inhabits it. Therefore, Jardín currently has a great infrastructure that allows tourists a comfortable and pleasant stay.

Supply analysis

For the commercialisation and execution of tourist products, the municipality has 67 travel agencies based in Jardín, Antioquia. Of those agencies, 44 are operator travel agencies and 23 are retail travel and tourism agencies. In this regard, it is worth clarifying that according to Colombian legislation, the Retail Travel Agency could also operate tourist products. After reviewing various sources, including OTA's, the municipality's tourism website and social networks, it was found that the municipality's Strategic Tourism Development PEDT is marketed in the municipality. It was found that they currently offer 17 tourism products in the municipality, some of which are marketed by 2 or more travel agencies but with similar characteristics. A summary of them is presented as follows.

Seven of its tourist products are cross-country hikes, three are horseback riding, two are extreme sports practices, one is a city tour, one is educational tourism, and one is bird watching. And only two are agrotourism experiences. In terms of their duration, most are day trips that are between 1 and 7 hours; the price varies between COP 30,000 and COP 926,000, but the majority ranges between

COP 110,000 and COP 120,000. Regarding the duration, a similar behaviour is observed. There are activities from 1 hour to experiences of 4 days, but most are outings that can last from 3 to 7 hours. This shows a disarticulation between the providers of tourist services. Although there are 15 places that offer accommodation, only 2 tourist products include spending the night at the destination.

Municipality tourist service providers

The municipality has a large number of tourist service providers. For their tracking, we resorted to both primary sources such as OTA's webpages and social networks and secondary sources such as the Strategic Plan for Tourism Development of the PEDT municipality and internet searches, with the following results. For the commercialisation and execution of tourist products, the municipality has six tourist guides and 19 travel agencies based in Jardín Antioquia, of which 16 are operator travel agencies and only three are travel agencies and tourism. In this regard, it is worth clarifying that according to Colombian legislation, a retail travel agency could also operate tourist products.

Supporting the different touristic products, the municipality has 60 restaurants of various categories, 15 lodging establishments and one transport company specialising in tourism. In this regard, it should be clarified that according to the Culture and Tourism Office, these are only the Providers of Formal Tourist Services, which are equivalent to 50% of the real offer except in the case of Tourism Guides, which there are around 60, of which 9 of them are formal, another 12 are in the process of formalisation, and the rest are informal.

Training for farmers

In the first stage of the project, a training action on the basic concepts of tourism was developed in which 145 farmers took part. An e-learning strategy was chosen, integrating synchronous and asynchronous activities that include synchronous video conferences, pre-recorded videos, and gamification, among others. As a result of the training action, the farmers designed four tourist products: *Chapolero* (coffee collector) for a Day, Literary Tour, Experience Tour of the Orellanas (Oyster Mushroom), and the Experience Tour 'The Power of Aromatic Plants'.

Description of tourist products

The four tourist products have similar characteristics; they are tourist experiences that integrate agrotourism and gastronomy, with an approximate 6 hour duration. They include a tour in Jeeps through the urban area of the municipality, followed by the trip to the farm, in the company of a professional tourist guide, and the peasant owner of each farm. Tourists will receive a snack and a traditional lunch that integrates the agricultural product according to the theme of the tour, and will have traveller's insurance. For the 4 tourist tours, the organisation *Campesinos Construyendo Futuro* established a price of COP 130,350; approximately USD 33.73.

Competitor analysis

The main competitor found is the *Organización Turística de Jardín, Antioquia*. Its main tourist product is called '*Los Tres Altos* Coffee Trekking'. It is an agrotourism walk full of landscapes between three paths. The tour has a cost of COL 110,000 (USD 28.56) and its characteristics are similar to the tour '*Chapolero* for a Day' of the organisation *Campesinos Construyendo Futuro*.

Their main competitive advantage is commercial and is based mainly on the strategic location of its offices and the alliances that they have with the hotels in the municipality. They are promoted mainly through online travel agencies such as TripAdvisor. Its value offer is based on agrotourism and they present themselves in the market as a peasant organisation similar to OCCF, but upon thorough investigation, it was discovered that it really is a traditional tour operator that cannot be considered community tourism.

Demand study

Due to the fact that directly interviewing tourists is complex, to facilitate the process, an expert survey was carried out with travel agencies. Respondents were asked to rate from 1 to 5 the level of innovation of each of the following tourist products; the average of the response for each tourist route is as follows.

According to the experts' response, it is clear that the tours of the Orellanas Experience Tour and the Aromatic Power Tour are considered more innovative. When asked which day of the week the tour would be best received, this was what they answered.

In this regard, it is evident that the experts prefer Friday, Saturday and Sunday for the tourist route, so that 85% of the preferences are concentrated on Saturday and Sunday. Based on the knowledge of the experts, the perceived value was

TABLE 15.1 Innovation level rankings

Chapolero for a Day	3,52
Literary Tour	3,97
Orellanas Experience Tour	4,14
The Power of Aromatic Plants	4,11
Number surveyed	195

TABLE 15.2 Preferred day of the week

Day of the week	Monday	Tuesday	Wednesday	Thursday	Friday	Saturday	Sunday
CHAPOLERO	4	0	6	8	19	91	67
LITERARY	2	10	9	20	47	56	51
ORELLANAS	0	2	6	17	22	78	70
AROMATIC	10	5	9	9	24	77	61
	16	**17**	**30**	**54**	**112**	**302**	**249**
	2,05%	**2,18%**	**3,85%**	**6,92%**	**14,36%**	**38,72%**	**31,92%**

TABLE 15.3 Perceived value by travel agencies

Tour	Value (COP)	Value (USD)
Chapolero for one day Tour	$143.800	$37,27
Literary Tour	$218.333	$56,61
Orellanas Experience Tour	$139.359	$36,14
The power of aromatic plants	$124.744	$32,35
Average	**$156.538**	**$40,59**

TABLE 15.4 Sum of the number of tourists that each travel agency can sell

Touristic product	PAX number	Average
Chapolero for a Day tour	2479	13
Literary Tour	1701	9
Orellanas Experience Tour	1187	6
The Power of Aromatic Plants	1982	10

Source: author created chart.

TABLE 15.5 Tour preferred by the interviewed travel agencies

Which is your favourite experience among the four offered?	Number	%
Chapolero for a Day Tour	86	44,33%
Literary Tour	51	26,29%
Orellanas Experience Tour	43	22,16%
The power of aromatic plants	15	7,22%
Total of interviewed travel agencies	194	100%

consulted, understood as the amount in dollars that they believe the public would be willing to pay, using as a criterion exclusively the description of the tourist route presented at the beginning of the survey; the most outstanding one is the Literary Tour.

The literary tour is the tourist product with the highest perceived value COL 218,333, (USD 56.61). Additionally, the *Chapolero* for a Day tour with COL 143,718 (USD 37.27) and Experience of the Orellanas COL 139,350 (USD 34.14) have a perceived value higher than the price proposed by the Corporación *Campesinos Construyendo Futuro*, which was COL 130,350 (USD 33.72), so we can preliminarily say that they are commercially feasible; however, the tour The Power of Aromatic Plants has a perceived value lower than the proposed price. The most important question that was used to estimate demand is the number of tourists that each travel agency estimates that it can sell on a monthly basis, as shown in Table 15.4.

As shown in Table 15.5, the tourist product with the best possibilities is the *Chapolero* for a Day tour, followed by the aromatic tour for an estimated demand of

7,349 tourists per month. However, this value does not make much sense if it is not compared with the load capacity of each one of the tourist attractions. This will be addressed in the analysis of the offer. Finally, the 195 experts were consulted about their preferred tourism product, with the following results.

The most positively perceived tourist product was the Chapolero for a Day tour; on the other hand, the Orellanas and aromas tours were also well received while the literary tour has very little response.

Analysis of the project capacity

To determine the capacity of the project, the capacity of some key resources, such as vehicles, and more importantly, the cargo capacity of the attraction was articulated, and the characteristics of the terms of sale. The Jeep Willys can only safely transport 10 passengers, and the cultural exchange experience must be carried out in small groups, to which are added the recommendations of the Ministry of Health where it proposes a maximum of 10 tourists per group, so this reference value will be used for the analysis of installed capacity of the project.

Due to the duration of each tour, you can take two tours per day, one in the morning and one in the afternoon, for a maximum of 20 passengers per day. It was established previously that the demand will focus on two days, Saturday and Sunday, because it was agreed with the OCCF that it will only be offered in an open group on those days, but it will be possible to offer during the week only to closed groups. Based on this information, a production capacity of 40 pax per week and 160 pax per month, 1,920 tourists for each farm each year, for each tourist route, is projected. For the execution of the aromatic tour, the literary tour and the orellanas tour, there is only one farm for each tour, while for the development of the *Chapolero* for a day tour, there are three farms, so in total there are 6 farms where tourists can be attended, which gives the project a capacity of 960 tourists per month, about 11,520 tourists per year.

This value is much higher than the value established in the demand analysis, which was estimated at 7,349 tourists per month only with 196 of the 8817 existing travel agencies only in Colombia, so if only the interviewed travel agencies complied with the 13% of the sales proposed in the interview, which allows us to conclude that the project is commercially feasible.

Income projection

Based on this information, a 5-year income projection for the projects was developed, as shown in Table 15.6.

Based on this value, a projection was made, assuming that it would take 18 months for each of the tourist products to reach its installed capacity. From that month on, 160 passengers per month will be sold, with the following income projection. The results are shown in Table 15.7.

TABLE 15.6 Value of the touristic product

Touristic product	Value (COP)	Value (USD)
Chapolero for a Day Tour	$146.476	$38
Orellanas Experience Tour	$219.783	$57
The Power of Aromatic Plants Tour	$139.359	$37
Literary Tour	$127.244	$33

TABLE 15.7 Estimated annual income according to tourist product

	Year 1	Year 2	Year 3	Year 4	Year 5
Chapolero for a Day Tour	USD 22.000	USD 67.260	USD 72.960	USD 72.960	USD 72.960
Orellanas Experience Tour	USD 33.060	USD 100.890	USD 109.440	USD 109.440	USD 109.440
Power of Aromatic Plants Tour	USD 21.460	USD 65.490	USD 71.040	USD 71.040	USD 71.040
Literary Tour	USD 19.140	USD 58.410	USD 63.360	USD 63.360	USD 63.360
Total	USD 95.660	USD 292.050	USD 316,800	USD 316,800	USD 316,800

Cost analysis

For the construction of the cost analysis, we started from the same sales projection in which the income was estimated, from which the following considerations were made:

The basic structure of each resort is the same. Due to the load capacity of the vehicle that transports them, each group must be of ten tickets, they must go with a tour guide, who receives a fee of USD 15.56 per group, the transport receives USD 2.59 per tourist, a traveller's insurance of USD 0.56 per tourist is paid, to the farmer who receives USD 7.78 for each tourist, and the traveller is given a snack and lunch that is also bought from the farmer who owns each Farm where the tourist tour takes place at a rate of USD 9.08 per person, only in the case of the orellanas tour and for biosecurity reasons for the plants, all attendees must enter with a disposable suit that costs USD 2.85 per person. The cost structure of a typical tour with 10 passengers is presented in Table 15.8.

Management expenses

The preliminary analysis of the annual administration expenses is presented in Table 15.9.

Payroll expenses

Next, the preliminary analysis of annual payroll expenses is presented; the calculation of social benefits is carried out according to Colombian legislation as shown in Table 15.10.

TABLE 15.8 Structure of cost per tour

Cost	Orellanas	Others
Transport	USD 25,90	USD 25,90
Tour guide	USD 15,56	USD 15,56
Travel insurance	USD 5,60	USD 5,60
Farm	USD 77,80	USD 77,80
Food	USD 90,80	USD 90,80
Disposable suit	USD 28,50	N/A
Total	USD 272,66	USD 244,16

TABLE 15.9 Expense structure

Expenses	Value
Office rent	USD 1.556,02
Public services	USD 155,60
Mobile phone plans	USD 933,61
Internet	USD 249.00
Stationery	USD 155,60
Accumulated depreciation	USD 435.00
Digital marketing plan	USD 1.556,02
Total	**USD 5.040,46**

TABLE 15.10 Payroll structure

Payroll	%	Value
General manager salary		$6.224,07
Commercial manager salary		$5.601,66
Operative manager salary		$5.601,66
Seller salary		$4.979,25
Community manager salary		$4.979,25
Core salary total		$22.406,64
Transportation assistance		$2.181,43
Layoffs	8,3%	$2.048,19
Layoffs interest	1,0%	$245,88
Service premium	8,3%	$2.048,19
Vacations	4,17%	$1.025,32
Health plan	8,50%	$1.904,56
Pensions	12,00%	$261,77
Professional risk management	0,52%	$10,65
SENA	2,00%	$4,92
ICBF	4,00%	$81,93
Family Welfare Fund	4,00%	$41,01
Payroll total		**$32.260,49**

TABLE 15.11 Cash flow

Investment	USD 18.000	Year 1	Year 2	Year 3	Year 4	Year 5
Initial balance		USD 18.000	USD 51.993	USD 246.152	USD 444.658	USD 598.164
Income		USD 95.660	USD 292.050	USD 316,800	USD 316,800	USD 316,800
Total cost		USD 24.367	USD 60.591	USD 80.994	USD 80.994	USD 80.994
Expenses		USD 5.040	USD 5.040	USD 5.040	USD 5.040	USD 5.040
Payroll		USD 32.260	USD 32.260	USD 32.260	USD 32.260	USD 32.260
Final balance		USD 51.993	USD 246.152	USD 444.658	USD 598.164	USD 796.670

Financial analysis

For the construction of the financial analysis, it was established in the first place that the start-up of the company requires an initial investment that was calculated at USD 18,000, which will be contributed by the *Corporación Campesinos Construyendo Futuro,* who expect a COK of 20% to be able to invest in social development programs. Table 15.11 displays a five-year cash flow analysis.

Internal rate of return (IRR)

For the calculation of the internal rate of return, the Excel functions were used, giving as a result an IRR of 44.1%.

Net present value (NPV)

For the calculation of the NPV, the minimum rate of return on investment (COK) of 20% is established, taking into account that the *Corporación Campesinos Construyendo Futuro* will be the one who contributes the necessary capital to develop the business model and expect a minimum return on it, with capital needed to finance other social projects.

Based on this requirement, the NPV was established using the Excel function, which resulted in a NPV of COP 1,062,221 demonstrating that the project is financially feasible.

Conclusions

In the formulation of the problem, the economic crisis that generated the coronavirus pandemic was revealed, which added to the difficult economic conditions that the agricultural sector is experiencing in Colombia. Therefore, this project aimed to determine if it is feasible to implement agrotourism products in the *Corporación Campesinos Construyendo Futuro* to complement their income and generate an economic recovery, and then sustainable economic and social development in the municipality of Jardín Antioquia. Once the political and legal aspects were analysed, it was found that there is a favourable context for the development of the project, due to the national, departmental and municipal policies about the development of tourism.

When analysing demand, it was found that the preferences of the post-COVID-19 tourist point towards nature tourism and rural community tourism, especially agrotourism, which is favourable for the project. This was confirmed by the consultation group of experts, demonstrating that the tourism product is innovative and will have excellent reception in the market. Finally, from the financial point of view, the analysis of the Net Present Value and the Internal Rate of Return allow us to affirm that the project is financially viable.

Additionally, from the social point of view, it is important to add that the project will generate at least 5 direct jobs, made up of 8 tourist guides and 5 people from the management area, to which are added the 4 families that own the farms where it is proposed to develop the tourist routes, additionally the drivers of the Jeeps who will carry out the transport will benefit, and the social benefit that the *Corporación Campesinos Construyendo Futuro* can achieve with the economic benefits generated by this project is immeasurable.

Once the legal, environmental, commercial, financial and social aspects have been analysed in the case of the *Corporación Campesinos Construyendo Futuro* of Jardín Antioquia, it can be concluded that agrotourism is an excellent alternative to complement the income of farmers and should be taken as an example to implement this type of program in other municipalities.

References

Aguilar Gavira, S., & Barroso Osuna, J.M. (2015). La triangulación de datos como estrategia en investigación educativa. Píxel-Bit. *Revista de Medios y Educación, 47*, 73–88

Álamo, M., Bagnulo, C., Cabanilla, E., & Molina, E. (2015). *Community Based Tourism Contribution to Strengthen the Food Sovereignty Principle in Ecuador Siembra.* Universidad Central de Ecuador, Quito DOI: 10.29166/siembra.v2i1.1440

Bernal, J.A.H. (2010). Desarrollo de habilidades cognitivas con aprendizaje móvil: un estudio de casos. *Comunicar: Revista científica iberoamericana de comunicación y educación, 34*, 201–209.

Cárdenas, M., Guzmán, J.J., & Hernández-Aguilera, J.N. (2020). *La Crisis del coronavirus: un llamado y oportunidad para inversiones más sostenibles.* New York: Centro de Política Energética global Universidad de Columbia.

García, C. (2016). *Turismo Comunitario en Ecuador ¿Quo vadis? Estudios y Perspectivas en Turismo, 25*(4), 597.

Jaime, P.V., Casas, J.C., & Soler, D. (2018). Desarrollo rural a través del turismo comunitario. Análisis del valle y cañón de colca. *Gestión Turística, 15*, 1–20. DOI: 10.4206/gest.tur.2011.n15-01

Morales Zamorano, L.A., Cabral Martell, A., Aguilar Valdes, A., Velzasco Aucly, L., & Holguin Moreno, O. (2015). Agroturismo y competitividad, como oferta diferenciadora:

el caso de la ruta agrícola de San Quintín, Baja California. *Revista mexicana de agronegocios, 37,* 185–196.

UN Brundtland Commission. (1987). *Report of the World Commission on Environment and Development: Our Common Future.* Washington, DC: United Nations.

Rendon, H.J. (2020). *Plan de desarrollo 2020–2023, Por Amor a Jardin: Bienestar para todos Alcalde, Jardin Antioquia.*

Tamayo y Tamayo, M. (2004). *El proceso de la investigación científica.* Chihuahua: Limusa.

16

RECOVERY OF HOTEL OCCUPANCY USING RISK MANAGEMENT OF SUPPLY CHAINS IN THE COVID-19 PANDEMIC CONTEXT AT THE US–MEXICO BORDER

Jesús Amparo López-Vizcarra, Jorge Carlos Morgan-Medina and Adriana Guillermina Ríos-Vázquez

Introduction

Tourism is a dynamic and complex phenomenon (Ceron & Silva, 2017; Ledhesma, 2017) and a very important one from the economic point of view, due to its growth in the last decades, seen in transport, catering, shopping and lodging (Monfort, 2002). Hotel occupancy can provide incomes and benefits through the number of occupied rooms (SECTUR, 2020), and can be affected by exogenous agents, such as violence, which weakens the state and conditions of insecurity for the population (Cisneros, 2014; Stopino, 2014), as well as the COVID-19 pandemic.

Whether during periods of violence or a pandemic situation, enterprises must be ready to confront risks in such a way that situations and certain factors must become the point of departure for decision making (Saavedra, 2015), analysing and interpreting information that allows planning on an adequate structure. Supply Chain Management (SCM) is a tool that can integrate, coordinate and manage organisational units in order to link processes and activities for such situations and produce value through products and services, accomplishing a competitive improvement to satisfy client needs (Calderón et al., 2017; Christopher, 1998; Stadtler & Kilger, 2005).

Background

The 2008 American economic slowdown enormously affected the US-Mexico border situation, with an important international finance crisis that diminished tourism flows (Alfonso-Rodríguez, 2016; Baba, 2016; Chacón, 2015; Maroto, 2017; Montes & Bernabé, 2020; Taboada, 2017; Tohry, 2016; Torres et al., 2014; Roldán et al., 2018). In spite of the decrease in violence in 2010, the scenario was not conducive to the 4–5 star hotel sector and reflected recession periods caused

DOI: 10.4324/9781003295839-19

by such economic deceleration (SECTUR, 2019). For Baja California, it was very difficult to overcome such a crisis, but it began to improve from 2010 with some accentuation in 2011 and with a very important year for tourism in 2013. According to Baja California's Tourism State Program 2015–2019, increased tourist flows were accompanied by historic levels of hotel occupancy.

The Tourist Destinations' Competitiveness Agenda (SECTUR, 2015) points out the existence of a problem for the lodging sector that coincided with the increase of violence, raising delinquency indicators at a national level. According to Baja California's State Guard of Security (Guardia Estatal de Seguridad e Investigación, 2020), Tijuana exhibited the highest levels of violence along the border. Mexico's economic growth in 2013 was only moderate, which is why the National Development Plan 2013–2018 focused on transforming the tourist sector through the Tourism Sectorial Program (PROSECTUR), trying to exploit tourist national potential and strengthening the competitive advantages of the offer. In spite of this effort, violence continued, and in 2018, the National Public Security Council (Consejo Nacional de Seguridad Pública, 2018) informed that 2017 was the most violent year of the new millennium, reporting 48,047 victims, situating Baja California in second place with 2,889 crimes reported to the Public Ministry. At the state level, Tijuana presented the highest levels of violence in 2017 (Guardia Estatal de Seguridad e Investigación, 2020).

Context of the US–Mexico border: the Tijuana–San Diego Region (TSDR)

Tourism, in a border context, goes beyond neighbourhood, hotels and restaurants due to the interaction by different actors that converge and integrate along a dividing line between two countries where experiences and practices are circumscribed by political, social, cultural, economic, demographic and technological factors (Vázquez, 2015). In this binational and regional context, the Ministry of Foreign Affairs emphasises that the US-Mexico border is one of the most active in the world with 14.6 million inhabitants, with daily crossings of one million people, 452 thousand cars (SRE, 2018), 30 thousand cargo trucks, and bilateral trade that reaches one billion dollars daily. It is important to mention that in the pandemic year 2020, the US-Mexico border was controlled and closed by the American government due to the COVID-19 pandemic, but the Mexican side stayed the same.

A complex scenario is perceived, especially in the Tijuana-San Diego Region (TSDR; RTSD in Spanish – Morgan-Medina et al., 2019), with the presence of economic slowdown and tourist trends variation and uncertainty. This has led to a change in the hotel sector and demands extraordinary measures and decision-making to guarantee stability and sustainability, with adjustments in strategy and established processes required (Chandler, 1977; Donaldson, 1987, 2006, 2015). Situational factors should be referred to in the design of a structure where efficient practices can take place, noticing eventualities with particular characteristics or contingencies that could put the enterprise at risk (Barrientos, 2007, 2013).

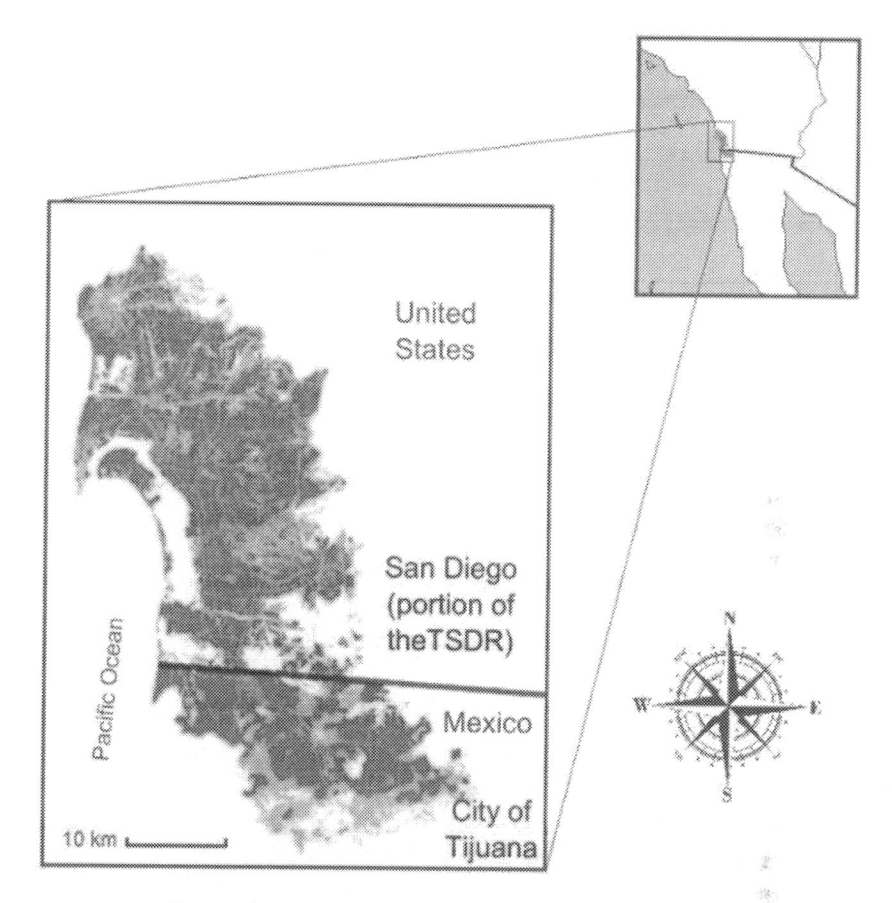

FIGURE 16.1   The TSDR

Source: Adapted from Trubetskoy (2016)

The city of Tijuana is relatively young, but it has a dynamic population. Despite being founded on July 11, 1889 (Piñera, 2021), it already had 1,922,523 inhabitants by 2020, becoming the most populated city of Baja, California, and the 4th in the country (INEGI, 2020). Its population is evenly distributed by gender, and two-thirds of the people older than 12 years old are economically active, with an economic participation rate of 76.2% for males and 54.7% for females (INEGI, 2020).

Tijuana, neighbouring San Diego, California (Bureau of Land Management, Esri, HERE, Garmin, USGS, NGA, EPA, USDA, NPS, 2022), is one of the most visited border cities in the world, receiving monthly 4,098,444 visitors averagely (Bureau of Transportation, 2017); this geographical situation has been strategically a booster for a permanent interaction with San Diego.

San Diego County's economy is characterised by the development of economic groups of business and industries that are related to each other, where tourism and entertainment stand at the same level as high-technology and communication industries, bio-tech and bio-medic products, as well as the aerospace sector. The diversification of the economic structure is high, and it is complemented by other economic activities that are also important for San Diegan dynamics. San Diego also has relevant economic groups in areas such as publicity, marketing, clean technology, and horticulture (San Diego Association for Governments, SANDAG, 2012).

Differences in both border urban areas are evident, mainly in aspects like culture, language and migration; nevertheless, according to specific circumstances of the border, both border areas received different impacts of economic integration (Niebuhr & Stiller, 2002); in fact, inequalities in both cities are boosting interchange, interaction and production, encouraging co-dependency on both sides of the border (Dilla, 2015). Similarly, the role of different economic activities, like tourism and culture activities, had increasingly fomented visits to the Mexican side (Kada & Kiy, 2004); e.g., health tourism in Tijuana had been growing until the COVID-19 pandemic, with a significant recovery in 2022, increasing medical and health services aimed at US citizens, due to the notoriously lower price (Vargas-Hernández & Reza, 2010).

According to Chang-Hee (2005), these economic activities are complementary in both cities, and this identifies this region as a trans-border metropolis. In this case, the Mexican side, as well as the American counterpart, have the common need to go across the border for shopping, work, family, tourism, etc. Due to the contingency perspective, relationships can be established between the global situation and the organisation (or enterprise), which allows the identification of events and factors that condition and determine processes, such as organisational behaviour. The study tries to determine whether violence, as a crisis, has a specific and temporal impact on the 4–5-star hotel sector slow-down. Additionally, due to the new normality caused by the COVID-19 pandemic, and analysing situational factors, it also diagnoses conditions of the climate where the hotel sector is developing, in order to pertinently understand the uneasy scenario that is expected, so an adequate structure can be designed from supply chain with the purpose of promoting a sustainable and competitive advantage.

Violence and delinquency frame at the world's busiest border

In this literature review, violence is analysed from 2017 to 2020, specifically regarding Tijuana's Zona-Centro (Downtown) 4–5-star hotels. The most important hotel zones are in violent environments, and the Zona-Centro is the most violent one. This characteristic diminished by 2018, and it has been characterised by less violence since the COVID-19 pandemic. Findings show that violence had been negatively impacting the tourist sector, mostly in the TSDR hotel industry, with a constant deceleration of occupancy, a problem that was detected and announced in the Tourist Destination Competitiveness Agenda (SECTUR, 2015). In this order of ideas, and assuming the effects of the COVID-19 pandemic, tourism confronts large economic losses, as opposed to what the WTO (2020) had foreseen, such as the 3–4% increase of international tourist arrivals, for example. At a global level, the impacts of the pandemic have been devastating; e.g., 320 thousands of billions of dollars in losses along the world, a 98% collapse of international arrivals, and 100–102 million jobs lost (WTO, 2020).

For Cervantes (2016), security is what tourists have as a main priority for travelling, agreeing with Taboada (2017) who points out that such a factor plays an important role. In 2019, INEGI published the Census of Perception on Public Insecurity, which shows that 2018 was perceived as the most violent year in Baja California. As well, the U.S. Department State emitted a risk category 2 security alarm in April 2019 (out of 4 different ranks of insecurity), which is defined as a raise of precaution and reconsideration of travel to Baja California. These types of actions are considered by Bringas and Verduzco (2008) as a negative amplifier, reflected in the increase in cancellations and increased security controls at the border, with economic implications. These alerts, emitted by the U.S. Government, affect Tijuana's image, inhibiting visits (Serrano-López et al., 2018), and according to Ríos-Vázquez and López-Vizcarra (2018) it also projects the image of an insecure and dangerous city; finding in a study that more than 50% of people feel insecure when transferring along different areas to get to the Tijuana–San Diego border crossing.

Along with this, Costa and González (2020), point out that tourism activity, in different spaces that are framed along the US-Mexico border (and therefore TSDR) end up influenced by American socioeconomic structures, with the creation, perpetuation and reproduction of unequal relationships, which are important for the American territory.

Risk management and supply chain as a response

Revising Correa and Gómez (2010), supply chain is where plans can be conceived to attend to existing conditions and contingency factors, due to structures that articulate all processes and links of the enterprise, beginning by its physical infrastructure, information flux, financial aspects, human talent and technological availability. These resources, according to Donner (2009), when managed integrally, the organisation focuses on identifying problems and preventing them from happening, avoiding risks, which is viable with the condition of detecting vulnerabilities and threats in time, identifying the weakest links in the chain (Arvis et al., 2010; Torres, 2019), promoting good fluxes, facilitating the enterprise trajectory towards competitiveness, and significantly influencing client satisfaction.

On the other hand, and relating this to violence, Berrones (2017) mentioned that risk factors in the supply chain (SC) are perceived through variables such as terrorism, robbery, theft (which also affects inventory), organised crime (using the border to commit crime), violence (e.g., assaults and kidnapping of haulers, who declined on considering driving to these type of destinations again), etc. Fisher et al. (2014); Gómez-Cedeño et al. (2015); and Schulz et al. (2014) had made systematic studies in different parts of the globe, in cases such as Mexico, U.S.A. and other industrialised countries, finding that for transport haulers nothing justifies facing insecurity; not an economic crisis nor unemployment are sufficient reasons retain qualified personnel, who are quitting their jobs, even though enterprises are applying different strategies like better salaries, schedules, equipment and bonuses. This situation has led to a severe human resource shortage, and therefore, there is a need to analyse these impacts on the SC.

Supply chain is more than just a logistic aspect (Johnson & Wood, 1996), because while logistics assume cooperation between buyers, suppliers and services focused on minimising costs during client attention, supply chain considers additional dimensions such as information systems, actors' behaviour, dependency levels, coordination power, planning and activity control. It can also be considered as the integrating trade process, through which management focuses on creating value to the enterprise, concentrating on client expectations, for which Johnson and Pyke (2000) suggest 12 elements: location, transport and logistics, inventory and prevision, marketing and channels' restructuration, catering and supplying management, product design and new product presentation, post-sale support and service, inverse logistics and ecological problems, outsourcing and strategic alliances, metrics and incentives, attention to global affairs, information and electronic environments.

Pereira-Moliner et al. (2016), points out that an important part of the operative processes of enterprises is the development of information systems, and when hotels use quality data and information to analyse and improve processes, then management introduces innovations centring efforts in tourist satisfaction, leading to a competitive advantage, which allows them to overcome competence and rivals. Planning for SC optimises resources that comply with satisfactory results and utilities to the enterprise, which means having a sustainable competitive advantage (Chakraborty, 1997; García-Santiago, 2006; Hoffman, 2000), and can be used by tourist establishments, especially hotels, as response to violence and insecurity, as well as in unexpected eventualities such a global health contingency, like a pandemic.

COVID-19 pandemic and its impacts on the tourism sector

According to the UN Conference on Commerce and Development 2021, falls in international tourism due to the COVID-19 pandemic could have caused the loss of 4 thousand billion dollars in global GDP during 2020 and 2021, causing a domino effect in sectors that are highly and directly linked to tourism, such as restoration industry, minority commerce, communications and transport (UN, 2021). Before the pandemic. Mexico was the 7th tourist destination in the world (WTO, 2020), and according to the National Tourist and Business Council (CNET, 2019) and Anahuac University, in 2019 tourism generated 25 billion dollars in incomes for the country, with approximately 45 million tourists. At the beginning of the pandemic, more than a million jobs were lost, 50 thousand restaurants stopped working, and more than half of the incomes in tourism disappeared (Duran, 2021). It is estimated that in September 2020, the pandemic could have put at risk more than 1.7 million jobs in the tourism and travel sector in Mexico (Statistics Research Department, 2021).

Methodology of the study

As mentioned before, the study analyses the viability of using SC in 4–5 stars' hotels in Tijuana and measures their ability to meet the needs of contemporary crises, with tools such as Risk Management (RM). On the other hand, it also tries to determine if violence and public insecurity imply a negative relation that slows down hotel occupancy.

In order to do so, the study was divided into three fundamental phases, where the first phase consisted of a literature review. The second phase used statistical analysis using an econometric model from six different factors and a regression technique. The last phase was a mixed study using both qualitative and quantitative techniques. Qualitative methodology evaluated the 4–5 to five-star hotel subsector boarding factors that are managed in the SC. Therefore, the interview was used as a technique and tool for the research that allowed significant data recollection, using the ATLAS.ti program, version 8, to interpret that data. A survey was conducted in the quantitative phase to examine possible relationships between violence and insecurity and the indicators of 4–5-star hotel occupancy in Tijuana, using the Statistical Package for the Social Sciences (SPSS), version 24.

Thus, this mixed study used a descriptive design, cross-section, diachronic and non-experimental; with instruments in the survey designed with the intention of measuring the impacts of violence and insecurity in the hotel subsector, with Likert-type scale items; while the interview was aimed at hotel representatives, in order to collect information for valuing SC. In addition, the analysis units considered in the quantitative technique were the guests of the hotels involved in the qualitative technique.

With information from the National Statistical Directory of Economic Units (DENUE – INEGI, 2020), and the support of the Tourist Observatory (El COLEF, 2020), nine 5-star hotels and nine 4-star hotels (18 hotels in total) were detected in the geographical space of the study. It was estimated that the number of guests was $N = 74{,}762$, using the hotel occupancy as a whole in the months related to the study, and then proceeded to calculate the sample in terms of proportions (Rea & Parker, 1991), determining values of p in 0.23 and q in 0.77, with a 93% confidence level ($Z = 1.81143$), and an error margin of $\pm 7\%$.

N = Population = 74,762
Z = 1.81143

S = Error = $\pm.07$
P = 0.23
Q = 0.77
n = Sample

Substituting Rea & Parker (1991) formula:

$$n = \frac{Z^2 N(p\,q)}{(p\,q)Z^2 + S^2(N-1)}$$

$$n = \frac{(1.81143)^2\ 74,762\ (0.23)(0.077)}{(0.23)(0.77)\ (1.81143)^2 + (.07)^2(74,762-1)}$$

$$n = \frac{6130401.56}{36633.8423} = 167.3425 = 168$$

According to the established sample size, the total of questionnaires to be administered to hotel guests in Zona-Centro Tijuana is 168.

Results

According to the econometric model from six different temps and regression techniques, the relationship between violence/insecurity and hotel occupancy slow-down is moderated, with a coefficient of 0.621, but sustained, with a coefficient of linear R^2 of 0.386, with a regression of 0.143 as a quadratic mean, with $F = 7.547$; which means that the violent status of the city is only a small part of the set of reasons why hotel occupancy is slowing down; it is also concluded that occupancy is steadily descending, sustaining the slowdown at least from the last period.

The third phase was divided into two techniques, a qualitative one based on interviewing hotel representatives, and another quantitative one consisting of a survey conducted with tourists. Situational factors are exhibited and identified as managed by the supply chain. In this sense, it is observed with different densities that 4–5-star hotels present strengths in the same variables that are managed from that supply chain, such as:

- Human resources training
- Service potentiation
- Technological infrastructure
- Products and services innovation
- Products and services design
- Processes optimisation
- Quality management
- Competitiveness

The factor identified with the most density is human resources, pointing out the importance of training the personnel in the field of hospitality, and nowadays is very

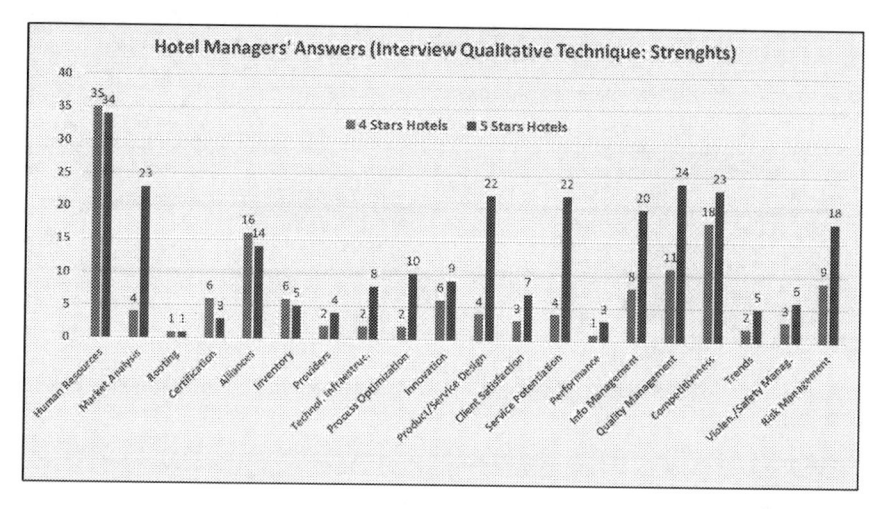

FIGURE 16.2 Hotel interview results

important to the same in the field of health contingencies, such as a pandemic. In the present, Tijuana hotels focus on training their personnel on issues like first aid and decision-making when a catastrophe happens, such as a fire or natural disasters. On the other hand, there is no training at all on matters of security, which shows a lack of attention that reflects risks in the links of an unmanaged supply chain. Service potentiation has no significance with all the activities that are developed in the organisation, and decision-making in this matter is fundamental in order to satisfy the guest needs. Technological infrastructure, innovation and product design are related to one another, and they are accompanied by process optimisation.

Hotel representatives agree on implementing technology, as well as innovation, for the optimisation of the communication process in case a risk related to insecurity shows up (e.g., security cameras, long range radio devices, etc.). In the meantime, processes that involve clients are applied to give them certainty when handling sensitive personal information. Products and services design are constantly watched over to meet the needs and requests of the guests.

On the other hand, data analysis detected weaknesses in the supply chain due to determined aspects that did not present a concurrence when addressing different informers (hotel managers), and this case density was too low or completely empty; therefore, carelessness was detected in issues like:

- Efficiency management (performance)
- Market analysis
- Settlement
- Marketing innovation
- Certification
- Supplies
- Inventory

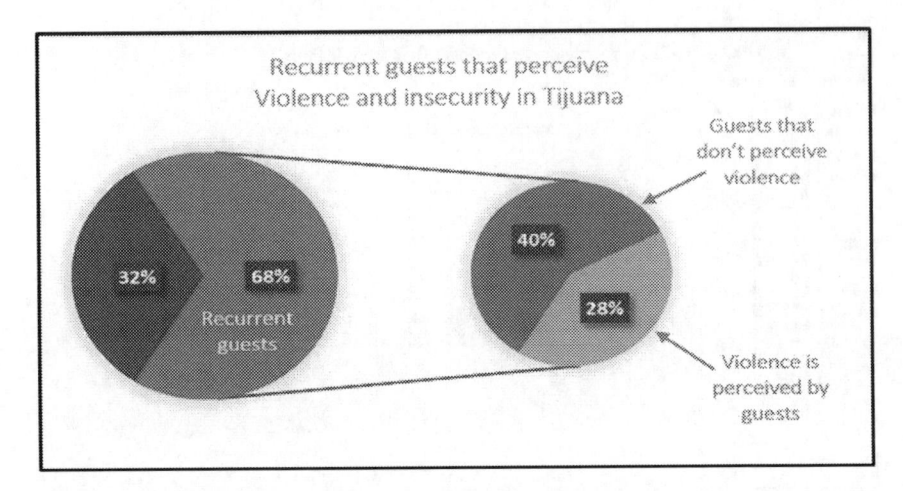

FIGURE 16.3 Tourist perceptions of violence and insecurity

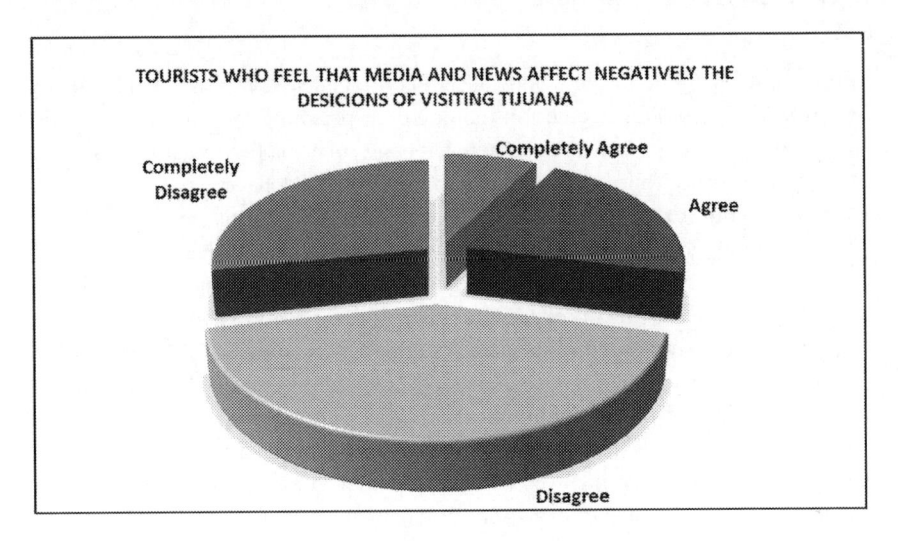

FIGURE 16.4 The influence of media and news reports on tourist decisions

According to the guests' opinions, a comparison was established between the near past and the present; 68% of the surveyed tourists were loyal to the destination (despite insecurity and violence in the city), and 28% of the 168 guests perceived violence and insecurity in Tijuana.

On the other hand, 29% of the 168 survey guests (49 in total) indicated that news and media influence their decision to visit the city, and 42% (71 guests, of the 168 involved) agreed that they do not feel protected by the authorities, and they do not trust the police. Nevertheless, this does not seem to affect in an important manner the decision of lodging in Tijuana, and only 17% (29 tourists) have at least one time discarded Tijuana as a destination because of the violence and insecurity experienced.

Conclusions

In conclusion, it can be said that a third of the tourists (29% of the 168 involved in the sample) feel insecure when they go sightseeing in the tourist areas of the city, and they perceive danger and fear, meaning that they put a great amount of interest in the location of the establishment based on the 88% (148 interviewed guests) that stated that they chose their hotel based on this. Meanwhile, four out of five people (145 surveyed guests) considered that use of technology and innovation when making efficient processes and services are very important elements for choosing where to stay in Tijuana, as well as the implementation of biosecurity protocols when preventing health risks (this was backed up by 145 guests, who represent 86% of the sample), especially when experiencing a pandemic scenario, like the one generated by COVID-19.

Summarising everything, constant violence was perceived during the 2006–2012 presidential administration in Mexico, which affected tourist activities, especially in Tijuana, along with repercussions for hotel occupancy in 4–5-star lodging establishments, as can be seen through documentary research.

Qualitative analysis demonstrated that supply chain management is not being exploited as a tool for decision-making. Information analysis shows a determined density on certain codes (Figure 16.2), but this will not necessarily support a recovery of establishments when confronting latent challenges as that experienced with COVID-19. Risk management, as well as the way of dealing with violence and insecurity, exhibited how weak 4- and 5-star lodging establishments are when confronted by these kinds of phenomena. It can be pointed out that supply chain risk management is not just an issue of logistics but also involves capacity for coordination, planning strategy, information management, processes and co-operation, which implies the management of distinct elements in the chain links through an internal and external context analysis, with the goal of accomplishing a structural design suited for different situations, using all resources to promote competitive advantages to deal with market changes and the risks that those changes imply.

References

Alfonso-Rodríguez, J. (2016). Evaluating the dynamics and impact of terrorist attacks on tourism and economic growth for Turkey. *Taylor & Francis Online, 9*, 56–81.

Arvis, J., Mustra, M., Ocala, L., Shepherd, B., & Saslavky, D. (2010). *Connecting to Compete. Trade Logistics in the Global Economy.* Washington, DC: World Bank.

Barrientos, J. (2007). *Teoría de las contingencias aplicada al diseño de las estructuras organizacionales: Taxonomía y nuevas contribuciones.* Argentina: UBA.

Barrientos, J. (2013). La gestión como variable interviniente en la teoría de las Contingencias. *Ciencias Administrativas, 2*, 21–32.

Berrones, L. (2017). Choferes del autotransporte de carga en México: investigaciones sobre condiciones laborales y la cadena de suministro. *Transporte y Territorio, 17*, 251–266.

Bringas, N. y Verduzco, B. (2008). La construcción de la frontera norte como destino turístico en un contexto de alertas de seguridad. *Región y Sociedad, 20*(42), 3–36. www.scielo.org.mx/scielo.php?script=sci_arttext&pid=S1870-39252008000200001&lng=es&tlng=es

Bureau of Land Management, Esri, HERE, Garmin, USGS, NGA, EPA, USDA, NPS. (2022). *Delegaciones Tijuana*. https://www.arcgis.com/apps/View/index.html?appid=e3 2b4f59544a450fbc3abfbeb3ef620c

Bureau of Transportation. (2017). *Transportation Statistics Annual Report 2016*. www.bts.gov/ content/transportation-statistics-annual-report-2016

Calderón, M., Roark, G., Urrutia, S., Paravié, D., & Rohvein, C. (2017). Metodología para la clasificación y Diagnóstico de Cadenas de Suministro. *Revista Ciencias Estratégicas, 25*(38), 279–298.

Ceron H., & Silva, U. (2017). La relación entre un proxi de la dinámica de la inseguridad pública y el turismo internacional a México: un análisis econométrico. *El Periplo Sustentable, 33*, 105–131.

Cervantes, A. (2016). Impacto de la imagen de México en el turismo y las inversiones: Evidencias contradictorias [Conference] XXI Congreso Internacional de Contaduría Administración en Informática.

Chacón, Y. (2015). *Colombia, la política de recuperación del turismo entre el 2002 y el 2014: el caso exitoso de arribo de turistas argentinos. [Trabajo de grado]*. Argentina: UBA.

Chakraborty, K. (1997). Sustained Competitive Advantage: A Resource-based Framework. *Journal in Advances Competitiveness Research, 1*, 32–63.

Chandler, A. (1977). *Strategy and Structure: Chapters in the History of the Industrial*. Englewood: Enterprise Press

Chang-Hee, C. (2005). *Tijuana-San Diego: Globalization and the Transborder Metropolis Department of Urban Design and Planning*. USA: UW.

Christopher, M. (1998). *Logistics and Supply Chain Management – Strategies for Reducing Cost and Improving Service*. 2da ed. London: Financial Times.

Cisneros, J. (2014). Cómo vivir en la violencia: Reflexión crítica sobre la violencia actual. *El Cotidiano, 187*, 83–99.

CNET. (2019). El turismo ante la cancelación de la inversión en promoción, Impacto macroeconómico y alternativas de políticas públicas. https://amdetur.org.mx/wp-content/ upload/2019/03/2019-estudios-cnet.pdf

Consejo Nacional de Seguridad Pública. (2018). *Informe de Actividades*. Mexico City: Gobierno de Mexico.

Correa-Espinal, A., & Gómez-Montoya, R. (2010). Seguridad en la cadena de suministro basada en la norma ISO 28001 para el sector carbón, como estrategia para su competitividad. *Boletín de Ciencias de la Tierra, 28*, 39–49.

Costa, J., & González, M. (2020). Criminalidad, seguridad pública y turismo en la zona fronteriza de ciudad Juárez, México. *Estudios Fronterizos, 21*, 1–26.

Dilla, A. (2015). Transborder Urban Complex in Latin America. *Revista Estudios fronterizos, 31*, 1–16.

Donaldson, L. (1987). Strategy and Structural Adjustment to Regain Fit and Performance: In Defense of Contingency Theory. *Journal of Management Studies, 24*(I), 1–24.

Donaldson, L. (2006). *The Contingency Theory of Organizational Design: Challenges and Opportunities*. Cham: Springer.

Donaldson, L. (2015). Structural Contingency Theory. In J.D. Wright (Ed.), *International Encyclopedia of the Social & Behavioral Sciences* (pp. 609–614). London: Elsevier.

Donner, M., & Kruk, C. (2009). *Supply Chain Security Guide*. Washington, DC: World Bank.

Duran, L. (2021). *La crisis de turismo*. Bogota: Red Forbes.

El COLEF. (2020). *Observatorio Turístico de Baja California*. El Colegio de la Frontera Norte. www.datatur.sectur.gob.mx/

Fisher, R., Mcphail, R., You, Y., & Ash, M. (2014.) Using Social Media to Recruit Global Supply Chain Managers. *International Journal of Physical Distribution and Logistics Management, 44*(8–9), 635–645.

García-Santiago, F. (2006). La Gestión de la Cadena de Suministros: Un enfoque de integración global de procesos. *Visión Gerencial, 1,* 53–62.

Gómez-Cedeño, M., Castán-Farrero, J.M. Guitart, L., & Matute-Vallejo, J. (2015). Impact of Human Resources on Supply Chain Management and Performance. *Industrial Management & Data Systems, 115*(1), 129–157.

Guardia Estatal de Seguridad e Investigación (2020). *Incidencia delictiva por zonas.* Rosarito: Gobierno de Baja California.

Hoffman, N. (2000). An Examination of the Sustainable Competitive Advantage Concept: Past, Present and Future. *Academy of Marketing Science Review, 4,* 1–20.

INEGI. (2020). *Censo de Población y Vivienda.* Mexico City: México.

Johnson, E., & Pyke, D. (2000). Supply Chain Management. In *Encyclopedia of Operations Research and Management Science* (pp. 1–31). Cham: Springer.

Johnson, J., & Wood, D. (1996). *Contemporary Logistic* (6th ed.). New York, NY: Prentice Hall.

Kada, N., & Kiy, R. (2004). *Blurred Borders: Trans-boundary Impacts & Solutions in the San Diego-Tijuana Border Region.* National City, CA: International Community Foundation.

Ledhesma, M. (2017). *Gestión de Crisis en Turismo. (Archivo PDF).* www.academia.edu/32256641/Gesti%C3%B3n_de_Crisis_en_Turismo

Maroto, J. (2017). La masacre de Gran Bassan: Impacto económico y social del terrorismo en Costa de Marfil. *Revista Brasileña de planeación y desenvolvimiento, 6*(3), pp. 445–468.

Monfort, V. (2002). Estrategia Competitiva y Desempeño en la Industria Hotelera Costera: Evidencias empíricas en Benidorm y Peñíscola. *Cuadernos de Turismo, 10,* 7–22.

Montes, G., & Bernabé, S. (2020). The Impact of Violence on Tourism to Rio de Janeiro. *International Journal of Social Economics, 47*(4), 425–443.

Morgan-Medina, J., Cuamea-Velázquez, O., Estrada-Gaxiola, A., Ferreira-Cury, M., & Stremel-Barros, L. (2019). *Caracterización del visitante transfronterizo y su consumo: comparativo entre Tijuana (México) y Foz do Iguaçu (Brasil)* (Unpublished research). Mexico: UABC.

Niebuhr, A., & Stiller, S. (2002). *Integration Effects in Border Regions, A Survey of Economic Theory and Empirical Studies.* Germany: HIIE.

Pereira-Moliner, J., Pertusa-Ortega, E., Tarí Maria, J., López-Gamero, D., & Molina-Azorin, J. (2016). Organizational Design, Quality Management and Competitive Advantage in Hotels. *Contemporary Hospitality Management, 28*(4), 1–43.

Piñera, D. (2021). Historia Mínima de Tijuana. XXIV Ayuntamiento de Tijuana 2021–2024.

Rea, L., & Parker, R. (1991). *Methods of Analysis in Public and Urban Affairs: Survey research, A Practical Guide.* San Diego: Collegiate Publication Service.

Ríos-Vázquez, A., & López-Vizcarra, J. (2018). Seguridad e Imagen en Garita Internacional de Cruce Peatonal: Retos para usuarios y turismo. *Revista Global de Negocios, 6*(6), 1–18.

Roldán, Andrés-Rosales, Sánchez-Mitre, L., & Cruz, J. (2018). Insecurity and its Impact on Tourism in Guerrero: A Spatial Approach, 1999–2014. *Revista de Relaciones Internacionales, Estrategia y Seguridad, 13*(1), 147–162.

Saavedra, R. (2015). *Contingencia o Planeamiento.* Lima: Asociados.

SANDAG. (2012). *Traded Industry Clusters in the San Diego region.* San Diego: San Diego Association for Governments.

Schulz, S., Luthans, K., & Messersmith, J. (2014). Psychological Capital: A New Tool for Driver Retention. (Online). *International Journal of Physical Distribution & Logistics Management, 44*(8–9), 621–634.

SECTUR. (2015). *La Agenda para la Competitividad de Destinos Turísticos 2013–2018.* México: Secretaría de Turismo.

SECTUR. (2019). *Reporte Monitoreo Hotelero. Resultados preliminares.* México: Secretaría de Turismo.

SECTUR. (2020). *Glosario de términos.* México: Secretaría de Turismo.

Serrano-López, A., Freire-Chaglla, S., Sanmartin, I., & Espinoza-Figueroa, F. (2018). Recesión en la ocupación hotelera a partir de tres acontecimientos: terremoto, cierre de aeropuerto, construcción de tranvía. Caso cuenca (Ecuador). *Cuadernos de Turismo, 42,* 465–479. https://dialnet.unirioja.es/servlet/articulo?codigo=6788190

SRE. (2018). *Hoja informativa, Frontera México-Estados Unidos.* México: Secretaría de Relaciones Exteriores.

Stadtler, H., & Kilger, C. (2005). *Supply Chain Management and Advanced Planning.* 3rd ed. New York: Springer

Statistics Research Department, (2021). *COVID-19 en México: impacto en el sector turístico 2020.* Secretaría de Turismo, Gobierno de México. Mexico: CDMX.

Stopino, M. (2014). *Diccionario de política.* Mexico: Siglo XXI.

Taboada, M. (2017). *Violencia, terrorismo y turismo: Hacia nuevos paradigmas a la hora de viajar.* [Trabajo de grado]. Argentina: UBA.

Tohry, F. (2016, March 21). Terrorismo: Las deficiencias del turismo. *On-line.*

Torres, E., Ramírez, R., & Rodríguez, B. (2014). La Crisis Económica en el Sector Turístico: Un análisis de sus efectos en la costa del sol. *Análisis Turístico, 18*(2), 11–18.

Torres, J. (2019). *La seguridad en la cadena de suministros como estrategia de competitividad de las organizaciones.* Colombia: UCC.

Trubetskoy, S. (2016). *US-Mexico Border Cities.* https://sashat.me/2016/12/14/mexicos-urban-pileups/Ciudades fronterizas EUA-México, de Oeste a Este. Dossier. Revista de la Universidad de México. July, 2018. www.revistadelauniversidad.mx/articles/b954fb99–4f98–484a-9621-dd3dea58899e/ciudades-fronterizas-eua-mexico

UN. (2021*). El impacto del COVID-19 en el turismo costará cuatro billones de dólares a la economía mundial. Asuntos Económicos.* Geneva: United Nations.

Vargas-Hernández, J., & Reza, N., (2010, January 27). *Study on Entrepreneurship and Role of Government in Enhancing Entrepreneurship by Establishing Small and Medium Enterprises, SMEs and Start-Ups.* https://ssrn.com/abstract=1543204 or DOI: 10.2139/ssrn.1543204

Vázquez, F. (2015). Repasando la frontera hispano-portuguesa: conflicto, interacción y cooperación transfronteriza. *Estudios Fronterizos, 16*(31), 65–89.

WTO. (2020). *Directrices Globales para Reabrir el Turismo.* Madrid: United Nations World Tourism Organisation.

17

VIRTUAL TOURISM AND DIGITAL COMMUNICATION IN THE CONTEXT OF THE POST-PANDEMIC SCENARIO

Bruno Barbosa Sousa, Carla Sousa Martins, Ana Carvalho Ferreira and Catarina Silva Pereira

Introduction

Despite the growing interest and discussions on Virtual Reality (VR) and Augmented Reality (AR) in tourism, we do not yet know systematically the knowledge that has been built from academic papers on VR and AR in tourism; if and how VR and AR research intersect; the methodologies used to research VR and AR in tourism; and the emerging contexts in which VR and AR have surfaced in tourism research (Yung & Khoo-Lattimore, 2019). According to Yung et al. (2021), in a post-COVID-19 landscape, there is growing interest and opportunity for cutting-edge technologies to contribute to destination recovery. During these unprecedented times, it is vital for destination marketers to communicate their tourism products in a clear and compelling format to potential visitors. In particular, the increase in interactivity, immersion and visualisation that VR is purported to provide suggests that technology may be an invaluable resource to communicate the intangible and experiential nature of tourism as a product or service.

The global pandemic caused by COVID-19 has changed not only the way we currently travel, but it has also highlighted the important role played by Virtual Tourism and Gamified Virtual Experiences. Faced with this scenario, several companies in the tourism sector had to reinvent themselves, using virtual environments and digital tools, as an opportunity to maintain and expand their business (López García et al., 2019). The need to invest in marketing and communication strategies was also highlighted in order to adapt to the new consumer behaviour that arose during the pandemic crisis and that will possibly endure. We live in the Age of Influence, in which the majority of the world's population is connected to the Web. New segments and market niches are generated by the use of Information and Communication Technologies (ICT), meeting and adapting to the needs of new generations, leading to the burst of new business models. According to

DOI: 10.4324/9781003295839-20

Subawa et al. (2021), and according to numerous studies, society needs to prepare for the changes associated with the new normal period, due to the inception of the COVID-19 pandemic, by implementing strict health rules. These behaviour changes include observing social distancing, avoiding crowds, minimising mobilisation, work activities, education and shopping, which are carried out from home using online media. Likewise, actors in the tourism industry used VR to carry out marketing activities for certain products or services. Thus, technology, COVID-19, and new consumer behaviour have brought to light a new type of tourism – virtual tourism. In this chapter, the authors propose to study this tourism segment and its role in mitigating the impact of COVID-19, both in tourism enterprises and tourist consumption.

Tourism marketing and virtual reality

Over the years, there has been an increase in competition among tourism destinations (Ferreira & Sousa, 2020), leading to the need for a deeper understanding about the tourism realm, impact and management. The field of tourism marketing, in particular, has faced increasing challenges in capturing market dynamics, such as market fragmentation and diversity. New habits, needs and trends in the global tourism arena create more sophisticated consumers who systematically look for different and specific experiences. Such a context calls for new market approaches (Sousa & Silva, 2019). Offering computer-generated environments with realistic images, virtual reality (VR) blends organic, intuitive technology with personalised information, allowing the user an experience in the virtual world that replicates physical presence (Adachi et al., 2020). According to Adachi et al. (2020), and responding to consumer interest, a number of VR-focused applications for travel are coming to the fore: for example, Ascape is a smartphone application giving users a platform to download 360-degree videos of various tourist locations that can be accessed at any time. Another world-famous example is Pokémon GO, an open, mobile multi-player AR-based game. Since its release in July 2016, it has taken the world by storm. It is an application with which players can collect points by walking around in the real world, holding up their smartphone in a quest to find, catch and collect virtual characters, called 'pocket monsters', which are located near and linked to specific geographical locations. For instance, Anjo et al. (2021), concluded that VR in literary tourism should be an object of in-depth studies, as it tends to be beneficial for cultural promotion of tourist destinations and products, specifically for literary tourists. VR and digital technology can be a fundamental aid to cultural heritage, since in addition to sharing information, VR promotes and sells its offerings, improving the visitor experience (Maurer, 2015).

Adachi et al. (2020) argues that with increasing interest in and use of VR, and to complement market-driven research into VR as a modality to engage tourists, a growing number of empirical studies examine users' psychological response toward VR travel experiences across media types (i.e., headsets and 360-degree videos). On a broad level, this corpus of research seeks to unpack how potential users think about VR technology in the context of travel (technology), the impact of VR use on the image of a destination in one's mind (destination image) and why VR experiences may offer a rich entre into tourism destinations (experience) (Adachi et al., 2020). In this context, Subawa et al. (2021) argues that tourism-related industries such as hoteliers, airlines, restaurants, tourist attraction managers, souvenir centres, travel agents, and tour guides experienced a decline in revenue.

According to the characteristics that virtual tourism has, the same in some pertinent examples may replace physical travel. For instance, Rafael and Almeida (2014) consider that tourists can learn more about a specific place through, for example, the online zooming platform. According to Martins et al. (2022), virtual tourism allows tourists to travel in time and to learn more about times and places that currently do not exist, taking as an example the Tower of London in the year 1255. The use of a smartphone and virtual reality equipment is essential for you to enjoy this trip to the past. Virtual tourism currently presents itself as the future of tourism. However, despite the numerous advantages in the implementation of virtual reality, there are some obstacles for some areas of tourism, namely travel agencies and for the consumer/tourist himself. Therefore, some barriers to virtual tourism will be presented (Martins et al., 2022): the human being is considered a sociable being, and thus, when opting for virtual tourism, the tourist may miss the real experience he has when he physically moves to a certain place, especially the social experience. However, Sussamann and Vanhegan (2000) argue that this barrier can be interpreted as a positive point since some tourists find it difficult to interact with local cultures, and by not enjoying the social experience, it will contribute to the nonexistence of cultural constraints. The consumer/tourist may come to overconsume this type of tourism and this can cause addiction; therefore, in these cases, there may be social consequences, making the consumer/tourist unwilling to communicate with other people (Martins et al., 2022). Since virtual tourism is carried out online, experiences and memories fall far short when compared to physical visits (Sussamann & Vanhegan, 2000).

Currently, there are also several amusement parks using this type of technology, namely the VR Time Machine Dinosaur Park and the Jurassic VR- Google Cardboard, and the Safari tours adventures VR 4D, which provides the experience of a safari, in a park designed by computer graphics (Taufer & Ferreira, 2019). According to Martins et al. (2022), virtual reality tries to transport users to the virtual environment using equipment in closed environments, while augmented reality does not have any type of restrictions about the environment. In the virtual environment coming from augmented reality, it is taken to the physical environment so that there is a more natural interaction among the users.

The hospitality and tourism industry received an impact on an unprecedentedly large scale. Therefore, tourism industry actors are required to utilise other marketing strategies to creatively market their products. One such strategy is the use of virtual reality marketing (VRM). Changes in the tourism industry are associated with the development of various marketing strategies, with VRM being used to offer services to domestic tourists. In addition, certain phenomena in the application of this technology include the emergence of niche market segments and sustainable tourism (Subawa et al., 2021). VRM is an alternative method used in the marketing of tourism products in a sustainable manner for community groups due to the imposed policy of the government restricting movements. Virtual reality marketing encourages tourists to visit attractions, despite being in different countries, and to see and enjoy them with the aid of technological devices used in different places.

Digital communication and tourism

One of the most significant developments in the field of information and communication technology (ICT) expected to greatly impact the tourism industry today is virtual reality (VR). Many recent innovations, such as VR platforms, devices and content production tools, have enabled the evolution of VR. As such, VR technologies nowadays offer unbounded potential for mass virtual visitations to actual tourism destinations. According to Pestek and Sarvan (2021), the marketing and promotion segments of the tourism sector have most often been used with the assistance of visual imagery. The intangible properties of tourism, as a service, constantly remind marketers that there is a need to continuously innovate the forms of visual imagery with the objective of promoting a positive destination image.

Internet marketing expands the possibilities available to attain this aim by allowing you to create and execute a plan that sends the appropriate message to the right people at the right time (Moita, 2017). In this context, and according to Ferreira and Sousa (2020), Facebook is the most widely used social networking site in the world, allowing businesses to reach many more people and more occurrences than companies using other means, such as calls, emails or meetings. Facebook is considered an attractive social network for digital marketing specialists and for online ads. These ads use social networks to connect customers to businesses, thereby creating new opportunities for customers to get to know their brands and products.

Following the trend of a world reality and a profile of the most technological tourist, Portugal realised the importance of increasing its online presence through digital strategies that give greater representation to the Destination. Since 2013, Turismo de Portugal has begun to review strategies, increasing the budget for internet campaigns to five million euros. This promotion was reflected in the increase in the number of tourists and the achievement of several awards and distinctions around tourism. In the Tourism Strategy 2027, there is a patent expansion of social networks, the redefinition of the business model according to the growing impact of the Millennium generation, and the definition of ICT as the engine of the economy. This strategic vision aims to affirm Portugal as a Smart Destination, with several digital measures of national and regional scope (Martins et al., 2022). To conclude, VR in marketing of tourism destinations can be associated with attachment (Wu et al., 2016), stimulation (Neuburger et al., 2018), evaluation (Gao et al., 2017), decision-making (Guo & Barnes, 2011) and experience (Pestek & Sarvan, 2021).

Social media networks in promotion

The use of social networks is one of the most popular activities and it is undeniable the impact that social media have had on society, a little all over the world (Silva, 2018). Since social networks are translated into online communities, where millions of users interact, these are now extremely important for the success of the activities of companies and tourism organisations. Social media marketing is used in all sectors and refers to the use of different technologies, channels and software to create, communicate, deliver and exchange offers that have their value to different stakeholders (Jacobson et al., 2020).

For companies, social networks are used as a communication tool to promote and sell products, while for the public, they are commonly used as a place for information sharing and interacting with other users. In this way, marketers use the information generated by social networks, with three main objectives: evaluation of the customers' opinion, through the collection and processing of data; develop a personalised offer; and enhance the relationship with the customer, since, through the generation of content per user, they can reach new customers, engage customers in a relationship with the brand and retain them through interaction with them and other users (Jacobson et al., 2020).

Concerning tourists and social networks or social media, they changed the way they think and make decisions and took the experience of planning and making a trip to a new level. Social media is the new place where tourists collect information about destinations and choose the destination through suggestions from other users. A new consumer traveller was born, more participatory in the act of consumption, to which tourism organisations should be attentive when planning their business model. In recent years, the presence of companies and destinations in social networks has provided an attraction for new tourists and maintained existing ones, with social media allowing greater reach and interaction.

Digital influencers

With the appearance of social media, the internet has become a participatory platform that allows people to collaborate and share information, turning normal people into globally-known influencers, attracting brands, and this has become a lucrative activity both to companies and influencers (Leung et al., 2022; Simas & Júnior, 2018). In this matter, influencers are individuals who can stand out on social networks due to their opinion or behaviour in each context (San Miguel, 2020) They are virtual opinion-makers, who exercise massive power since they hold a lot of influence over their followers. The use of social networks stimulates the idea of belonging to a group, and the amount of information to which the new consumer is exposed daily makes him rely only on the F Factor (family, friends, Facebook friends, and followers) and this favours the role of digital influencers (Ramalho, 2019).

In tourism, influencers have become the new travel guides, either by reporting their first-person experience, creating a greater proximity, credibility and authenticity that travel brochures do not have, or because visitors today seek a more personal and creative approach that conveys emotions to them. The individual is subjected to social influence before the trip when they receive feedback through comments or other content about travel, on social media and creates expectations about it. Because of their travels, digital influencers utilise their social media platforms to promote not just products, businesses and services, but also tourist locations through photo and video uploads. As a result, the image serves as a motivator for tourists to want to learn more about a location (Perinotto et al., 2018). According to this, the information that opinion leaders provide directly affects consumer's purchasing decisions and drives the consumption of tourism products/services.

VR to mitigate the negative impact of COVID-19 on the tourism sector

During mandatory confinement, due to COVID-19 and borders closed in almost every country in the world during March and April 2020, museum platforms and websites emerged and destinations that allowed people to travel without leaving home, which helped combat anxiety because of isolation, uncertainty and loneliness. AirPano, Google Arts and Culture, Era Virtual, Go tours, You visit, British museum and Oceanarium of Lisbon are just some of the many examples of sites that transported us on virtual trips. It is even possible to book a trip on schedule, with a tour guide, for a symbolic value, and on the day and time scheduled, through video conference, you will be accompanied on a visit entitled to know all the history and all curiosities about the chosen destination, as if it were a conventional tour. Digital technologies bring potential to tourism, such as enhancing the preservation of historical sites and educating visitors to this end. The virtual experience can also generate revenue for destinations, reducing the impacts of seasonality and promoting economic sustainability, since it will be available for purchase online. This experience will stimulate the desire to visit the destination, functioning as a marketing tool (Bec et al., 2021). Whether virtual tourism will be the way to travel in the future is not yet known, and studies emerge on its possible impacts to understand whether conventional tourist demand will suffer a decrease or increase, attracting tourists for certain trips. The dynamics of society directly affect tourist activity, which has become one of the most important economic and social activities of the century. The tourist is becoming increasingly demanding, looking for more knowledge and authentic experiences, which leads him to look for new services, products and markets.

Conclusions

Despite the growing interest and discussions on VR and AR in tourism, we do not yet systematically know the knowledge that has been built from academic papers on VR and AR in tourism, if and how VR and AR research intersect, the methodologies used to research VR and AR in tourism, and the emerging contexts in which VR and AR have surfaced in hospitality and tourism research. It is possible to conclude that new technologies have led to the appearance of new forms of tourism marketing, revolutionising in a certain way the physiognomy of how to travel. The hospitality and tourism industry received an impact on an unprecedentedly large scale. Therefore, tourism industry actors are required to utilise other marketing strategies to creatively market their products. One such strategy is the use of virtual reality marketing (VRM). Changes in the tourism industry are associated with the development of various marketing strategies, with VRM being used to offer services to domestic tourists. Tourists are increasingly demanding and technologically capable, designing new products and niches. In this sense and responding to the needs of new generations, namely millennials and generation z, who are increasingly technological experts and concerned with the sustainability of destinations, virtual tourism has emerged. The COVID-19 pandemic positively provided an opportunity for virtual tourism, since, due to confinement, borders were closed and for health reasons, tourists were afraid to travel. Motivated by the lack of jobs and income, workers and tourist companies created online solutions and took advantage of existing solutions to overcome the crisis in the sector, such as visits to museums, visits to cities, and online tourist guides, among others. For instance, in the context of destination marketing, researchers have suggested that presence is a necessary part of DMO website performance (Choi et al., 2016; Hyun & O'Keefe, 2012). Destination marketing websites have to be engaging to enhance users' sense of presence, which then leads them to feel that they are actually at the destination and perceive that time spent as enjoyable. When online visitors feel present in a destination through web-mediated virtual information, studies have shown that users vividly remember what they experienced on the website, leading to familiarity, knowledge, interest, and positively influencing intention to visit the destination.

Virtual tourism is gaining more and more notoriety in the market as it allows an individual, without moving, to experience unique sensations. According to information from the literature, it is understood that virtual tourism currently consists of immersive environments and experiences of various types, which include digital and face-to-face tools, namely, virtual games that are already part of young people's routine, who use digital technologies to create unique sensory experiences such as virtual tours created using 3D glasses, among others. Although there are still many questions regarding the evolution of the tourism sector, it is possible to identify positive aspects for the adoption of this new segment in the most diverse aspects. In the future, there will still be much to explore about this segment, namely about the new products and services that may arise from it, outline the profile of its consumer and quantify what economic impacts it will have on destinations. VR is considered a promising technology for the hospitality and tourism industries that has the powerful effect of fooling the senses into believing one is present in a virtual world by providing interactive 3D surroundings simulated by a computer. These simulations can depict any tourist location or attraction reproduced as 3D imagery, controlled by powerful computers creating a complete Virtual Environment (VE) (Nayyar et al., 2018). This chapter covered a description of the history of VR/AR enabling technologies, the currently popular VR/AR equipment, and several use cases of VR/AR applications for the tourism & hospitality context. In an interdisciplinary perspective, the present chapter aimed to present contributions to marketing, virtual tourism and pandemic management.

References

Adachi, R., Cramer, E.M., & Song, H. (2020). Using Virtual Reality for Tourism Marketing: A Mediating Role of Self-presence. *The Social Science Journal*, 1–14.

Anjo, A.M., Sousa, B., Santos, V., Lopes Dias, Á., & Valeri, M. (2021). Lisbon as a Literary Tourism Site: Essays of a Digital Map of Pessoa as a New Trigger. *Journal of Tourism, Heritage & Services Marketing (JTHSM)*, 7(2), 58–67.

Bec, V., Moyle, B., Schaffer, V., & Timms, K. (2021). Virtual Reality and Mixed Reality for Second Chance Tourism. *Tourism Management*, 83, 104256.

Choi, J., Ok, C., & Choi, S. (2016). Outcomes of Destination Marketing Organization Website Navigation: The Role of Telepresence. *Journal of Travel & Tourism Marketing*, 33(1), 46–62.

Ferreira, J., & Sousa, B. (2020). Experiential Marketing as Leverage for Growth of Creative Tourism: A Co-creative Process. In Á. Rocha, A. Abreu, J. de Carvalho, D. Liberato, E. González, & P. Liberato (Eds.), *Advances in Tourism, Technology and Smart Systems. Smart Innovation, Systems and Technologies* (pp. 567–577). Singapore: Springer.

Gao, L., Bai, X., & Park, A. (2017). Understanding Sustained Participation in Virtual Travel Communities from the Perspectives of is Success Model and Flow Theory. *Journal of Hospitality and Tourism Research*, 41(4), 475–509.

Guo, Y., & Barnes, S. (2011). Purchase Behavior in Virtual Worlds: An Empirical Investigation in Second Life. *Information & Management*, 48(7), 303–312.

Hyun, M.Y., & O'Keefe, R.M. (2012). Virtual Destination Image: Testing a Telepresence Model. *Journal of Business Research*, 65(1), 29–35.

Jacobson, J., Gruzd, A., & Hernández-García, Á. (2020). Social Media Marketing: Who is Watching the Watchers? *Journal of Retailing and Consumer Services*, 53, 101774.

Leung, F.F., Gu, F.F., & Palmatier, R.W. (2022). Online Influencer Marketing. *Journal of the Academy of Marketing Science*, 1–26.

López García, J.J., Lizcano, D., Ramos, C.M., & Matos, N. (2019). Digital Marketing Actions That Achieve a Better Attraction and Loyalty of Users: An Analytical Study. *Future Internet*, 11(6), 130.

Martins, C.S., Ferreira, A.C., Pereira, C.S., & Sousa, B.B. (2022). Virtual Tourism and Challenges in a Post-Pandemic Context. In C. Ramos, S. Quinteiro, & A. Gonçalves (Eds.), *ICT as Innovator Between Tourism and Culture* (pp. 122–137). London: IGI Global. DOI: 10.4018/978-1-7998-8165-0.ch008

Maurer, C. (2015). Digital Divide and its Potential Impact on Cultural Tourism. In *Cultural Tourism in a Digital Era* (pp. 231–241). Cham: Springer.

Moita, P. (2017). *e-Business em Turismo*. Em F. Silva & J. Umbelino (Eds.), *Planeamento e Desenvolvimento Turístico* (pp. 159–171). Lisboa: Lidel.

Nayyar, A., Mahapatra, B., Le, D., & Suseendran, G. (2018). Virtual Reality (VR) & Augmented Reality (AR) Technologies for Tourism and Hospitality Industry. *International Journal of Engineering & Technology*, 7(2.21), 156–160.

Neuburger, L., Beck, J., & Egger, R. (2018), The 'Phygital' Tourist Experience: The Use of Augmented and Virtual Reality in Destination Marketing. In M. Camillieri (Ed.),

Tourism Planning and Destination Marketing (pp. 183–202). New York: Emerald Publishing Limited.

Perinotto, A., Mota, D., & Ferreira, H. (2018). As Mídias Sociais e os Influenciadores Digitais na Promoção de Destinos Turísticos. *Anais Brasileiros de Estudos Turísticos.* DOI: 10.34019/2238-2925.2018.v8.3213.

Pestek, A., & Sarvan, M. (2021). Virtual Reality and Modern Tourism. *Journal of Tourism Futures,* 7(2), 245–250.

Rafael, C., & Almeida, A. (2014). Impacto da informação online na formação da imagem de destino virtual. *Dos Algarves: A Multidisciplinary E-journal, 23,* 27–50.

Ramalho, B. (2019). *O Papel dos Influenciadores Digitais Portugueses na Promoção de um Destino Turístico.* Vila do Conde: Politécnico do Porto.

Silva, J. (2018). *Marketing digital e Redes Sociais no Turismo: O caso do Município de Ovar.* Aveiro: Universidade de Aveiro.

Simas, D., & Júnior, A. (2018). Sociedade em Rede: Os Influencers Digitais e a Publicidade Oculta nas Redes Sociais. *Revista de Direito, Governança e Novas Tecnologias, 4*(1), 17–32.

Sousa, B., & Silva, M. (2019). Creative Tourism and Destination Marketing as a Safeguard of the Cultural Heritage of Regions: The Case of Sabugueiro Village. *Revista Brasileira de Gestão e Desenvolvimento Regional, 15*(5), 78–92.

Subawa, N.S., Widhiasthini, N.W., Astawa, I.P., Dwiatmadja, C., & Permatasari, N.P.I. (2021). The Practices of Virtual Reality Marketing in the Tourism Sector, A Case Study of Bali, Indonesia. *Current Issues in Tourism, 24*(23), 3284–3295.

Sussamann, S., & Vanhegan, H.J. (2000). Virtual Reality and the Tourism Product: Substitution or Complement? *ECIS 2000 Proceedings. 117.* http://aisel.aisnet.org/ecis2000/117. Accessed 1 January 2021.

Taufer, L., & Ferreira, L.T. (2019). Realidade Virtual no Turismo: Entretenimento ou Mudança de Paradigma?. *Rosa dos Ventos, 11*(4), 908–921.

Wu, D., Weng, D., & Xue, S. (2016), Virtual Reality System as an Affective Medium to Induce Specific Emotion: A Validation Study. *Electronic Imaging, 2016*(4), 1–6

Yung, R., & Khoo-Lattimore, C. (2019). New Realities: A Systematic Literature Review on Virtual Reality and Augmented Reality in Tourism Research. *Current Issues in Tourism, 22*(17), 2056–2081.

Yung, R., Khoo-Lattimore, C., & Potter, L.E. (2021). Virtual Reality and Tourism Marketing: Conceptualizing a Framework on Presence, Emotion, and Intention. *Current Issues in Tourism, 24*(11), 1505–1525.

18

COVID-19 AND CHANGING REALITIES IN THE FOOD & BEVERAGE SECTOR

Exhibiting the Indian chefs' perspective

*Anubha Mahender Singh, Priyakrushna Mohanty,
Sarah Hussain and Mahender Reddy Gavinolla*

Introduction

Chefs are considered the artists of the kitchen (Dornenburg & Page, 1996) and often their roles stretch far beyond the colloquial duty of cooking (Ruhlman, 2006). Modern-day chefs are involved in many complex operations concerning culture, policies, safety, sustainability and nutritional issues of food (McBride & Flore, 2019). With stringent norms of conduct and growing customer demand for a higher level of sophistication, chefs' roles have become more challenging than ever. While some of these challenges have contributed to making the chefs efficient, improved and multitaskers, others have proved to be too harsh on them in the face of drastic changes in the food ordering, preparation and delivery processes. Among all these challenges, perhaps the most radical is the COVID-19 outbreak.

It has been more than a year since the outbreak of the COVID-19 virus, which has ravaged the world entirely. With multiple economic, social and environmental implications, this disease has materialised as the worst pandemic the world has seen in the last 100 years (Rosenthal, 2020). Almost all economic activities have come to a standstill and the global economy is at its lowest point. In these dire situations, the tourism and hospitality industry is estimated to be one of the hardest-hit industries (WTO, 2020). At the beginning of 2021, global tourist arrivals had shrunk by 86% since January 2020 and 100 million people employed in the tourism and hospitality industry were at risk of losing their jobs (UNWTO, 2021). The American Hotel and Lodging Association (2020) highlights that the hotel business was the front-line industry to be most negatively affected and will also be the last sector to recuperate, with approximately 3.9 million total job loss across the industry. Measures like mass lockdowns, stay-at-home orders, restrictions on travel, and social distancing have greatly affected the mobility of people, the outcome that has been percolated as waves of despair for the hospitality industry since tourists and people in general

DOI: 10.4324/9781003295839-21

are confounded to the boundaries of their houses to stop and/or reduce further infection (Gursoy & Chi, 2020).

Further, the impacts of this pandemic are not evenly distributed in terms of geography and demography (Higgins-Desbiolles, 2020) such that people from a specific sector (such as tourism and hospitality) or specific countries are going to suffer more than their counterparts. Consequently, the Indian tourism and hospitality sector is one of the most sternly hit industries and has been pronounced to be going through the worst crisis ever (Confederation of Indian Industry, 2020). Currently, the Indian hospitality sector is experiencing a 30–50% decline in the revenue earned per room while operating at a critical 10–15% occupancy rate (IANS, 2020). Further, 70% of the total workforce employed in the Indian tourism and hospitality sector are expected to lose their jobs if situations do not improve (IANS, 2020).

The condition of Indian restaurants, a sector of the hospitality industry, is similar or worse (Agarwal, 2021). Government-enforced measures like lockdowns, social distancing, restrictions on dine-in services, limited operations, and lower mobility have paralysed the Indian F&B sector (Lakshmi & Shareena, 2020). The demand for cuisine experiences is at an all-time low and so is the revenue generated from their operations. The melancholy is exacerbated by the staggering amount of job loss as a cost-cutting measure to control the losses from the pandemic and to keep businesses alive (Agarwal, 2021). Despite several pleas from the industry side, government financial support is far from adequate (Tiwari, 2021). Further, the limited success and hindrances in distribution as well as supply chains of the vaccines are adding fuel to the fire, as COVID-19 is reportedly to stay longer than expected. All these negative influences have changed the reality of the Indian F&B sector, which once enjoyed the repute of being a continually growing industry.

Against this backdrop, the opinions of various stakeholders, especially the hotel staff involved in the food ordering to delivery process, hold special importance in devising strategies for the future (Agarwal, 2021). The growing importance of chefs makes a lot of sense in the background of the current COVID-19 outbreak, as chefs are regarded as the principal actors in the field of gastronomy with both culinary and managerial skills (Zopiatis, 2010) and are known to have a great influence on food experiences (Batat, 2020b). The pandemic has also drastically changed the way chefs perform their operations in the kitchen, especially the usage of their sensory perceptions. Times like these are challenging and unprecedented. Chefs are wearing masks and are putting their flavour perceptions to rest to ensure food safety and safeguard guest health. Also, with a majority of restaurants resorting to laying off manpower, cooking is becoming challenging more than ever. Academic papers discussing changing paradigms in the F&B sector from the customer's perspective have risen sharply with the breakout of the COVID-19 pandemic. However, since the emergence of the pandemic, very few academic works have highlighted the chefs' perspective on the operations of the F&B sector, especially in developing countries.

This chapter is an attempt to fill that critical gap by revealing the opinions of chefs across India about the issues and challenges of cooking in these new realities of COVID-19. This chapter also discusses additional measures taken by chefs as food handlers to ensure the safety of their guests during the current COVID-19 outbreak. The work is exploratory and a qualitative research approach has been adopted for this study. An unstructured questionnaire was administered to 15 chefs from nine popular five-star establishments serving at different locations in India. The interviews were transcribed and coded, following which thematic content analysis was applied to the data collected from the interviews and observations.

Literature review

A thorough analysis of the previous literature on the crisis-stricken service industry will reveal that F&B businesses were one of the most affected industries in case of a crisis with a decrease in demand and revenue generated from business (Alonso-Almeida et al., 2015). Irrespective of the nature of the crisis, which may be financial (Esteves, 2014) or social (Askey et al., 2018) or environmental (Jeffery et al., 2006), restaurant businesses suffer from higher vulnerabilities from crises mainly because they are often regarded as tertiary sectors. So, when any crisis strikes, customers often refrain from activities like going to restaurants and spend most of their resources on basic needs (Ghiani et al., 2020). Also, in case of an infectious disease-related crisis such as the COVID-19 pandemic, restaurants are often the first sectors to be closed down by the government, as they involve volumes of public gatherings that may also turn out to be one of the mediums of spread (Boakye et al., 2020).

When it comes to the impacts of the crisis on restaurant businesses, the implications are multifaceted. A study by Kim et al. (2020) confirms the significant negative effects of the crises on the financial performance of restaurants. In these adverse conditions, restaurants, which are by default a labour-intensive industry, often get pushed into the misery of cutting down manpower to survive (Fernandes, 2020). In their topical chapter on employment in restaurants during the COVID-19 pandemic Nhamo et al. (2020) argued that the government-enforced shutting down of sit-in-meals services in restaurants and limited operations (~20%) of the fast-food outlets were the primary reasons for job loss in the restaurant industry. Another sad truth of these job cuts is the fact that more often than not, these layoffs happen at the bottom of the employment chain; that is, staff belonging to vulnerable sections of society doing the menial jobs are the first ones to lose their jobs (Marat, 2009). These facts not only underline the higher vulnerability of the F&B sector, but also emphasise the importance of crisis management in the industry.

The state of affairs of the Indian hospitality and F&B sectors is still worse. The second wave of COVID-19 disease has had devastating impacts on India, as the country has now become one of the most COVID-affected countries in the world (Menon, 2021). With daily growth in the number of cases regularly reaching a record high, Indian state and central governments have imposed nationwide lockdowns to contain the rapid spread of the disease. Norms such as social distancing and lower mobility have become everyday rituals. With all these restrictions in place, the hospitality industry in India is far from the recovery process (Kaushal & Srivastava, 2021). The lack of announced relief packages has left the entire Indian hospitality sector in great shock and despair (Tewari, 2020). Consequently, in the Indian Food & Beverage (F&B) industry, which accounts for about 3% of the total Indian GDP and is the single biggest employer in India, the impact of the COVID-19 pandemic has been tragic. One estimate suggested that many restaurants would close altogether by December 2020 (IBEF Knowledge Centre 2020). The National Restaurant Association of India (NRAI) underlines that the restaurant business in India is expected to lose ~US$9 billion in 2020 (Holland, 2021). Adding to this, more than the sustenance of the industry, the safety and security of consumers has been set as the top priority for the Indian F&B sector. Therefore, many new innovative and adaptive measures have been taken in this regard to safeguard the interests of both the F&B industry and its consumers.

The aspect of changing realities in the F&B sector in the context of the COVID-19 pandemic has been considered in the existing literature (see Byrd et al., 2021; de Freitas & Stedefeldt, 2020; Hakim et al., 2021). However, the majority of these works have focused on the customer or management perspective of the pandemic's effect on the industry. For instance, Batat (2020a) delves upon the French Michelin-starred chefs' perspective while Bucak and Yiğit (2021) work highlight views of the chefs from Turkey. Both studies have been conducted in the context of developed countries, which are showing great signs of recovery thanks to the sizeable financial assistance provided for assisting the revival process. However, as stated previously, the case of India is entirely different if not opposite. Further, the inequitable and unprecedented nature of this pandemic makes it harder to generalise any findings. Therefore, it is imperative that, as the situation for Indian chefs is harsher, a detailed investigation of this phenomenon is required. Hence, the authors of this paper have made a meticulous enquiry into the standpoint of the chefs employed in high-end Indian hotels regarding their views on the new realities in operations during and post-COVID-19.

Methods

An online qualitative research approach was adopted to gain insights about the difficult chapter in the professional lives of chefs in the current scenario of the COVID-19 outbreak. The study intends to highlight the main issues faced by chefs in various tourism cities in India and how the pandemic has influenced the profession. A qualitative research methodology was adopted to explore the perceptions of chefs in a holistic way in their natural workspace/work environment. The chefs were engaged through our network using a purposeful sampling technique. Participating chefs are located in major tourism cities in India. The sample consists of male chefs majorly working as kitchen managers in the positions of executive chefs, executive sous chefs, chef de cuisine and restaurant entrepreneurs. Table 18.1 offers an overview of the chef's profile and the tourism cities in which they are working.

TABLE 18.1 Sample of chefs

Participant	Gender	Experience	Position	Location
Chef 1	Male	18	Executive Chef	Delhi
Chef 2	Male	15	Executive Sous Chef	Bangalore
Chef 3	Male	15	Executive Sous Chef	Jaipur
Chef 4	Male	18	Executive Chef	Chennai
Chef 5	Male	28	Executive Chef	Hyderabad
Chef 6	Male	15	Chef de cuisine	Hyderabad
Chef 7	Male	15	Pastry Chef	Jaipur
Chef 8	Male	19	Executive Chef	Bekal
Chef 9	Male	20	Restaurer	Hyderabad
Chef 10	Male	18	Executive Chef	Delhi
Chef 11	Male	18	Pastry Chef	Mumbai
Chef 12	Male	18	Executive Chef	Hyderabad
Chef 13	Male	18	Executive Chef	Dharamshala
Chef 14	Male	22	Pastry Chef	Mussoorie
Chef 15	Male	16	Executive Chef	Bangalore

Respondents were asked a set of questions, and data was collected through online interview forms and analysed by the researchers using Braun and Clarke (2006) thematic manual analysis. To bring out concrete evidence, the verbatim responses and researchers' comments were reanalysed by experts from the hospitality industry.

Findings and discussions

Our study provides insight into the views of Indian chefs and their multilevel response strategies to mitigate the downturn faced by the hospitality industry due to the upheaval of the current pandemic. The responses cluster into six main categories: 1) Changes in the chef profession; 2) Sensory deprivation/sensory disarmament; 3) Personal well-being, psychological and physical challenges; 4) Factors determining the future of professional kitchens; 5) Operational challenges; 6) Positive effects of the pandemic. In each section, an indicative quotation is presented from the interviews carried out for this research to give voice to the industry participants from whom this data was collected.

1. Changes in the chef profession

The current pandemic has changed the dynamics of chefs' profession. There is a paradigm shift in the way chefs operate in professional kitchens. Lockdowns and import restrictions to curb the spread of the virus have significantly disrupted the supply chains in the world and have affected the availability of imported ingredients (Rizou et al., 2020). Though the responses are very optimistic and the chefs across India are exploring various resources (local ingredients) and working with the best of their capabilities (expertise, innovation, creativity), the challenge is novel and requires changes in the regular style of working in professional kitchens. Another major advancement is the inclination of customers towards immunity boosting foods and reinventing and curating menus on these lines.

> *The new normal and the call of the day and priority being to serve safe food first, followed by making best use of seasonal products, keeping food as fresh as possible. Using immunity boosting vegetables and fruits has become a regular thing while planning menus. For the time being, the attention is split into well plated mini portioned foods and basic healthy, immunity boosting plates of food.*
>
> *(Chef 5)*

As per the guidelines of FSSAI, in India, it is advised to all food and beverage outlets to avoid buffets and shift to a la carte service of food to minimise crowding on buffets and to follow social distancing between tables in a restaurant. As the study focuses on kitchen managers, it was observed that they are operating on tight budgets and restrained manpower due to the shortfall in revenues due to reduced business as compared to pre-COVID-19 times.

2. Sensory disarmament

Sensory experience is a culmination of multiple sensory inputs and contributes to our experience of food flavour (Delwiche, 2004; Keast et al., 2004; Small et al., 1997). Hedonic and sensory experience plays an important role in curating new food preparations on the menus by professional chefs, wherein a dish passes numerous food tastings/sensory evaluations before making it to the menu to be presented to the customer. However, with the pandemic, with the chefs wearing masks, it is a challenge to experience food while preparing it and presenting it to the customer. The changing times have changed the sequence of food tastings, with small portions served to chefs for evaluation following the norms of social distancing. Needless to say, most chefs are finding it extremely challenging.

> *It has indeed a big challenge as evaluating food is done on the basis of smell and taste. Taking off the mask every time to smell and taste food exposes the food to a greater risk of being infected or contaminated. Alternatively, we have dedicated sous chefs in every section, sent for a COVID test every fortnight to ensure he is not infected; tasting and evaluating food is the responsibility of these particular sous chefs. Any other staff apart from these cannot taste the food. This ensures we minimise the risk of contamination.*
>
> *(Chef 12)*

3. Personal well-being: psychological and physical challenges

The COVID-19 pandemic has devastated livelihoods and has given rise to negative psychological responses and emotions and its manifestations like depression, anxiety, panic and psychosomatic disorders across large populations (Qiu et al.,

2020; Tandon, 2020). The nature of a chef's job is physically demanding, but the current pandemic has also given rise to uncertainties, with the fear of getting infected on the job and also the underlying fear of losing jobs, as major hospitality companies are reducing their employees in India. Further, psychological well-being is often ignored; hence, building a holistic intervention system is essential to prevent psychological stress and future mental health consequences (Paul & Devi, 2021).

> *Being in a kitchen is challenging, especially when it's busy and when you're covered up in masks and gloves 24*7, it does take a toll on your mental and physical health. Getting rashes on the skin due to gloves has become a normal part of our life now!*
>
> *(Chef 14)*

4. Factors determining the future of professional kitchens

Food safety has always been an integral part of the food and beverage industry, even before this pandemic. For a food and beverage outlet to achieve commercial success, following food safety standards is crucial (Tuncer & Akoğlu, 2020). This outbreak has further strengthened the existing system of food safety being followed by chefs in various star category hotels across India from where the responses were collected.

> *'Precaution is always better than cure, following cleaning & sanitation at work station, personal hygiene like frequent cleaning of hands, wearing masks in kitchen are must, increasing awareness through training, following physical distancing in kitchen, use of right chemicals and sanitizers for disinfecting the workplace, following FSSAI guidelines for food safety measures etc. are effective ways to ensure safety at work place.'*
>
> *(Chef 3)*

Also, the chefs are observing a change in the eating habits of customers and are curating immunity boosting menus in line with the AYUSH recommended ingredients, and reintroducing ayurvedic cuisine. The kitchen managers also believe that the industry in India can only be revived through vaccination drives and only then can the industry operate at its full potential as it was in pre-COVID times.

5. Operational challenges

As social distancing remains the key policy in controlling the spread of the virus, restaurants globally are operating at half of their original capacity, making it difficult to operate with small profit margins and huge operational costs. The direct effect of reduced capacity results in reduced revenues, which in turn affects the operational allocated budget cuts.

> *Management is not generating revenues and considering the fact that this would be for the certain time, their first priority is to cut down the cost. The management is*

replacing not even quality manpower against the average skilled manpower but they are doing the same with different products and the facilities provided to the guest.

(Chef 6)

There is also a significant decline in demand, with fewer potential customers preferring to dine out. This has led to the flourishing of the online food delivery business, but this does not compare to the extent of the business of the food and beverage sector in the pre-pandemic times.

6. Positive effects of the pandemic

The pandemic has had catastrophic effects on the hospitality industry and culinary professionals. However, there are some positive effects of the pandemic as well.

Yes, the pandemic has a few good sides as well. Let me be blunt and tell the truth: this situation has taught people to think unconventional. It has pushed people into entrepreneurship.

(Chef 1)

There is a growing awareness in society about personal health and hygiene, which would have a positive effect on society as a whole. Also, it emerged as a response from culinary professionals that now the customers would prefer places with good hygiene conditions. Although star category hotels are already following standard operating procedures (SOPs) for food safety and hygiene, with this pandemic, good food hygiene will attract customers and also result in repeat business.

Conclusion

The COVID-19 pandemic has affected the chef profession tremendously, with multidimensional factors resulting in adversities in the professional lives and personal well-being of culinary professionals. The responses collected from chefs are diverse and present their strategies to keep businesses afloat in these troubled times. There are growing physical, mental and socio-economic adversities faced by culinary professionals due to the downturn in hotel revenues, which in turn is pushing even corporate hospitality giants like Marriot and Hyatt to reduce their workforces. The hospitality industry is trying to revive itself, but as there is an underlying connection between travel, tourism and hospitality and without the revival of travel and tourism, it is impossible to revive the hospitality industry. The worldwide spread of the COVID-19 pandemic has affected tourism demand and has successively affected the hospitality industry, which is one of the largest employers in the world.

This chapter presents the spectrum of changes brought in by the pandemic in the lives of culinary professionals in India, ranging from the sensory disarmament of culinary professionals to ensuring the food safety of customers. The researchers have also tried to identify the positive effects of pandemic, though most of the chefs in their responses have preferred not to answer the question. The responses were collected from the organised hospitality sector in India, and the reverberations of the pandemic were quite pronounced.

The current study outlines the occupational changes in the profession of culinary professionals during the current outbreak and is expected to contribute to the literature. However, the findings cannot be generalised to unorganised F&B sectors, as the responses are collected only from the culinary professionals employed in the organised hospitality sector working in major Indian tourism cities. We suggest further strengthening the study by conducting further research on the unorganised food and beverage sector.

References

Agarwal, P. (2021). Shattered but smiling: Human resource management and the wellbeing of hotel employees during COVID-19. *International Journal of Hospitality Management, 93*, 102765.

Alonso-Almeida, M. d. M., Bremser, K., & Llach, J. (2015). Proactive and Reactive Strategies Deployed by Restaurants in Times of Crisis: Effects on Capabilities, Organization and Competitive Advantage. *International Journal of Contemporary Hospitality Management, 27*(7), 1641–1661.

American Hotel & Lodging Association. (2020). *COVID-19's Impact on the Hospitality Industry.* www.ahla.com/covid-19s-impact-hotel-industry

Askey, A.P., Taylor, R., Groff, E., & Fingerhut, A. (2018). Fast Food Restaurants and Convenience Stores: Using Sales Volume to Explain Crime Patterns in Seattle. *Crime & Delinquency, 64*(14), 1836–1857.

Batat, W. (2020a). How Michelin-starred Chefs are being Transformed into Social Bricoleurs? An Online Qualitative Study of Luxury Foodservice during the Pandemic Crisis. *Journal of Service Management, 32*(1), 87–99.

Batat, W. (2020b). Pillars of Sustainable Food Experiences in the Luxury Gastronomy Sector: A Qualitative Exploration of Michelin-starred Chefs' Motivations. *Journal of Retailing and Consumer Services, 57*, 102255.

Boakye, E.A., Zhao, H., Ahia, B.N.K., & Damoah, M.A. (2020). Mitigating the Socio-Economic Impacts of COVID-19; Role of Governments in Sub-Saharan Africa, Fiscal and Monetary Policy Perspectives. *Open Journal of Social Sciences, 8*(11), 300.

Braun, V., & Clarke, V. (2006). Using Thematic Analysis in Psychology. *Qualitative Research in Psychology, 3*(2), 77–101.

Bucak, T., & Yiğit, S. (2021). The Future of the Chef Occupation and the Food and Beverage Sector after the COVID-19 Outbreak: Opinions of Turkish chefs. *International Journal of Hospitality Management, 92*, 102682.

Byrd, K., Her, E., Fan, A., Almanza, B., Liu, Y., & Leitch, S. (2021). Restaurants and COVID-19: What are Consumers' Risk Perceptions about Restaurant Food and its Packaging during the Pandemic? *International Journal of Hospitality Management, 94*, 102821.

Confederation of Indian Industry. (2020). *Impact of COVID-19 on Hospitality Sector -Estimated Revenue Losses.* www.cii.in/PublicationDetail.aspx?enc=6/lnlra7c1XlKPU0O5MvJtWcrtv6LPYFaLAzELIKJ5I=

de Freitas, R.S.G., & Stedefeldt, E. (2020). COVID-19 Pandemic Underlines the Need to Build Resilience in Commercial Restaurants' Food Safety. *Food Research International, 136*, 109472.

Delwiche, J. (2004). The Impact of Perceptual Interactions on Perceived Flavor. *Food Quality and Preference, 15*(2), 137–146.

Dornenburg, A., & Page, K. (1996). *Culinary Artistry.* Canada: John Wiley & Sons.

Esteves, J.M. (2014). Economic Crisis and the Image of Portugal as a Tourist Destination: The Restaurants' Perspective. *Worldwide Hospitality and Tourism Themes, 14.*

Fernandes, N. (2020). Economic Effects of Coronavirus Outbreak (COVID-19) on the World Economy. IESE Business School Working Paper No. WP-1240-E

Ghiani, E., Galici, M., Mureddu, M., & Pilo, F. (2020). Impact on Electricity Consumption and Market Pricing of Energy and Ancillary Services during Pandemic of COVID-19 in Italy. *Energies, 13*(13), 3357.

Gursoy, D., & Chi, C.G. (2020). Effects of COVID-19 Pandemic on Hospitality Industry: Review of the Current Situations and a Research Agenda. *Journal of Hospitality Marketing & Management, 29*(5), 527–529.

Hakim, M.P., Zanetta, L.D.A., & da Cunha, D.T. (2021). Should I Stay, or Should I Go? Consumers' Perceived Risk and Intention to Visit Restaurants during the COVID-19 Pandemic in Brazil. *Food Research International, 141*, 110152.

Higgins-Desbiolles, F. (2020). Socialising Tourism for Social and Ecological Justice after COVID-19. *Tourism Geographies, 22*(3), 610–623.

Holland, S. (2021, February 15). 2021: The Year When the Customer is Not Always Right. *ET Hospitality World.* https://hospitality.economictimes.indiatimes.com/news/speaking-heads/2021-the-year-when-the-customer-is-not-always-right/80921939

IANS. (2020). *Coronavirus Impact: The Impact of COVID-19 on the Hospitality Sector.* https://timesofindia.indiatimes.com/business/india-business/the-impact-of-covid-19-on-the-hospitality-sector/articleshow/75290137.cms

IBEF Knowledge Centre. (2020, December 3). *Future of Indian Food and Beverage Industry Post-Pandemic.* www.ibef.org/blogs/future-of-indian-food-and-beverage-industry-post-pandemic

Jeffery, R.W., Baxter, J., McGuire, M., & Linde, J. (2006). Are Fast Food Restaurants an Environmental Risk Factor for Obesity? *International Journal of Behavioral Nutrition and Physical Activity, 3*(1), 1–6.

Kaushal, V., & Srivastava, S. (2021). Hospitality and Tourism Industry Amid COVID-19 Pandemic: Perspectives on Challenges and Learnings from India. *International Journal of Hospitality Management, 92*, 102707.

Keast, R., Dalton, P., & Breslin, P.A. (2004). Flavor Interactions at the Sensory Level. In A.J. Taylor & D.D. Roberts (Eds.), *Flavor Perception* (pp. 228–255). Oxford: Blackwell Scientific.

Kim, J., Kim, J., Lee, S.K., & Tang, L.R. (2020). Effects of Epidemic Disease Outbreaks on Financial Performance of Restaurants: Event Study Method Approach. *Journal of Hospitality and Tourism Management, 43*, 32–41.

Lakshmi, B., & Shareena, P. (2020). Impact of COVID 19 on the Restaurants. *Journal of Interdisciplinary Cycle Research, 12*(8), 1327–1334.

Marat, E. (2009). *Labor Migration in Central Asia: Implications of the Global Economic Crisis.* Silk Road Studies Program. Washington, DC: Institute for Security and Development Policy.

McBride, A.E., & Flore, R. (2019). The Changing Role of the Chef: A Dialogue. *International Journal of Gastronomy and Food Science, 17*, 100157.

Menon, S. (2021, May 8). India COVID: How Bad is the Second Wave? *The BBC.* www.bbc.com/news/56987209

Nhamo, G., Dube, K., & Chikodzi, D. (2020). Restaurants and COVID-19: A Focus on Sustainability and Recovery Pathways. In *Counting the Cost of COVID-19 on the Global Tourism Industry* (pp. 205–224). New York: Springer.

Paul, M.T.V., & Devi, U.N. (2021). Managing Mental & Psychological Wellbeing Amidst COVID-19 Pandemic: Positive Psychology Interventions. *arXiv preprint arXiv:2104.11726.*

Qiu, J., Shen, B., Zhao, M., Wang, Z., Xie, B., & Xu, Y. (2020). A Nationwide Survey of Psychological Distress among Chinese People in the COVID-19 Epidemic: Implications and Policy Recommendations. *General psychiatry, 33*(2), e100213.

Rizou, M., Galanakis, I.M., Aldawoud, T.M., & Galanakis, C.M. (2020). Safety of Foods, Food Supply Chain and Environment within the COVID-19 Pandemic. *Trends in Food Science & Technology, 102*, 293–299.

Rosenthal, M. (2020). *Fauci: COVID-19 Worst Pandemic in 100 Years.* www.idse.net/COVID-19/Article/10-20/Fauci – COVID-19-Worst-Pandemic-in-100-Years/60937

Ruhlman, M. (2006). *The Reach of a Chef: Beyond the kitchen*, Vol. 1. New York: Penguin Books.

Small, D.M., Jones-Gotman, M., Zatorre, R.J., Petrides, M., & Evans, A.C. (1997). Flavor Processing: More than the Sum of its Parts. *Neuroreport, 8*(18), 3913–3917.

Tandon, R. (2020). The COVID-19 Pandemic, Personal Reflections on Editorial Responsibility. *Asian Journal of Psychiatry, 50*, 102100.

Tewari, S. (17 May 2020). Travel and Tourism Industry in Shock with No Relief Measures from Govt. *The Mint.* www.livemint.com/news/india/travel-and-tourism-industry-in-shock-with-no-relief-measures-from-govt-11589722537599.html

Tiwari, A. (2021, April 26). Tourism and Hospitality Industry Urges Centre to Release SEIS Aid. *CNBC.* www.cnbctv18.com/business/tourism-and-hospitality-industry-urges-centre-to-release-seis-aid-9063881.htm

Tuncer, T., & Akoğlu, A. (2020). Food Safety Knowledge of Food Handlers Working in Hotel Kitchens in Turkey. *Food and Health, 6*(2), 67–89.

UNWTO. (2021). *International Tourism and COVID-19.* www.unwto.org/international-tourism-and-covid-19

WTO. (2020). *Tourism and COVID-19.* www.unwto.org/tourism-covid-19

Zopiatis, A. (2010). Is It Art or Science? Chef's Competencies for Success. *International Journal of Hospitality Management, 29*(3), 459–467.

INDEX

Note: Page numbers in *italics* indicate a figure and page numbers in **bold** indicate a table on the corresponding page.